JACK'S BOOK

Jack Kerouac in the Lives and
Words of his Friends

JACK'S BOOK

by Barry Gifford & Lawrence Lee

HAMISH HAMILTON

LONDON

First published in Great Britain 1979
by Hamish Hamilton Ltd.
Garden House, 57–59 Long Acre, London WC2E 9JZ

Copyright © 1978 by Barry Gifford and Lawrence Lee

Remarks attributed to Gary Snyder are
copyright © 1978 by Gary Snyder

Designed by Laurel Marx

British Library Cataloguing in Publication Data
Gifford, Barry
  Jack's book.
  1. Kerouac, Jack – Biography   2. Novelists,
  American – 20th century – Biography
  I. Title
  813'.5'4   PS3521.E735Z/
  ISBN 0–241–10066–6

Printed in Great Britain by
Redwood Burn Ltd, Trowbridge and Esher

CONTENTS

To Marshall Clements,
the book we always wanted

And to Mary Lou, as always
—B.G.

To John and to the memory
of Robert Goodman
—L.L.

The authors wish to thank all of those persons who participated in this project—"An Adventurous Education" as surely as was Jack's *Vanity of Duluoz*—and thank especially those who personally assisted us: Carolyn Cassady, James Grauerholz, Les Pockell, Marshall Clements, Pat and Liz Delaney, Ken and Tony Anderson, Lorna Goodman, Don Ellis, Deirdre Tabler, Dennis McNally, Duane BigEagle, Ray Neinstein, Sarah Satterlee, Bill Alexander, Paul DeAngelis, Mary Lou Nelson, the offices of KSAN-FM radio and Julie Lyon, for her indefatigable transcription of the nigh-untranscribable. Our very special gratitude to Sara Bershtel of St. Martin's Press, a late entry who came out of nowhere and brought it all home in style.

—B.G. and L.L.

"All your America...is like a dense
Balzacian hive in a jewel point."

—Jack Kerouac
in *Doctor Sax*

PROLOGUE

America makes odd demands of its fiction writers. Their art alone won't do. We expect them to provide us with social stencils, an expectation so firm that we often judge their lives instead of their works. If they declare themselves a formal movement or stand up together as a generation, we are pleased, because this simplifies the use we plan to make of them. If they oblige us with a manifesto, it is enforced with the weight of contract.

So it happens that, from Henry James on, Europe is regarded by Americans as a large lending-library of inspiration, and expatriation becomes something of a duty, whether fulfilled or not. Ernest Hemingway makes a market for wineskins. Mr. and Mrs. Scott Fitzgerald certify a dip in the Plaza Fountain as apt behavior for young Americans of a certain class and time.

Having derived an etiquette from their works, we hold these writers in our minds as creatures of the moment in which we noticed them. If they abandon our expectations, the literary critics and chroniclers put them in their place, like stamps that have been stuck onto the wrong page of the album. In this way we sometimes deny artists the ordinary chances at growth and change that are among art's bare necessities.

This book is about a man who was a victim of this spirit of literary utilitarianism. Jack Kerouac is remembered as the exemplar of "The Beat Generation." But the Beat Generation was no generation at all. The label was invented as an essay in self-explanation when journalists asked questions, but it was accepted at face value. Kerouac used the phrase above one of the first samples of *On the Road* to reach print ("Jazz of the Beat Generation," 1955) and his friend John Clellon Holmes, who had described the same world in his novel *Go*, obliged the *New York Times* Magazine and *Esquire* with think-pieces about this new generation written in the style that the readers of those journals expected.

Kerouac was a writer whose belated success depended upon a new prose method, which he applied to a sturdy old form, a young man's varied adventures. It was Kerouac's misfortune that his fame—as distinct from his literary standing, a matter yet to be determined—owed more to the people and events he portrayed than to the way in which he portrayed them, as he later insisted he would have preferred.

Cutting away the amateurs, the opportunists, and the figures whose generational identification was fleeting or less than wholehearted on their own part, the Beat Generation—as a literary school—pretty much amounts to Kerouac and his friends William Burroughs and Allen Ginsberg. In life and in art the three relied upon each other in strong and complex ways, and, a decade after his death, Kerouac's prose style lives on in the forms Ginsberg adopted to become the world-poetry voice he is today. Ginsberg shed his role as the earnest, necktie-wearing "Ginsy" of the 1940's and managed to utilize the dangerous energy of publicity in projecting an image useful to his motives as a poet. Burroughs, whose frosty distance and Coolidge-like silences evidently have been in his repertoire since boyhood, saw to it that he was let alone. A fourth figure, Gregory Corso, entered the circle late, and continues to play the *poète-maudit*, lately in France, where that role is a matter of accepted tradition. Kerouac's failure to adopt any of his former cohorts' survival tactics or to find a successful one of his own is the sad heart of the last part of this book.

When *On the Road* appeared in 1957, after languishing in Kerouac's rucksack for years, Jack won the literary and commercial success he had wanted desperately, but had failed to achieve with his first novel, *The Town and the City*, published in 1950. Ginsberg asked him to write a brief explanation of his technique, and it was printed in *The Black Mountain Review*, the journal of that resolutely advanced Southern college, as "Essentials of Spontaneous Prose." Kerouac's method was a war on craft, but his notes were adopted as the excuse for a torrent of bad stream-of-consciousness prose and poetry. Kerouac, unwillingly, was set up as the avatar of a movement that he had no desire and little ability to advance. Suddenly, he found himself placed by the media at the center of a stage dressed with props from French existentialism (black sweaters, berets), late romanticism (footloose hedonism) and the whole race-hoard of ideas about drugs, from De Quincey to Anslinger.

Kerouac realized the threat of this role at once, but he reacted with an odd mixture of shyness and belligerence. He accepted the attention, at first, as a compliment. Its focus was an insult. Why didn't the journalists examine the books as well as the man? As he told *The Paris Review* in 1967:

> I am so busy interviewing myself in my novels, and I have been so busy writing down these self-interviews, that I don't see why I should draw breath in pain every year of the last ten years to repeat and repeat to everybody who interviews me what I've already explained in the books themselves....It beggars sense.

He began to say forthright things about his essential conservatism and religiousness, and they were duly quoted with the feature-writer's skill at synthetic irony. *Esquire* portrayed him as a pathetic class-traitor, a hipster-as-Bircher. Although that particular insult was delivered only after his death, Kerouac did live long enough to recognize the imminent fulfillment of this prophecy he had delivered in 1951 across a midnight kitchen table to Neal Cassady:

> A Ritz Yale Club party where I went with a kid in a leather jacket, I was wearing one too, and there were hundreds of kids in leather jackets instead of big tuxedo Clancy millionaires...cool, and everybody was smoking marijuana, wailing a new decade in one wild *crowd*.

He saw it coming before anyone else, and he got blamed for its coming at all.

This confusion between some of the social forms of the late sixties and the content of Kerouac's work continues to do his reputation damage. In *Exile's Return*, his book about the social side of American letters between the world wars, Malcolm Cowley describes *The Saturday Evening Post's* thirty-year grudge against Greenwich Village, a vendetta replicated by the *New York Times,* which still maintains a specialist in critical attacks on "the Beats." Students of English literature waited twenty years for the first scholarly edition of

On the Road, and only just now has Kerouac's work begun to prevail over what poet Jack Spicer called "the great, gray English Department of the skull."

But despite the gap on the assigned-reading list, students at any school of a certain size, whether in Ann Arbor, Chapel Hill, Austin, or Cambridge, have always been able to step across the street and find a big selection of Kerouac novels, often in British paperback editions. The books live. New American Library's Signet edition of *On the Road* has never gone out of print. Ginsberg and fellow poets have created a Jack Kerouac School of Disembodied Poetics at the Buddhist college in Colorado, Naropa Institute. Movie companies are looking at Kerouac's novels again, and a play based on his life was produced in New York in 1976 and in Los Angeles in 1977.

As with Scott Fitzgerald, another drinking Catholic who gave out at the midpoint, there is a threat that Jack Kerouac's legend may supplant his work, rather than merely overshadow it. Had he lived unto silvery literary senior-statesmanship, it is possible that one publisher or another would have fulfilled his wish for corrected and uniform publication (with the names straight, once and for all) of his "one vast book...an enormous comedy, like Proust's." He would have called it *The Duluoz Legend*. As it is, the one-vast-book notion cannot accommodate his first novel, *The Town and the City*, a fact Jack acknowledged. He would have set it aside. There are other problems. Tidy-minded publishers forced him to give the same characters exasperating strings of pseudonyms masking pseudonyms and even, in *The Subterraneans*, to disguise New York as San Francisco in a hedge against libel suits. His work is scattered among foreign and American houses, individual volumes popping in and out of print. Finally, we may expect a long wait for a first look at his unpublished material, which includes *Some of the Dharma*, his rendering of classic Buddhist texts, and his letters.

The idea of this book is to provide the framework for a first or fresh reading of Kerouac as a man who succeeded in giving us his one vast book, but in the bits and pieces the marketplace demanded. The authors are men born during or shortly after World War II who at first knew their subject only through his work, where they found the energy for the undertaking of learning as much as they could of his life.

Kerouac died in 1969 at the age of forty-seven, young in the terms of our time. Most of his friends survived him. Our idea was to seek them out and to talk with them about Jack's life and their own lives. The final result, we hoped, would be a big, transcontinental conversation, complete with interruptions, contradictions, old grudges, and bright memories, all of them providing a reading of the man himself through the people he chose to populate his work.

The job took us back and forth across the country twice, mostly by airplane. The very roads have been replaced since Jack's travels by the homogenized culture of the Interstate Highway system, but the people of Kerouac's novels have survived. We talked to seventy or so individuals, thirty-five of whom speak here. We had no "Rosebud" to ask them about, like the friends and victims of *Citizen Kane*, nor, although more than one interviewee proposed the metaphor, did we feel much like the field investigators in the Roman Catholic Church's saint-making procedures. Much of what we learned from these conversations has been used in the text that binds the excerpts from them together. We have let Kerouac's friends speak a good deal about themselves because it seemed to us both possible and proper to provide a group portrait as well as a close-up of the man who stands at its center. Because the cast reached Russian-novel proportions, we provided the character key as an aid to following their appearances in this book and those of their fictional shadows in Kerouac's.

In what follows you will read again and again, in many voices, that Kerouac's novels were fiction, not reportage. We agree. It is fascinating to see the way in which real people, places, and events are utilized in the books, which then fed back to alter reality, but the technical leaps and the heartbreaking beauty of Kerouac's prose take his novels into a realm far beyond that of the reporter or diarist. His books are the product of a genius at recollection. When he was a boy in Massachusetts Jack's friends nicknamed him "Memory Babe." To the editor who brought *On the Road* to light he was the recording angel. To his friend and fellow novelist, John Clellon Holmes, he was "the great rememberer." And to a great many of those with whom we spoke, memories of Jack were mixed up with notions of sainthood. If miracles are required as evidence of his life, his books themselves should suffice.

1 THE TOWN

The tenements were, and are, Little Canada. There are others like it in Burlington and Nashua and Portsmouth, neighborhoods in which the shop signs are in English but the French language and ways prevail. You can still see the young French-Canadian men lounging by the front door of the Pawtucketville Social Club, the bowling alley and beerhall where Jack's father, Leo, went on afternoons when business was light at his Spotlight Printshop in the "crowded metropolitan business section" across the river.

Like many New England towns, Lowell has swallowed up a collection of villages, each with its own history. Jack Kerouac was born in Centralville and grew up in a succession of rent-houses and flats in Dracut and Pawtucketville, all of them north of the Merrimack and the now-vanished mills that multiplied the Merrimack's power by that of the leisurely Concord, a river which is a river only as Lowell is a city, on an old scale—New England's.

During the early years of the industrial revolution Lowell was a wonder-town, literally a capital of industry. The mills spun Boston fortunes that survive to this day. Charles Dickens, a stern critic of factory slavery in his own country, visited Lowell and wrote home an approving report. He was impressed by the looks of the place and by the deportment of the farm girls who had come there to tend the looms, and he found no fault with their wage, two dollars a week. The mill owners gave the town a Textile Institute on the north bank of the Merrimack, but they were less generous with their workers. As the nineteenth century rolled on, the "operatives" became

3

relatively less and less well-paid. The farm girls went to Boston, instead, to work as stenographers or telephonists. Their places at the looms were taken by immigrants from Ireland, France (via Canada), Poland, and Greece.

The mills hummed until the end of World War I, when imported cloth and southern factories provided competition that began to close them down. By the time Jack was born— March 12, 1922—Lowell's splendid century was over. A hundred years of immigrants drawn by the mills had sorted themselves into a loose constellation of ethnic groups bound by a common Catholicism but separated by their loyalties to a particular parish or language. Every one of them was caught in an economic depression such as the rest of America would endure only ten years later.

Leo Alcide Kerouac and Gabrielle Ange L'Evesque met and married in New Hampshire, where their families had immigrated from Canada. Leo was a job printer who had tried his hand at selling insurance before he got the money to open his own press. As a youth he had worked in New Hampshire sawmills. Jean-Louis Lebris de Kerouac was the third and last child. His sister, Caroline, "Nin," was three years older and his brother, Gerard, five when Jack was born.

Leo and Gabrielle lived in separate worlds when they were away from their rented hearth. Leo was a hearty, outgoing burgher whose shop was crowded with his friends. They found little difficulty in luring him away for an afternoon of billiards or political talk. At one point they proposed that he run for mayor of Lowell, but he declined the draft. Leo passed on to Jack a complicated notion of his ancestry on the Kerouac side, explaining that his own father, a carpenter who had immigrated from Brittany, was descended from Cornish Celts. Leo supplied a nobleman for one branch of the family tree, a coat-of-arms with three carpenter's nails and a motto which translated as "Love, work and suffer." Jack's father counted Greeks and Poles and Irishmen among his friends and cus- tomers, and he was entirely comfortable with English, the language that all of them could share. Gabrielle preferred French and conducted her household in that tongue, which was also the language of the parish where she performed novenas and sent her children to be taught.

When Jack was four, Gerard, then nine, died of rheumatic

fever. Gerard was a bright, frail child who had treated Jack, his sister Nin, his pet cat, and the mice he rescued from traps with the same extraordinary kindness. Jack worshipped him and emulated him and was entirely bereft at his death, which was marked by ceremonious mourning by the teaching sisters. Gerard had been a favorite of the nuns. When he died, they thought over things that he had said and done in his brief life and spoke of him as a saint-in-the-making. The boy was buried with Gabrielle's family in Nashua, New Hampshire, his soul consigned to a heaven which she sought to make comfortable and at-hand to Jacky and Nin. To Gabrielle there was no question that Gerard was a saint, and Jacky was told so again and again. The implication was that Jack, perhaps, was not.

The special, official saint to whom Jack was taught to pray was Thérèse of Lisieux, whose life provided something of a stencil for Jack's memories of Gerard's saintliness. Thérèse was the consumptive daughter of a watchmaker in Brittany, the region of France the Kerouacs considered their ancestral home. In 1888, at the age of fifteen, she took the Carmelite habit. When it became plain that Thérèse would die of tuberculosis, her Mother Superior instructed her to keep a journal, which the girl crowded with bright, simple memories of a bourgeois childhood. At her death the Carmelites edited the diary into an obituary pamphlet, *The Story of a Soul*, which swiftly gained hundreds of thousands of readers around the world. In a section of the journal that came close to a campaign speech Thérèse had promised to "spend her heaven doing good upon earth," and had forecast a "shower of roses" for those who prayed to her after her death, Gabrielle Ange L'Evesque among them. The Carmelites were deluged with letters about the resulting miracles, but the Vatican was adamant about the required waiting period before canonization could begin. Finally, having confessed his certainty of her sainthood to a visiting bishop, Pius X relented in 1914 and prepared the way for her recognition. In 1923, twenty-five years after she died at twenty-four, Thérèse was accorded beatification by Pius XI and immediate ranking with Joan of Arc as co-patroness of France.

She is known today as St. Thérèse of the Infant Jesus, and the chromolithographed iconography of her is rich in images of the Holy Child, of baby lambs, of roses, and of yolk-yellow

5

shafts of light piercing back-lit clouds to illuminate her simple, adoring face. Forty years after the canonization of Thérèse, Jack Kerouac, literally hung over from success, would sprawl in a San Francisco park and explain to the poet Philip Whalen the comfort and refuge he felt in praying to Thérèse and "little lamby Jesus" to ease his woes.

Jack harbored bitter memories of the strict sisters at parochial school, an ordeal that ended when he was sent to public school at seven. Gerard's coffin, the dark glade where the Kerouacs made the stations of the cross, the cheaply-printed portraits of the weeping Christ—all of these images stayed in his mind and his mind stayed on Lowell, or "Galloway," as he called it in his first novel, *The Town and the City*. The hard times would make Jack and his family wanderers throughout the crescent of poor neighborhoods north of the Merrimack, but despite the shadows, Jack remembered and spoke of a childhood that was full and rich, a time in his life that he never tired of reconsidering and recreating in his writing, approaching it again and again from different angles.

In *The Town and the City* Jack multiplies himself and uses elements of his friends' characters to create a large and complicated family he calls the Martins. Martin was St. Thérèse's family name and an important mercantile name in Lowell. Jack gives his fictional family a sprawling, many-porched house that he had passed on summer-evening walks with his mother and his sister. The Martins of the novel are indifferent Catholics,

The Twelve Stations of the Cross—"I knew Doctor Sax was there flowing in the back darks with his wild and hincty cape . . ." (*Doctor Sax*, pp. 122-123). Photo by Marshall Clements.

and given the economic realities of Lowell in the thirties, almost unaccountably comfortable. Only Mrs. Martin, the mother, is of French descent, a trait Kerouac uses to shade her character, but not to define it. The Martins probably represent an amalgam of all the wealthy families on Varnum Road with whom Gabrielle wished her son could associate.

Later in his writing career, when he was striving to set down his true feelings, Jack's French self surfaced, as in *Visions of Gerard,* the thirty-five-year-old man's prolonged meditation on the brother who had died when he was four. A world of steaming puddings and rainy afternoons home from school is keenly evoked. Jack portrays conversations with Gabrielle—Mémère—in French, and then translates them. "When I read of Proust's teacup," he wrote, "—all those saucers in a crumb—all of literary history by thumb—all of a city in a tasty crumb—I got all my boyhood in vanilla winter waves around the kitchen stove."

Jack painted and drew and cocked an ear for gossip, and he was a faithful reader of the sports pages of the *Lowell Sun* and the Boston newspapers. By the time he was eleven he was amusing himself by writing sports coverage chronicling the fortunes of his racing stable, a box of marbles. In another season the marbles became the players in an elaborate statistical baseball game that Jack continued to play in one form or another for the rest of his life.

Children's tickets for the movies cost eleven cents in those days, but Jack and Nin could attend for free because Leo printed the theater programs. Jack was seven when the pictures began to talk, which made him a member of the first generation to secure its fantasy in this noisy, American way. Until the talkies Lowell's main theater, the Keith, was a stop on the Keith-Albee vaudeville circuit, and Leo's connection with the theater provided his son with glimpses of the Marx Brothers and W.C. Fields as stage performers, before their movie fame. As stars of the talking pictures they became full-scale comic heroes for Jack and his friends. The men of *The Big Parade* were real heroes, models in case the Kaiser decided to march again. The villainess of *Murder by the Clock* was frightening to Jack because she was only a shadow, never seen full-face.

At parochial school Jack's catechism and his first reading of the Bible had been in French. After he began attending public school he read the popular children's books of the day: *The Little Shepherd of Kingdom Come*, *Rebecca of Sunnybrook Farm*, and the adventures of *The Bobbsey Twins*, three brace of bland siblings whose existence defied statistical common sense. All of these books were case-bound volumes of great popularity, accepted by teachers and school librarians despite their lack of literary merit, because of their uplifting moral lessons. But Jack's tastes soon led him to the pulp thriller magazine-novels that Street and Smith and other publishers produced weekly, which were sold on newsstands or in the little grocery-and-sundry shops called "spas" in Lowell. The character Jack followed devoutly was The Shadow, Lamont Cranston, who knew "what evil lurks in the minds of men," and had the power to cloud men's minds in order to triumph over that evil. The Shadow, the creation of the pseudonymous Maxwell Grant, had established beachheads in several media by the time Jack was twelve. The Shadow appeared in a magazine, in theater serials, and in a radio program.

On snowy days Jack came home from school and cranked up the phonograph to play thick, gutta-percha discs that provided the soundtrack for the race-meets, the ballgames, and the movies of mystery and adventure that played continuously in his head. But in spring and summer his fantasies spread to a wider stage, the sandbanks of the Merrimack, the woods of Dracut, the grounds of the mansion on Wannalancet Street, and the orphanage on the hill that he would consolidate into a single Castle and populate with a cabal of vampires and hangers-on, the arch-enemies of his shadow hero, Doctor Sax.

In *Doctor Sax*, Jack's novel about the last weeks of childhood, Lowell's ordinary, small-town shadows deepen and spread to contain a counter-world in which Doctor Sax, a shrouded figure with a green complexion, is pitted against the forces of evil, acting through comic and banal agents. Jack wrote the book when he was thirty-five and visiting William Burroughs in Mexico. Sax himself contains elements of Burroughs, and W.C. Fields appears under the name Bull Balloon, along with a good deal of intellectual décor that was no part of Kerouac's boyhood world. There is, for example, a funny set-piece portrayal of Bohemianism, à la Isadora Duncan or Amy Lowell. But all of this material is identified with Kerouac's fantasy subplot, a titanic struggle between good and

8

evil played out under the unsuspecting noses of the Lowell townspeople. The sounds and smells and tastes of a Massachusetts boyhood are here, and the underground bungalow where Doctor Sax hides out is located on the real road that Jack and his friends walked to reach their playing field at the edge of the Dracut woods, just north of town.

The same small circle of boys—"a summer baseball team, a winter basketball team, and an invincible autumn football team"—populates all of Jack's writing about Lowell. The boys do ordinary things, play ball, pull pranks, swim in the raw, and talk to each other in a code language designed to confuse their elders while cementing their alliance. But in all of his books and stories about boyhood Jack makes a clear distinction between himself and the others. He looks down on those who found their heroes in the pages of Alexandre Dumas instead of in Maxwell Grant's chronicles of The Shadow. It is Jacky alone who can see and speak with Doctor Sax. There is a suggestion that the other boys do not realize what evil lurks in the hearts of men, but that Jacky does. He gently indicts his friends for the crime of insufficient imagination. As it turned out Jack was the only one of the circle to leave Lowell to seek his fortune.

George J. Apostolos was Jack's closest boyhood friend. In the books, as in life, he is "G.J.," sharp and aggressive. There is a well-thumbed copy of *On the Road* on the shelf behind his desk at the insurance agency he owns in Lowell.

G.J. Apostolos:

Everything hurt the guy. Just a drizzly November day would zing him. I guess if you read his books, I guess somewhere you'd find the answer.

Jacky's mother wanted so very much for him. Jack had everything. His mother tried to get him to associate with "better" people.

"I can never be what she wants. I can't live with her. I'm disappointing her," he'd say. Jack always tried to please his mother. It seemed to eat away at him. He went off with the Beat Generation, but he always worried about his mother.

Roland Salvas stayed in Lowell, too. He is the Albert "Lousy" Lauzon of Jack's novels, a member of a teeming

French-Canadian family that Jacky Duluoz (Kerouac) encounters in crowded kitchen parties or accompanies on summer picnics by the river.

Roland Salvas:

I always thought Jack was going to get up there somehow. I mean, being a writer—*wanting* to be a writer— you don't become a writer in your own town. You have to go out and give what you can and learn what you can. But you don't do that around your own town or city. You get the education step by step. That's what he did.

He was a clean-cut kid—clean-cut and clean-shaved. He was a hard-nosed backfield man. Right halfback or left halfback, I don't remember which one. He liked football. He used to tell the quarterback, "Pete, let me take the ball next. I know I can outrun that guy." He was a speeder, a real speeder.

In the neighborhood there was all French. His mother spoke French. I don't think the father did much of it, but his mother was a true Frenchman. Jack's father was a big man and a chain smoker. A tremendous man, really big. He liked to joke with you. I can't say anything bad about that family at all.

I think Jack wanted to be something out of life rather than just normal. He did talk much about the Shadow. He liked that kind of stuff, you know: "Mwee-hee-hee-hee-hee!"

He really did like the Shadow.

G.J. Apostolos:

I remember one time he was the Silver Tin Can. If there was a window open, or a door, he'd throw a tin can through it with a note: "The Silver Tin Can Strikes Again!" He'd wear a cape and give his Doctor Sax laugh. "Mwee-hee-hee-hee-hee!"

Everybody thought it was the dirty Greek, me. Jack's mother just couldn't believe Jack would do anything like that. He'd be in his cape—thirteen years old—jumping over fences and running, always running.

I'll tell you something about Doctor Sax's castle.

We met an old man walking along Textile Bridge, and he was drunk and we took him home to this big old house, and he kept saying, "There's Chinamen under the floors." We put him on the cot and he rolled off the other side and hit his head. This house was off Riverside Street, down in Dracut.

Writing about that incident in *Maggie Cassidy* Jack recalled that G.J. was convinced that the old man had died of his head injury. The next day the three boys waited in suspense for the afternoon edition of the *Lowell Sun*. To their relief the old man's obituary was missing.

Joseph Henry "Scotty" Beaulieu, Scotty Boldieu of the novels, was nicknamed for "his thrift among five cent candy bars and eleven cent movies." Jack described him in *Dr. Sax* as "a very heroic-looking boy in the morning." He was a bit older than Jack and something of an idol, especially when it came to sports.

Scotty Beaulieu:

Jack was hard as a rock, a great athlete. When I tackled him, or tried to, once, when I grabbed his legs—man, I saw stars! He plowed right through me.

He was a funny guy. His family had a lot of problems and bad luck, but Jacky never mentioned them. Of course, we all had problems, but us boys never talked about them, so maybe it wasn't so unusual.

Me and Jack and G.J. were like the Three Musketeers. We were always together and never had no fights. Jacky's parents didn't like us hanging around him, though, like we wasn't good enough for him. But his mother was a very nice woman. His father was nice, too, but never had much to do with us.

In the spring of 1936, the year that Jack turned fourteen, floods swept New England. Safe on the Pawtucketville hill, Jack and his family watched the Merrimack rise out of its banks, covering the sandbars that were the boys' usual playground and, finally, the Textile Bridge itself, isolating Little Canada from downtown Lowell. One of the old locks protected the business section from thorough destruction, but as it was Leo's shop was filled with water to a depth of six feet. The flood drowned his prospects as an independent businessman. From that point on he made his living working for whatever printer would hire him, picking up extra money by tending the bowling concession at the Social Club.

At first, Jack, G.J., and the others regarded the flood as a wonderful adventure. For a moment Lowell was important. Photographers came up from Boston to record the devastation. Interesting flotsam from New Hampshire rushed downstream, and Jack watched it drifting out of sight, out of Lowell. Remembering the occasion twenty years later as he wrote *Doctor Sax,* Jack more or less ignores the effect of the flood on his family's fortunes, recording instead his fear that the high water would prevent his weekly walk downtown to the public library for a fresh armload of books.

But by Saturday morning the water had receded. Jack and Nin went downtown as usual, passing the movie house where they had gone together before either could read properly, "—now we are grown up, we read books." Kerouac's record of this day and night is one of his most brilliant acts of remembrance. The events no doubt were selected from many weeks or months of real experience, but it was this particular Saturday that Jack chose to regard as marking the end of his boyhood and the beginning of his young manhood. (This threshhold had nothing to do with sexual discovery. That was another occasion, the night when he idly invented masturbation while pondering the death of a pet dog.) It was, instead, a subtle and profound change in the way that he looked at the world.

Jacky spends the day alone, climbing "Snake Hill" and exploring the grounds of the empty mansion that shelters the forces of evil. After dinner, standing on the sandbank, he is joined by Doctor Sax, who speaks to the boy for the first time: "'The Flood,' said Doctor Sax, 'has brought matters to a head.'" Sheltered by Sax's cloak of invisibility, Jacky joins the phantom on a tour of the neighborhood, unobserved by his friends and family. Gabrielle hurries home from a late shopping trip for cold cuts; Leo is planning a party. Nin catches up with her mother, to tell her about a dress she has seen downtown. A dance band on the radio plays a Gershwin tune. A shed-door slams. A woman laughs raucously at a dirty joke.

The boy and the phantom vault fences to spy on neighbors: Scotty pensively eating a candy bar, G.J. surveying the dusk, Gene Plouffe in bed with the covers up to his chin, reading a Street and Smith pulp western. An older boy strides confidently home. Jacky knows, without knowing how, that the story that the youth will tell his parents about working late will be a lie, that he is returning from an episode of furtive love-making with his girl in a barn in the Dracut woods. Lowell goes about its night business, but Jacky is no real part of it. With his Shadow by his side he is, this night for the first time, quite self-consciously the bystanding recorder. He watches. He listens. He files it all away. Sax's running commentary provides an infuriatingly muddled obbligato, and then, this sentence, pronounced upon Gene Plouffe, abed with his thriller:

> Bye and bye you'll rise to the sun and propel your mean bones hard and sure to huge labors, and great steaming dinners, and spit your pits out, aching cocklove nights in cobweb moons, the

LOWELL LOWLANDS in the Rosemont section saw 2000 flee their homes as the Merrimack rose about their houses. Boston *Globe* photo by Callahan.

mist of tired dust at evening, the corn, the silk, the moon, the rail—that is known as Maturity—but you'll never be as happy as you are now in your quiltish, innocent book-devouring boyhood immortal night.

Rainclouds obscure the moon, and presently Sax and the boy are at the castle, where the satanic world-snake stirs from its sleep to stage a direct assault. During the titanic struggle that follows, an amalgam of all the scenes in all the B-movies in which the peasantry destroy the mad scholar's laboratory, Sax whips off his cape and hat, revealing himself to the terrified boy as a bit-player wholly inadequate to deal with the forces he has helped to unleash. It doesn't matter. As the storm gathers the snake is subdued in a manner Kerouac borrows from the mythology of Mexico, where he was living when *Doctor Sax* was written, and it is for Sax himself to deliver the moral: "I'll be damned.... The Universe disposes of its own evil."

To regard the mature writer's vision of this watershed Saturday is not to conclude that its lessons were clear or even available to the fourteen-year-old Jacky, but it does seem that behind many of Kerouac's later choices and actions, some of which could be regarded as impulsive and destructive, there lay an essential reliance on the universe as a self-regulating mechanism. The wealthy Presbyterians up Varnum Road could comfort themselves with their doctrine of predestination, but that doctrine wasn't available to the Kerouacs of St. Jean-Baptiste parish. Much later the Buddhist notion of *dharma* would supply Kerouac with a name for this attitude.

Jacky was Jack now, that season and each season for three more years, a little sturdier, a little more certain of his skill as an athlete. He was good at all sports, but football was his game. For all his life Kerouac regarded October as the kindest month—"Everybody goes home in October," he wrote—and in those years of the late 1930's, each October promised four or five Saturdays when the boys and a gallery of their fathers and brothers would troop up Snake Hill to the Dracut Tigers' Field, conducting their games in at least three languages, sometimes four. Some of the boys were taller, but Jack was heavily muscled—and quick. His thick legs belied the speed and the startling changes of direction that he could command whenever he got the ball.

14

There were girls now, too, but not a great many. Some of them read Jack's shyness as conceit. He was quick in class, he was a skilled athlete, and he was becoming a classically handsome young man. The boy–girl gap was probably no wider then than now, but Jack appears to have had less ease in bridging it than his friends. The resulting distances and silences were enough to ratify his image as stuck on himself.

However, one girl, Mary Carney, captured his heart. She was a year ahead of Jack in school, a girl from the Irish neighborhood across the river. Her little brother was enlisted as a matchmaker, and Jack became a familiar fixture on the Carneys' front porch. Mary's father was a railroad man, an occupation that fascinated Jack, and it may be that the Carneys supplied a warmth and closeness that Jack found difficult to demand or accept from Leo and Gabrielle. Jack and Mary had long, soul-baring talks. G.J., Scotty, and Roland had listened to Jack talk about his complicated perceptions and ambitions, but Mary Carney appeared to understand them. Like those three, Mary Carney never left Lowell, either.

Mary Carney:

There was something deep between Jack and me, something nobody else understood or knew about. After that book *Maggie Cassidy* came out I had a lot of trouble. People calling me and the neighbors talking. It was awful.

Jack was so sweet. He was a sweet, good kid, and the people in Lowell didn't understand him. They never did. Nobody ever reads here. They wouldn't even put up a plaque for him.

Jack was so sensitive. All he wanted was a house and a job on the railroad. Jack used to tell me everything.

Nobody would understand anyway, so I'm not going to talk any more. I made up my mind a long time ago I wouldn't, so I'm going to stick to it. Nobody listens anyway.

G.J. Apostolos:

There was no connection between Maggie Cassidy and Mary Carney. Jack invented her. I remember Jack came back after the war and made me call up Mary Carney.

He wanted to see her. She said all right, for ten minutes, so we went over there: me, Jack, and a couple of my buddies.

Mary was sitting on the porch Jack talks about in *Maggie Cassidy*. She was surrounded by her fiancé, her mother, and her father.

Jack and she just stared at each other. He didn't say anything. He was frozen. There wasn't anything between them. It was all in Jack's mind, his imagination. There really wasn't anything between them in the first place.

After Leo lost his shop in the flood the Kerouacs moved to the top floor of a tenement over a lunch counter on Moody Street. One night as Jack sat in his room reading, he heard a stranger's voice calling his name from the street. The caller was Sammy Sampas, a boy a year older than Jack who lived on the other side of town. He had heard of Jack by reputation—not as a halfback, but as a voracious reader, and as a writer. Like Jack, Sammy was studying serious authors according to his own syllabus, but his tastes were a little loftier and a good deal surer. Perhaps most important of all, Sammy was certain that he would be able to make his living as a writer, and his personal vision of success included Broadway, where he hoped to be a producer as well as a playwright.

Roland Salvas:

That guy Sammy was a smart person. I met him through Jack and George. Their vocabulary was much higher than mine, so when they'd talk, the three of them, there's lots of times when I'd shake my head. Even Scotty and I couldn't understand. But it didn't matter, you know. It didn't matter.

When you talk of Sampas, you're talking of Sampas, Jack, and George, those three. They were more serious-minded.

By the fall of 1938, the first semester of Jack's senior year at Lowell High School, Gabrielle had returned to her old trade as a skiver, or cutter, in a shoe factory. Aside from his duties at the social club Leo had a more or less regular income from his job in a printshop owned by an Irish family. Roland Salvas had

16

dropped out of school to work in the Boston Navy Yard. George Apostolos had enrolled in the Civilian Conservation Corps and was in Colorado, helping to build Estes National Park.

"I wanted to go to college and somehow knew my father would never be able to earn the tuition," Jack wrote. Football offered a way. Despite his swiftness and his solidity Jack was smaller than his compatriots on the Lowell varsity, boys who had played against one another in the sandlot games in Dracut Woods. The coach had held Jack on the bench for most of the 1937 season, and Jack's jealousy of the starters was intense. But in the fall of 1938 he made a series of brilliant, last-quarter appearances that caught the attention of the Boston sportswriters—and of scouts for Boston College, Duke, and Columbia.

In one game Jack ignored the coach's direct order, and attempted his flashy, one-handed carry. He fumbled, and his conscience was stung. But in the game that really counted, the Thanksgiving Day meeting with Lawrence, Jack scored the only touchdown. From that moment his college scholarship was secure. The question was, which offer to accept?

Leo's bosses at the printshop were enlisted by the recruiters from Boston College to help them get Kerouac for their team. Jack resisted. He didn't want to be taught by Jesuits, and Boston wasn't far enough away. He was in love with the New York City of the movies, and the visions of high life there that he had shared with Sammy Sampas. Gabrielle sided with Jack, sketching a fantasy of the whole family following him to New York. Jack chose Columbia. Soon afterward Leo was fired from the printshop, and ever after, Jack believed he had been responsible for Leo's misfortune by refusing to go to Boston College.

The Lowell High School yearbook for 1939 shows Jack in his track uniform: dark, clear eyes; a tangle of black hair; powerful legs that permitted him to elude all but the craftiest defensive players. That spring he began to cut classes one day a week, spending the morning in the library looking at chess books and whatever else caught his attention: "Goethe, Hugo, of all things the *Maxims* of William Penn, just reading to show off to myself that I was reading." Afternoons he went to the Rialto to "study the old 1930's movies in detail." To Jack the

Manhattan that Don Ameche and Alice Faye toured by limousine was a real place with real penthouses, and he would visit them soon.

G.J. Apostolos:

In '38, '39 the letters he wrote me were books. I was in the CCC's in Estes Park, Colorado, where we were digging ditches, painting barracks. But it was The West to Jack. To him, I was breaking stallions. I had to walk bowlegged when I got off the train, to go along with him.

I remember one day I made the mistake of going down to see *Wuthering Heights* with Laurence Olivier. I had a beer, and thought I was the hero. We went to Canolie Lake and went on the dodge-ems. So I went over to this girl and Jack said, "There's Heathcliff!" I whispered in her ear, "Why can't there be the scent of heather in your hair?"

I got panicked. A cop came over and asked me what I'd said, and I told him. I did it for Jack. He flipped over it. He was so impressionable when he was young. He never forgot his buddies.

Despite his starring runs on the football field and his excellent grades the Columbia recruiters decided that Jack needed a year of prep school before he would be ready for the Ivy League, athletically or academically. His scholarship was arranged to begin with a year at Horace Mann School for Boys, where trainers would introduce him to the theories and methods of Columbia's famous coach, Lou Little, while the teachers, most of them Ph.D.'s, prepared him for Columbia's tough version of a liberal arts program. Horace Mann is at 246th Street on Van Cortlandt Park, the northernmost reaches of New York City. Jack was to live with Gabrielle's stepmother, her new husband, and their family, in Brooklyn. It was two hours each way by subway, a journey that would sweep Jack beneath the Manhattan he had dreamed about.

G.J. Apostolos:

When he went to Horace Mann Jack's mother told me, "Now Jack's going to meet the people he should have grown up with. Jack's much better off."

18

2 THE CITY

The key to the whole thing was boredom.

—HAL CHASE

< Hal Chase, Jack Kerouac, Allen Ginsberg, William Burroughs —Columbia University, ca. 1944. Photo courtesy of Allen Ginsberg.

Horace Mann School for Boys is a satellite of Columbia University Teachers College and in 1939, like Columbia itself, was overseen by the redoubtable Nicholas Murray Butler, friend of Presidents (Harding), of world figures (Mussolini), and president of the university from 1889 until his replacement in 1946 by Dwight Eisenhower. Had he lived to deliver the advice, it is likely that Butler would have counseled Eisenhower to remain at Columbia instead of quitting to seek a lesser post. For all his long reign Butler strove to see that his school instilled the old values. Columbia began by grounding a man in the classics, exposed him to the whole range of the humanities through large lecture courses, and, finally, afforded him a chance at individual growth through small seminars. Many of the very best teachers were democratically available to graduate student and undergraduate alike.

Most of Jack's classmates in Lowell ended their educations with a high school diploma, if that. Those who did go further were not likely to progress beyond Textile Institute. Horace Mann School, named for the great fighter for free, public education, prepared young men for a costly, private education. Run along the lines of its more arcadian counterparts, its methods were formal and severe, its standards exceeding anything Jack had encountered at Lowell High. Because the Horace Mann diploma provided a foot in the door to many Ivy schools, the rolls were crowded with wealthy young day students from Manhattan, including the heirs to freshly-made Irish and Jewish fortunes. Some of the boys arrived each morning by limousine, carrying lunches packed by the family cook. Jack boarded the subway in Brooklyn each morning at six, carrying a paper bag with a peanut butter sandwich prepared by Gabrielle's stepmother. Gabrielle—if she knew—probably was pleased that the day at Horace Mann began with mandatory chapel services. But Jack, who calculated the student body as "96 percent Jewish rich kids," noted and shared their discomfort at being made to sing such Protestant anthems as "Onward, Christian Soldiers!" and "Lord Jeffrey Amherst."

That fall Jack's history classroom overlooked Van Cortlandt Park, and the outlines of the bare trees reminded him of the Dracut woods. But if Jack was homesick, he had to look no further than Brooklyn, where Gabrielle's stepmother and her new husband kept a household identical in every respect to that of a French-Canadian family in Lowell or Nashua. Each night Aunt Ma and Uncle Nick sat in the parlor listening to such radio programs as Father Coughlin's controversial sermons, which were not sermons at all, but homegrown fascism cloaked in religion. Upstairs in his room Jack struggled to keep up with the course-load of a Horace Mann senior, despite the fact that he was of college age.

Football was a disappointment, too. In Lowell Jack had been—finally—a star. At Horace Mann he was one among many boys from unheard-of high schools who were being primed by Lou Little's coaching disciples while their minds were being honed to survive Columbia. New York columnists attacked Little that season for using Horace Mann in this way, but the controversy soon was forgotten because, by design, Lou Little made copy. His real name was Luigi Piccolo. He was a Bostonian, a Catholic, who had begun his rise to fame at Georgetown University in Washington, D.C. Little was one of the first technician-coaches, full of ideas about psychology and deception. Jack's skills were perfect for Little's style of football, and that season Kerouac's reverse ("Reverse is too slow a word, I *jack off* to the left") won a game. But he still didn't make the starting line-up. Surely once he reached Columbia itself, Lou Little would recognize Jack's talents.

That first fall in New York the city provided an expansive campus. Jack played hookey the second day of classes and took the subway only as far as Times Square. He spent the rest of the day seeing movies and watching the crowds and the changing light in the heart of the city he had dreamed about. When he chose his friends among his Horace Mann classmates he chose boys who could serve as tutors and guides to all of the city's secrets and delights. Most Saturday nights Jack's bed at Aunt Ma's house in Brooklyn was empty. Jack was staying over with a friend on Park Avenue or Riverside Drive—one of "the people he should have grown up with." Kerouac met the young William F. Buckley, Jr. during a reconnaisance of the Columbia campus, and in *Vanity of Duluoz* Jack wrote of one wealthy young friend he fictionalized as "Ray Olmsted." They met at lunch one day when "Ray" shared his chicken sandwich with Jack.

Ray is slight and bookish, Jack muscular and outgoing. When Jack goes to the Olmsteds' one night for dinner he charms Ray's mother with his perfect manners, and Ray's father with stories of his athletic exploits. He is asked to come again. (Ten years later, in one of his false starts to *On the Road*, the character representing Kerouac would turn his back on just such a wealthy home to begin his long journey.) In short order Jack became accustomed to wealthy friends and surroundings and uncomfortable around the other jocks, who razzed him for spending his time with Jews and "grinds," helping them with their term papers.

During his high school years in Lowell Jack had been interested in the big band shows sent by radio from the ballrooms of the great New York hotels. At Horace Mann he met Seymour Wyse, who shared that interest and knew the city's music scene first-hand. Wyse introduced Jack'to a recent Horace Mann graduate, George Avakian, who had begun his career as a producer and musicologist by running a Greenwich Village jazz club called Nick's. In an interview for the school paper Jack treated Avakian as the scholarly authority in the field that he was to become. Kerouac wrote a detailed analysis of the way the Count Basie band functioned, and he sought out an interview with Glenn Miller, who surprised him by cursing as would an ordinary man. These were dance bands, working from written arrangements, but their choirs contained individual voices whose solo choruses forecast a new jazz, which would be a form of personal expressiveness. In 1940 Jack wrote in the *Horace Mann Record* that Lester Young was likely to popularize the neglected tenor sax as a solo instrument. This is exactly what happened. Jack understood the degree of

23

emotion that the instrument was capable of conveying, a skill that he envied.

The music pieces Jack wrote that year at Horace Mann were workmanlike reporting and criticism. The two short stories he published were clumsy and mannered. "The Brothers" is narrated by a young detective, Watson to the Holmes of Henry Browne, who is "lean and angular, with the generous features of a Saxon." Vacationing in Browne's hometown, the pair drop by a general store, where vivid clues to a planned fratricide are dropped into their laps. Browne thwarts the criminal, and the narrator chides himself for failing to note the pertinent facts: poison, gas tubing, an inheritance. "Une Veille de Noël" is a vignette set in a Greenwich Village tavern on Christmas Eve. The barkeep announces at the outset that his establishment is meant to represent the universe. As soon as the regular customers are sketched in, a bearded visitor, unmistakably Christ, pays a sobering call. Both stories owed more to the popular magazine fiction of the thirties than to the masters Sammy had recommended to Jack as apt models.

In June 1940 Jack was an eavesdropper at his own graduation. He could not afford the necessary white suit, but he was within earshot of the ceremony, lounging on the lawn behind the gym, chewing a blade of grass, and reading Whitman.

Jack returned to Lowell that summer under an obligation to make up the courses he had failed at Horace Mann: chemistry and French. (Gabrielle's patois and classroom French were separate tongues.) Instead he ran around with his buddies, who now called him by a new nickname, Zagg, after the village drunk who periodically threw up his hands and cried "Woo! Woo!" as he ambled the streets of Pawtucketville. One night Jack, George, and Sammy, inspired by beer, collared townspeople with the information that each was, truly and individually, God. The boys then staggered down to the sandbanks by the Merrimack and whooped at the news.

Jack saw little of Sammy that summer, and he never made up the missing credits, but it didn't matter. He was under Lou Little's protection. Jack was leaving Aunt Ma's in Brooklyn for dormitory life, and Leo accompanied him to New York, where they toured the final season of the New York World's Fair, a pageant of post-Depression marvels that the war was about to defer.

24

Like any other freshman Jack was assigned a two-man room in Hartley Hall, the oldest dormitory. He didn't like the cockroaches, or his roommate, and he used his pull as a scholarship athlete to get a single room in Livingston Hall, the slightly more elegant building where most of the graduate students lived.

Gabrielle had saved up to get Jack a collegiate sports jacket, and he bought himself a pipe. He puffed it as he did his homework, classical music playing on WQXR in the background. Now he was a college man. But there were disappointments. Fresh from his lazy summer Jack was faced with a daunting load of assigned reading, daily football drill, and the job that paid for his board—washing dishes in the student cafeteria.

Scotty Beaulieu:

In September 1940 G.J. and I went to visit Zagg in New York City. He showed us around Columbia University, the Lion's Den in the basement, his room. We went to Madison Square Garden and Zagg said, "Let's go up to Glenn Miller's office." We were amazed. "Sure," said Jacky. "Why not?" So we went up and found Miller's offices deserted. Such a famous guy, and not a soul in his office.

Zagg fixed me up with a girl named Lucille in the New American Hotel. This was the first time I'd ever been to a whorehouse. I was the last of the three to have her, all dressed up in my green suit and tie. Jack called me "Kid Faro" because of my green suit and hat, green tie and green pipe—and gold tooth. Lucille was dressed only in a bathrobe. When we went into the room she said, "Are you from Oklahoma, too?" I wondered what the hell those crazy guys had told her, but then she took off her bathrobe and I forgot about the Oklahoma bit. You never saw anybody get out of his clothes so quick.

We also had a seven-course meal somewhere fancy. When the chickens came they had a string tied around them, and Jack picked up the butter knife and was trying to cut the string with it. What did we know about such things? And so the waiter tapped Jacky on the shoulder and said, "Pardon me, sir, but you're using the butter knife."

"That's okay, Mac," Jacky says. "I've got a strong arm."

And he sure did, too.

When the freshman coach made out his roster that fall, Jack wasn't in the starting line-up. But he did see action, and Lou Little was on hand to see him play in the game against St. Benedict's. Little cheered as Jack made a ninety-yard kickoff return. A few plays later two men tackled Kerouac as he caught a punt. He twisted to free himself, and heard a sharp crack. The trainer dismissed it as a simple sprain, and every afternoon that week Jack limped through a full practice, hating Little and the others who accused him of malingering. Finally he was sent to the infirmary, where an x-ray revealed the hairline break. His leg was placed in a cast.

Jack used the injury to buy leisure. Instead of washing dishes he went each evening to the Lion's Den and ordered a steak and a sundae, which he charged to the athletic department. Instead of making practice he plunged into the novels of Thomas Wolfe, who, he wrote, "woke me up to America as a Poem instead of America as a place to struggle around and sweat in."

The men of Phi Gamma Delta asked Jack to join their fraternity, which he did, but he refused to wear the pledge beanie. In the elections that spring Jack was chosen vice-president of the sophomore class, an honor that came as a surprise to him. When he went home to Lowell for the summer of 1941 he was under orders to make up his failing grade in freshman chemistry, but the coaching staff secured permission for him simply to take the course again.

It was the summer before America entered the war, and Jack and his friends spent it drinking beer, camping in the Green Mountains, and dreaming about distant adventures such as becoming merchant seamen. Jack and Sammy hitchhiked to Boston, where Sampas declaimed improvised Leninist speeches from the soapbox in the Common. Leo had found a steady printshop job in New Haven, and now Jack's parents planned to leave Lowell, too.

26

One night that August, while Mémère talked in the kitchen with her niece Blanche, Jack sat on the back stoop, looking up at the sky. He enjoyed—or suffered—one of those flashes of cosmic consciousness that literary critics call an epiphany and religious types regard as enlightenment. After watching the stars for so long that he imagined them watching him back, Jack staggered into the parlor, where he fell into Leo's easy chair and daydreamed a future of athletic, literary, and financial triumph. Then he returned for another look at the stars, which "just stared at me blankly. In other words, I suddenly realized that all my ambitions, no matter how they came out ... wouldn't matter anyway in the intervening space between human breathings and the 'sigh of the happy stars.' ... It just didn't matter what I did, anytime, anywhere, with anyone."

Recalling this experience Jack linked it in his mind with the war, which already had begun in Europe and Asia. Pearl Harbor was still four months away.

Late that summer he helped Leo and Gabrielle move to their rented house on Long Island Sound, near New Haven. Somewhere between Lowell and New Haven the Kerouacs lost Ti Gris, "Little Gray," the latest in the line of pet cats that reached back to Gerard's. The death of a cat always struck Jack as a particularly bad omen.

America's entry into the war was so plainly on the horizon that September that Lou Little's quarterback enlisted in the Marines. But enough senior men remained to fill out the backfield, and Jack, who was only a sophomore, resented the idea of another season on the bench. His relationship with Lou Little degenerated into open and mutual hostility. The coach finally accused Jack of being unable to run the KF-79, the fake play that had secured Little's reputation in the Rose Bowl five seasons before. The KF-79, which survived for years with minor variations as the TNT, the FDR, or the LS/MFT, involved a faked quarterback feed to the right halfback, who in turn faked a short pass over the opposing tackle. Of course, the quarterback retained the ball throughout this rigamarole, which, by the fall of 1941, was no surprise at all but a ritual anticipated by everyone in the stadium, especially Columbia's opponent. The legend of Lou Little was in fact merely that: a legend. The war would explain away another decade of mostly losing seasons, and by the time of Little's forced retirement in the fifties, Ivy League football would be a different sort of sport. Jack disliked the fact that Little had disowned his Italian ancestry, and he mocked the coach's reputation as a sharp dresser. The rumor around Columbia was that Little owned more than a hundred suits and sports jackets, but the official number, released by Little's own publicists, was approximately forty. Finally, to make his disenchantment complete, Jack believed that Columbia had reneged on a promise to help Leo find work in New York City. It is likely that one of Little's recruiters did make such a pledge in the process of bargaining for Kerouac, perhaps in response to Jack's story of Leo's bosses in Lowell who had fired the elder Kerouac when his son refused to enroll at Boston College.

The Saturday evening after Little embarrassed Jack in front of the other players by accusing him of being unable to run the KF-79 play, Kerouac packed his things and left Livingston Hall. When Little stopped him on his way out to ask where he was going—and Jack had made sure that he bumped into the coach—Kerouac told him to his Aunt Ma's place in Brooklyn. In Brooklyn, as he dumped his possessions, Jack told Uncle Nick that he was returning to campus. Instead he went to the Greyhound station and bought a ticket that would take him "into the American night."

It was a ticket to Washington, D.C., where he spent a single night in a flophouse before returning to New Haven and his family. Leo was bitterly disappointed that Jack had abandoned Columbia, deaf to Jack's argument that he could make a living as a writer. Jack took a job as a tire hemmer in a nearby plant, but he walked away at lunchtime the first day. Then a friend told him about a grease monkey job at a service station in Hartford. Jack took it.

In Hartford he rented a room and a portable typewriter, and, through October and November of 1941, he came home each night to write two or three stories for a collection he had entitled in his imagination *Atop an Underwood*. None has ever been published.

When Thanksgiving came Jack was expected to pump gas as usual. Sammy Sampas turned up at the rooming house, begging Jack to explain why he had abandoned Columbia. To

28

write, Jack told him, but the answer didn't satisfy Sammy. They ate a blue-plate Thanksgiving dinner in a diner, quarreled about which movie to see, and went to separate theaters, meeting afterwards in a bar.

A week or so later Leo wrote that he had secured a steady job in Lowell and was returning there with Gabrielle. On Sammy's advice Jack applied to the *Lowell Sun* for a sportswriting job and was accepted. The Kerouacs were reunited.

Jack's newspaper job required punctuality and a necktie, and it paid fifteen dollars a week. Jack soon discovered that he could finish his assignments by noon and spend the rest of the day sneaking pages of the novel he had begun. He called it *Vanity of Duluoz*, the same title he chose in 1967 for the last of his major novels to be published. By his own word the stories he had written on the rented Underwood mimicked Hemingway, Saroyan, and Wolfe. Now he was reading Dostoevski's *Notes from Underground*, and had begun *Ulysses*. In the novel he attempted in the fall of 1941 Jack was trying to deal with Lowell and its people as Joyce had written of Dublin. His subject was the everyday, not the adventures of an imaginary detective; and his fictional persona of Duluoz already was at work, although here he was called Bob, not Jack. Each night at nine when the library closed, Jack met Sammy Sampas to talk. It was to please Sammy, whose ambitions for him never had dimmed, that Jack was writing.

The first Sunday in December Jack went to see the new Orson Welles movie, *Citizen Kane*. When he stepped out of the theater he heard a newsboy hawking an extra edition announcing the Japanese attack on Pearl Harbor. For America the war began the next day. Jack already had applied for the V-12 program, under which the Navy utilized colleges to generate gentleman officers at an accelerated pace. Leo saw the Navy program as a way for Jack to return to Columbia. Jack and Sammy pledged to join the same service, whatever it might be, and to fight the war together.

Within a few weeks Jack chafed at his sportswriting job on the *Lowell Sun*. One morning his assignment was to interview the basketball coach at Textile Institute, but instead of walking the few blocks between his flat and the school, Jack sat at home pondering the reasons why he was going to leave the newspaper. Leo was enraged, telling Jack he was a ne'er-do-well who would be unable to support Gabrielle in her old age. Gabrielle sided with Jack, chastising Leo for an uncontrollable temper. Jack bolted for Washington, where G.J. was working on the Pentagon construction project and had written for Jack to join him.

Kerouac signed on as a sheet-metal man, a task for which he was unskilled. He spent his few days at the Pentagon site hiding out from the foreman, and then quit to work in a diner in the northwest section of the capital. There he met and moved in with a pretty brunette from Georgia, but the affair was brief, and within a month Jack caught a bus back to Lowell. Now, going off to war seemed to him exactly the right thing to do. Forgetting his pledge to Sammy, Jack hitchhiked to Boston with boyhood pal Jim O'Day and, in a single afternoon, enlisted in and was accepted by both the Marines and the Coast Guard.

Jim O'Day was satisfied to join the Marines and to return to Lowell to await the call to basic training, but Jack was more impatient. He stayed in Boston that night, drinking around Scollay Square, where he met a gang of merchant seamen. These men were technically civilians. Their seamen's cards exempted them from military service, although their supply runs to Murmansk and Liverpool were made in defiance of the German Navy. Jack's new friends explained the ins and outs of the hiring hall, where, the following morning, he claimed a scullion's job on the *S.S. Dorchester.*

Sammy was stricken when he learned what Jack had done. Kerouac advised him to get his own papers and sign up for the same ship, but Sammy wasn't as lucky as Jack had been. Jack tried to soothe Sammy's feelings by joking that he had seen the flowers of death in the eyes of his shipmates, as indeed he might have. On a later run, minus Kerouac, the Germans sank the *Dorchester,* an incident fixed in the popular imagination, and upon a wartime commemorative postage stamp, by the story of the four chaplains who gave their life jackets to young sailors and went down with the ship.

Aboard the *Dorchester* Jack kept up his writing. "Death hovers over my pencil. How do I feel? I feel nothing but dim acceptance." He was proud that his wages carried a hazardous-

30

duty bonus; the cargo included ammunition.

One morning as Jack fried two thousand strips of bacon for the crew's breakfast, he heard the booming sound of the *Dorchester* and her escorts laying depth charges against German submarines. As he describes the incident in *Vanity of Duluoz* it evokes a vision of his blond German counterpart drowning as he fries bacon for the crew of his U-boat. This was Kerouac's closest brush with action for the duration of the war. Reconsidering that morning near the end of his life, Kerouac has Duluoz pause to formulate a pacifist creed that owes more to simple reverence for life than to any conventional religious expression of the idea: "I dont see it, I dont get, I dont want it. Why couldnt our two ships just meet in a cove and exchange pleasantries and phony prisoners?"

During his summer at sea Jack climbed a mountain during the call at Greenland and spent a brief, drunken leave in England. He sketched his impressions into his journal each night, including his hatred for a black steward who pulled a knife on him one morning for sleeping past his duty call. Kerouac never threw away his carbon copy of the order docking his pay by two days for going AWOL in Nova Scotia.

When he got home in October 1942 there was a wire from Lou Little asking him to return to Columbia, which Jack did the following morning. A few days later Sammy came to New York to visit, and Jack felt only a twinge of guilt about abandoning his assignments to join him on long, conversational walks. Then Leo, once again without a steady job, materialized to confront Little personally with the recruiter's broken promise to help him find work. Jack stood outside the coach's office as the two men shouted at each other. Earlier that week the Army coach had visited a Columbia scrimmage and had asked Little to see Kerouac in action. Jack was certain that he would play in the Army game that Saturday. After the argument with the coach Leo suspected otherwise, and he told his son that if Little once more kept him on the bench, he would sympathize with Jack's decision to leave Columbia, as Jack had done a year before. As it turned out Jack did not play. Now he prepared to leave Columbia for good.

Jack informed his teammates of his decision to quit, and then retreated across the street from the campus to the house of a wealthy young Detroit woman named Edie Parker, who was living with relatives there while she studied art at Columbia with George Grosz. Jack had met Edie through Henri Cru, a Horace Mann friend who had also become a merchant seaman.

A few days later Jack was back in Lowell, working on a second attempt at a serious novel while he waited for the Navy to call him. He put Shostakovich's Fifth Symphony on the phonograph, and began hand-printing a manuscript he called *The Sea Is My Brother*. In March he took the notebook with him to boot camp in Newport.

Jack had failed in a last-minute effort to join the Army Air Force, and he resented the fact that, at twenty-one, he was three years older than the other recruits, whom he regarded as "war fodder." But most of all he resented the ordinary discipline demanded of a recruit: guard duty, the rules against smoking. "Who was this gentleman who had the nerve to tell me to wipe a speck off my foot? I am a descendant of very grand gentlemen who were in the Court of King Arthur and weren't told to be as clean as that. . . ." During close-order drill one morning Jack laid his rifle down and marched off in his own direction.

He wound up in the mental section of the Navy hospital in Bethesda, where psychiatrists pored over *The Sea Is My Brother* for clues to his state of mind. He was confined to a barracks which also held a manic boy from West Virginia and a man who had attempted suicide. Leo visited him there, muttering condemnation of the whole war. Sammy appeared in an Army uniform. Kerouac read the pain in Sammy's eyes as he took in the scene, and then he recalled for Sammy the time that Sampas had run alongside the train carrying Jack back to New York and Horace Mann, singing "I'll See You Again." This visit at the hospital was the last time the two men saw each other. Sammy was killed the next January at Anzio.

After two months Jack told a Navy psychiatrist in a final interview that he conceded cowardice, but perceived his malady as an inherent inability to accept discipline. He received an honorable discharge—"indifferent character"— and returned to New York, where Leo and Gabrielle had now moved. Leo was running a typesetting machine in a printshop off Canal Street, and Gabrielle was a skiver in a Brooklyn factory that made Army shoes. Their apartment was over a drugstore in Ozone Park, Queens.

Jack tracked Edie Parker to her family's summer place in New Jersey, and there he promised her that they would live together after he shipped out one more time. He signed aboard the *George Weems* as an ordinary seaman on a Liverpool run with a cargo of bombs. He worked on a new version of *The Sea Is My Brother*, and read Galsworthy in his bunk. Jack was unskilled as a deckhand, and in short order he found a target for his hatred of authority, the chief mate. "It was close to being a Billy Budd and Master-at-arms Claggart situation," he wrote.

When he returned in October 1943 he began spending the night at Edie's apartment, and when he took her home to meet his parents the four spent a happy night drinking together. Gabrielle was displeased at the notion that Jack and Edie lived together without benefit of clergy, but for the first time since he had left Lowell for Horace Mann, her son was happy.

Edie and her friend Joan Vollmer, who also liked Jack, shared an apartment near Columbia at 118th Street and Amsterdam Avenue. Edie and Joan did not keep a *salon*, but they were more than tourists in Bohemia, and it was in and around their rooms that, in the late autumn and early winter of 1943, Jack became part of a constellation of friendships with the men and women who would remain close to him for the rest of his life and who would provide the *dramatis personae* for much of his mature work.

Allen Ginsberg had enrolled in Columbia that year at the age of seventeen. He was the son of Louis Ginsberg, an academic poet who taught high school in Paterson, New Jersey, and night courses at Rutgers. Allen's mother, Naomi, had undergone hospitalization and shock treatment for paranoid schizophrenia. In her calm moments she was an ardent theoretical leftist. Allen was gawky, brilliant, and struggling with the intensity of his sexual desires, which happened to be homosexual. He had chosen Columbia—his scholastic record permitted a choice—because of his unrequited attraction for a high school friend who had enrolled there. Allen was uncomfortable with his sexual nature for years, but his consistent strategy was to resist identification with, or a plunge into, any of New York's insular homosexual subcultures.

Instead he cultivated a talent for friendship that cut across all barriers of station and circumstance, a predilection that led to his life among "junkies and geniuses," as he was later to recall it.

Allen Ginsberg:

New York in the forties. Well, the main scene, I think, where everybody met—that is to say, Burroughs, Kerouac, myself, Herbert Huncke, Neal Cassady, Joan Vollmer Adams Burroughs, Ed White, Hal Chase, Clellon Holmes, Ed Stringham of *The New Yorker* magazine, Alan Harrington, started around Christmas '43...

Lucien Carr moved into the seventh floor of the Union Theological Seminary on 120th Street, which during wartime was used as a dormitory for Columbia, which was filled with V-8 Navy students. I moved in across the hall in my second term at Columbia, on the seventh floor, and Lucien was at the end of the long, old wooden corridor. And I met him 'cause there was some music coming out of his door. It was very beautiful— Brahms Trio No. 1, which I'd never heard. So I knocked, and he opened the door, and we immediately were struck with each other and started talking.

And he took me down, for the first time, to Greenwich Village, and that Christmas I met Burroughs, who was a friend of Lucien's from St. Louis. Then, around the same time, Lucien met Edie Parker, who was Kerouac's girlfriend, Kerouac was still at sea. Edie, when Kerouac came back from shipping, I think, to Greenland, introduced Lucien to Kerouac at the West End cafeteria, or else at the apartment they had on 118th Street near Amsterdam Avenue. Then Lucien took me over to see Edie, maybe at the West End, or took me over to see Jack, or else gave me the address to go see him.

He described Kerouac in very romantic terms as a seaman who was a novelist or a poet, or writer, Jack Londonesque in style. I don't know what our reference point was then, actually. Soulful.

So I went up to visit Jack one morning when he was eating breakfast, eleven or twelve, and we got into some kind of funny conversation, I don't know what it was about any more. I remember being awed by him and amazed by him, because I'd never met a big jock who was sensitive and intelligent about poetry. Not that I knew anything about poetry, because my idea was A.E. Housman and Shakespeare, or something, I hadn't read any Eliot or Pound or any modern poetry, I didn't have any idea what I was doing, I was writing little rhymed lyrics. And he had just finished a book called *The Sea Is My Brother,* which was written, I guess, aboard the ocean liner. I don't know what we talked about, except prose versus poetry, or something—

That memory is mixed up with another memory, maybe of the same time. I was moving out of the room at the theological seminary. I think I'd moved my stuff out and was going back to pick up the dishes, and Jack walked me down through the Columbia campus, down along 120th Street, I guess, to Union Seminary. And we were talking about the phantomlike, ghostly nature of moving from place to place and saying farewell to old apartments and rooms. And so we walked up the seven flights, and I picked up whatever gear I hadda get, and then turned and bowed and saluted the door as I left, and then saluted the hallway and said, "Goodbye, beautiful steps. Goodbye, second step. Goodbye, third step," and so on, as we went down the seven flights. And so we got into a rapport over the sense of mortal transience, because he said, "Ah, I do that, too, when I say goodbye to a place."

... He was aware when he was saying goodbye to a place or when he was passing through the world, that it was a melancholy mortal tearful moment, constantly. Saying goodbye was like arriving or something. I don't know. It was a little poem idea that we had. The conversation was a discovery that we both felt the same sensitive, personal self-farewell toward the world, and the occasion was moving out of this college dormitory where I'd fallen in love. So I think that from that conversation we became friends...

Jack was introduced to Burroughs by Lucien, I think. We didn't know Burroughs. We just met him once, and I think that was Christmas, '43. David Kammerer, Burroughs' friend, was living at forty-four Morton. So Lucien took me down to visit David's flat, and Burroughs was there that Christmas. I remember Burroughs describing a fight that he'd seen on the floor of some dyke bar, in which this guy had bit somebody's ear. And

35

I think Bill had said, "Tis too starved an argument for my sword." It was the first time I ever heard Shakespeare quoted with intelligence. "In the words of the immortal bard, 'Tis too starved an argument for my sword.'" So I wondered who this intelligent aristocrat was. He hasn't changed at all. I mean, his demeanor is the same now as it was then.

Jack must have met him with Lucien at some point or another, or at the same time, but neither of us knew him. It wasn't until about a half year later, after Lucien left town, that Jack and I decided we ought to go look up Burroughs together and pay him a formal visit and examine his soul and find out who he was and what he was, because he was so interesting and intelligent and worldly wise that he seemed like some sort of international spiritual man of distinction to us. But we couldn't figure out what his secret mystery was, so we decided we'd go find out in his apartment on Riverside Drive.

So Jack and I made a formal visit to Bill, and I remember that he had copies of Yeats' *A Vision*, which Lucien had been carrying around. Shakespeare, Kafka: *The Castle* or *The Trial*, *The Castle*, I think; Korzybski's *Science and Sanity*, Spengler's *Decline of the West*, Blake, a copy of Hart Crane, which he gave me and I still have, Rimbaud, Cocteau's *Opium*. So those were the books he was reading, and I hadn't read any of those. And he loaned books to us...

So we had a long conversation with Burroughs, probably about Spengler and Korzybski. He was pointing out that words were not things that they represented, were not identical...Of course, Burroughs was interested from the viewpoint of general semantics, since he studied with Korzybski in Chicago. From his own point of view, also being involved in psychoanalysis, he was interested in..."original mind...preconceptual primordial mind."

Lucien and Jack remained the closest of friends until Kerouac's death, but many of the circumstances of that friendship were exempted from Kerouac's books, or heavily disguised in them, because of the strict terms of Carr's parole from his sentence for killing David Kammerer. Lucien had known Burroughs when both were boys in St. Louis, and later they were together when Lucien was a student at the University of Chicago and Burroughs was working in that city as an exterminator. Kammerer also came from a well-to-do St. Louis family. He was fourteen years older than Carr, whom he met as a teenager enrolled in a series of nature hikes David conducted while he was a physical education instructor at George Washington University.

Lucien Carr:

Bill Burroughs told me that if you're cursed with literacy, which is the greatest curse of mankind, you should read Spengler, Korzybski, and Pareto.

I can remember Bill in East St. Louis. I must have been about fourteen. I borrowed Bill's car. I said, "Bill, I gotta have your car, because I want to go over and see what all those whores are doing in East St. Louis." They had dirt roads over there, with big potholes, and then as you tried to ease the car through these things the whores were all over the car.

This is one of the reasons why I really will always love Burroughs—*always*.

It must have been an old 1936 Ford. In the middle of the fucking winter. And I got over to East St. Louis, and when we went back to the car, the car was cold, and I said, "Well, I'll heat up this car." I was gonna get it *warm* in there—until the fuckin' front of the car *exploded!* And the hood comes up to let the head out, right? I mean the car was fucked up, that was it for the car. Leave it where it was.

So we went and stayed in some fuckin' place and got back across the river in the morning, and then I began to think about this. And when I thought about it for a week I thought "Jesus, I oughta call that guy and tell him that I fucked up his car and it's over there across the river...."

So I call him, and I say, "Hey Bill, you know your car—"

And he says, "Yasss—"

I said, "Well, let's see. I had it across the river, and I think I blew the head off it, anyway it all came flying out the hood, and...it's over there and I don't think it's worth goin' over to pick up."

And he said, "All right."

And I said, "Well I thought I better tell you," and he

Jack Kerouac and Lucien Carr, Columbia University, 1944. Courtesy Allen Ginsberg

said, "Fine."—Click click. Hang up. And that was it.

But later the word got back to me that Burroughs really appreciated that I hadn't bothered to apologize. I really didn't *feel* any apology. I thought I oughta tell the guy where his car was—y'know. Ever since then Burroughs and I have been real friends.

Allen Ginsberg:

Kerouac and I decided that Burroughs was a big seeker of souls and searcher through cities. I think Kerouac said "the last of the Faustian men." He was taking the terminology from Spengler, and it was from Spengler that Kerouac got his idea of *fellaheen*—the word *fellaheen*.

We all got our whole conception, certainly different from my original, liberal, *New York Post* background, of some kind of spiritual crisis in the west and the possibility of Decline instead of infinite American Century Progress—The idea of an apocalyptic historical change.

Bill moved downtown to an apartment on, I think, Sixtieth Street and Ninth Avenue, above a bar called Riordan's, where he sat around in a vest, as he sat around for the last thirty years since, having tea or coffee and smoking and conversing in his room...

So Jack would come in from Long Island and visit him, and I would come down from Columbia and visit him, and I think around that time, he met Huncke and Bill Garver. And so we—living around Eighth Avenue, we all started exploring Eighth Avenue from Fifty-ninth down to Forty-second and the Times Square area, hanging around Bickford's under the Apollo Theater marquee on Forty-second, when it was still there—an all-night population of hustlers and junkies, and just sort of wandering... Street wanderers—intelligent, Melvillean street wanderers of the night.

Lucien Carr:

It must have been the summer of '44 when Jack and I were going to get a ship. It was very difficult to get your papers, unless you had a Union card. You couldn't get your Union card unless you had a ship. We finally got seamen's ratings, and we kept sitting in the Union hall waiting around—going to Paris, going to France, right? Two ordinary seamen, and then we never could get it.

So finally Jack decided he had to be an A.B., which means you are able to navigate the ship—which he got by just going in and talking to Phil Stack, who was a big wheel in the Union. He just went in and said "Yeah, I wanta be an A.B., I don't want to be an ordinary any more." So the guy said "Yeah well that's alright."

So he signed for a ship in Brooklyn—in Red Hook. We went toodling down to get on this ship, with all our gear, and as we walked out on the pier all the crew was leaving, just like ants—saying "Don't get on that ship any possible way, don't get on that ship, the mate is a son of a bitch."

We went bravely aboard this abandoned ship, man there wasn't *nobody* on it. So we picked our bunks, in the fo'c'sle, and started to look around, and found a food locker, and drank some milk and ate some raw meat. We were in good shape.

And somebody started yellin' down the gangway, "Who's on my ship! Who's on it?" So we came chuckling out and here was this son-of-a-bitch who must have been about seven feet tall—red-haired, bad-lookin' man. Bad-lookin' man. And he said, "What're you doing on here?"

We said, "We're signing on."

He said, "You're signing on as crew?"

And we said, "Yes, sir. Ordinary seaman. Ablebodied seaman—but we're not signing on until you take this ship up to Albany and bring her back, 'cause we've heard some bad things about you."

And he said, "If you're not signing on till we take this ship up to Albany, then you're gettin' *off!*"

He was pretty big, and pretty mean. So we picked up our stuff and left the ship.

Allen Ginsberg:

Then a friend of ours from Denver, Hal Chase, told us about Neal Cassady, a bright young poolhall cocksman who was sort of orphaned at thirteen and had gone through the Denver Public Library and read all through Kant and a lot of philosophy. And Chase, on a summer vacation, had told Neal that there were a bunch of poets in New York and that poetry was superior to philosophy, which immediately clicked in Neal's mind. It suddenly delivered him from bondage to rationalistic thinking and to a realization of creative humor, romance. That conversation apparently—according to Neal years later— was crucial. So he told Neal about the poets he met around Columbia, and he told us about the car-thief "Adonis of Denver" with his head full of philosophy. I think there's a line in Yeats about somebody who read all of Immanuel Kant while tilling the field—some Irish peasant or Premier.

So this was all between '44 and '46, these engagements and alliances. And then, around '45, Kerouac's girlfriend Edie Parker's roommate, Joan, who had a baby—newborn—* had an apartment on 115th Street between Morningside Drive and Amsterdam Avenue and was broke and needed people to share the apartment with her. So Hal Chase and myself moved in, and Jack would hang around, and so would Ed White and various other people'd visit occasionally.

Then Jack and I decided that Joan, who was very

---

*By her first husband.

intelligent, should meet Burroughs, it was a match we decided we'd arrange. They were older than us, slightly, and we thought they were kind of intellectual, sardonic equals, because they both had a laconic sense of humor and both were completely untyrannized by normative American stereotypes. They hadn't internalized any of that, as I had, certainly. They both seemed more sophisticated to us, so we thought we should bring these two sophistications together.

So we went to see Bill and he had to move out of his... apartment on Riverside Drive. There was an extra room at Joan's, and we were all living there, and so we invited him to come over, and apparently he and Joan hit it off and were very witty together and enjoyed each other's company.... Soon Bill had moved in there.

The apartment was a nice, big, old-fashioned apartment with big rooms—six big rooms. Living room facing south, so we got nice light in the daytime. It was me in the first room by the door, staying with Hal Chase, or Hal Chase in another room sometimes... Burroughs staying with Joan; a room of his own, but staying with Joan, relating to her, sleeping with her occasionally but very much sort of friends and lovers, actually. Huncke visiting and Kerouac visiting.

I was still taking classes at Columbia, which was right across the street, so I'd go from class to Burroughs' and Kerouac's conversation and back to class. So it was kind of funny, because the conversation in the house was a lot more elegant than the classroom conversation, a lot more curious and investigative and psychically moving.

Jack had nothing to do with Columbia, he was just living there because he had a girl friend on 118th Street, and he had gone there. He wasn't living at home, he was living with his girl. His home base was Ozone Park, and then he'd come for the weekend or two or three days, or just take the subway in and hang around with us and write. Or he'd use the Columbia library occasionally. He had friends at Columbia: myself, Hal Chase, Ed White.... And then Burroughs moved up there, so it just became our social center, between there and Times Square.

He'd been away at sea, so he already had had a break, years. He'd already had a change of life from

41

being a student at Columbia to being out on the ocean on his own.

He had written *The Sea Is My Brother*. That we brought to Raymond Weaver, a professor at Columbia who was Mark Van Doren's office-mate. Weaver had lived in Japan and had some experience in Zen and was a kind of Gnostic.... A very powerful man who taught a strange course called Communications 13—ahead of its time. He'd present *haikus* or Wyatt or Crazy Jane poems or *koans,* what's the sound of one hand clapping? as part of the class. And all the football players and all the sensitives took his class for some reason or other, 'cause it was an easy class. He didn't fail anybody.

But at the same time it was very tough to be in, because it was like being with a Zen master: pitiless, unremitting intelligence, accepting no dumb stupidity answers for the sound of one hand clapping.

I think he loved the football players. That's why he liked to have them in the class. He was a good teacher for them, 'cause he related to them really directly, inside their skin. So he had a lot of special students, like John Tagliabue, who's a poet around now, and Ted Hoffman, who teaches drama. There was a whole group of students that really dug him. But as an academic man his real glory was that he had written the first biography of Melville, and he personally discovered *Billy Budd* and other manuscripts in a trunk in an attic in New York City. So he really was an historically important scholar.

The Sea Is My Brother was just a lot of reverie prose about the sea is my brother. Some description of the ocean in Greenland. Either that, or another sort of symbolic novel that Kerouac wrote, the title of which I have forgotten, which was modeled on Gide's *Lafcadio's Adventures,* or some disguised version of Rimbaud Lucien Carr...Some symbolic novel, a completely obscure symbolic novel, very brief novella, which he brought to Weaver.

And Weaver read it very sympathetically and he gave Jack a little reading list—suggestions of what to read: The Egyptian *Book of the Dead*, the early Gnostics, Plotinus, I've forgotten what else. Maybe something Chinese or Taoist, but it was a Gnostic reading list, because it was a Gnostic novel that Kerouac gave him, and Weaver was the only Gnostic at Columbia. I mean someone who was acquainted with Chinese and Japanese Zen and Western Gnostic traditions, and Melville's Gnosticism, and the American Transcendentalist tradition. So Jack comes up to Weaver with a big book, and it's not full of obscure symbolism, but obviously beautiful prose of some kind or other, but not clarified, not focused or particularized in this world. Probably he was by then already doing *The Town and the City*, because in the mid-forties, his father was ill.

Leo had cancer of the stomach, a slow and painful death that entrapped Jack as a helpless bystander. Gabrielle continued to work as a skiver while her son pursued his new friendships and the notion of a writing career. He was living through the period from which he would eventually cull selectively as he composed his mature novels, but the novel that came to his mind now was of Lowell itself, and of his family, a story that would take them from a big, happy house on the banks of the Merrimack to disillusionment and dispersal in New York.

In the summer of 1944 there was a brief experiment with marriage, to Edie. The circumstances were bizarre.

David Kammerer had become obsessed with his friend Lucien. Kammerer did odd jobs to pay the rent on his Morton Street apartment and told his neighbors that he was a writer, but Carr was his main pursuit. Kammerer was a muscular six-footer. Lucien, at nineteen, was slight and blonde, with finely-featured good looks.

In the wee hours of Monday morning, August 16, 1944, Carr and Kammerer were walking along the Hudson in Riverside Park near Columbia, when David made what the newspaper reports described as "an indecent proposal." Carr defended himself with a Boy Scout knife, stabbing Kammerer twice in the chest. Then he weighted Kammerer's body with rocks and rolled it into the Hudson.

Lucien went to Burroughs with what he had done, and Bill advised him to tell his family, and to get a lawyer.

Instead Lucien went to Kerouac, who watched him drop the knife down a sewer grate and bury Kammerer's eyeglasses in the park, and then spent the rest of the day with him. They went to the movies (Zoltan Korda's *Four Feathers*) and to the Museum of Modern Art. Finally, late that afternoon, Lucien turned himself in. At first the police would not believe his story, but when Coast Guardsmen hauled Kammerer's body from the river, Carr was booked for murder.

The police went to Edie's apartment and arrested Jack as a material witness. Kerouac was held in lieu of $5,000 bail, and Leo was unable to pay for a bond to secure his son's release.

At his arraignment Jack told the judge, "I only watched him bury the glasses."

"You came very near becoming an accessory after the fact," the prosecutor said.

Kerouac pleaded with the judge that his bail was too high, and that he and Edie had secured their license and planned to be married that day.

"They'll take very good care of you in the new city prison," the judge told him. Jack was granted an hour's leave from jail to marry Edie. The police who escorted him from Bronx prison to the Municipal Building served as witnesses to the ceremony.

Burroughs, meanwhile, had left New York for his parents' home in St. Louis. His bond as a material witness was set at $2,500, which his parents posted. He returned in time for Lucien's arraignment on a charge of second-degree murder.

Carr was held without bail, but Edie posted Jack's, and the two went to her family in Grosse Pointe, where Jack once more found himself comfortable in the company of the well-to-do. To fulfill his duties as a husband Jack took a job in a ball-bearing plant, but by October the marriage was over, and he was back in New York.

The New York dailies treated Kammerer's death as an "honor slaying," and the Columbia *Spectator* editorialized, "We only know that there is a complexity to the background of the case that will defy ordinary police and legal investigations. The search for motive will dig deep into the more hidden areas of the intellectual world."

In mid-September Lucien entered a plea of guilty to a reduced charge of first-degree manslaughter, and three weeks later he was sentenced to an indefinite term in Elmira Reformatory. Throughout the hearings and pleadings Lucien carried with him his copy of *A Vision* by William Butler Yeats.

In their earnest talks about creating a literary movement of their own Allen and Lucien had spoken of calling it "The New Vision." Yeats' *Vision* is a quirky souvenir revealed when, on their honeymoon, his wife, Georgie, began producing texts in automatic writing. This resulted in a scheme of classifying individuals—and entire historical eras—into twenty-eight categories. It is likely that the Lucien Carr of 1944 would have felt comfortable as Category Seventeen, Daimonic Man, characterized by a fate of impersonal action.

Yeats himself saw similarities between this odd work, which he felt only partly responsible for, and the massive reconsideration of all human history which Spengler had attempted in *The Decline of the West*. In the Spengler study, the world's poor, the *fellaheen* (Arabic for "peasantry") inherit by default the remains of the world for which the great powers were at war in 1944.

Sitting in their rooms across the street from Columbia, where the mind of Nicholas Murray Butler still reigned supreme, Kerouac and his new friends looked beyond the end of the war and saw defeat for the classical culture for which their teachers had failed to enlist them. These young men's attitudes were different from those of their European counterparts, for whom there was no escaping the war. For these Americans, the war was a symptom of their pessimism, not its proximate cause. They were thinking about ancient and immutable cycles of change involving every soul on the planet, and much of what these strange young men read and discussed they read and discussed because of its utility to this general thesis. There is a thread that runs from Plotinus to Korzybski, of which shadows may be seen in Taoist texts. When Professor Weaver told Jack to read the Gnostics he was recommending a heretical gospel that tells of liberation from a doomed world created by a perverse and joking deity, the worship of whom foreclosed the prospect of glimpsing the world of light that lay beyond.

Leo was dying, his swollen stomach drained daily by catheter. Jack's brief attempt at marriage was a failure. Kerouac now began in earnest to compose a publishable novel. *The Town and the City* is a progression from scenes of an idealized New England boyhood to a family's death, as a family, in the big city. The sense of ultimate loss that informs it came from Jack's own life to that point. Weaver and the others made it possible for Jack to express his sense of loss.

Lucien Carr:

I was never really interested in writing. Jack was—Jack wasn't just *interested* in writing, I mean, whatever else Jack was doing, he had to write. It's like you gotta breathe, or shit, or eat. He was always writing. And no matter how much of his life was having a job—or riding around in a car, or traveling or this or that—he always found some time to scrawl in the little books. And he didn't have to do it right away, which was a great virtue that he had. He really had a memory like few men that you meet. Like he used to say—"That's why they call me Memory Babe," which is what they used to call him in Lowell.

He had a *fantastic* memory.

Allen Ginsberg:

...I knew Jack was a poet-genius, but I didn't realize that he had that enormous volume of patience and sit-down ability to create like a big, huge, huge, huge, long novel...I didn't realize he was that fluent and vulnerable...I was astounded when I read the whole thing, 'cause it seemed like a reproduction of life as it was. It was like a great romance and family story reaching back into the past and coming up to the post-war present. Like a regular novelist but more—with poetry in it. So I thought some great accomplishment had taken place, some great fusion of poetry and novel in America.

He'd read me little pieces here and there, but I had no idea of the extent of it, and the power. I was so exalted by the idea...I was so moved by it that I wrote the first poems that I published actually, in a book, the first poems in *Gates of Wrath,* in Solitude of New York City. It turned me on to being an artist, too...really take myself seriously as a poet...to accomplish something, I realized that it was within ourselves to write something immortal, I guess.

46

Lucien Carr:

I saw a lot of stuff that Jack had written—it must have been six or eight months after I met him. A lot of stuff he had written down on little pieces of paper. One was a novel about the sea, and one was *The Town and the City*. They were on little handwritten notebook pages. But what I saw then had to do with people that I didn't know.

Allen Ginsberg:

It seemed immortal, that book, in the sense of having recreated his whole childhood and his whole youthtime. A lot of our conversation around then was recollections of childhood, recollections of epiphanous moments of childhood—confessing out secrets of the childhood soul, in a way. Where we first realized that the universe was infinite—at what point, or at what time in our life, on what street corner or under what hedge we realized that the universe was infinite. Or what conceptions we had. Like it might be bounded at the other end by a big rubber ball or something. But then, beyond that, would have to be more space and rubber, so therefore... there was no wall around the universe. We were considering the infiniteness of space and when we were beginning to be awed by that.

And then when Neal came in, in '46, there was a lot of recollection of childhood adventure-fantasy. Kerouac was already conscious of that—that is, the Doctor Sax mythology, and I was having dreams about the Shrouded Stranger, which was my equivalent.

... When Burroughs was living on Sixtieth Street, over Riordan's Bar, Jack and Burroughs wrote a novel together called *And the Hippos Were Boiled in Their Tanks*, which was taken from a radio broadcast about a fire in a St. Louis zoo which ended, "And the hippos were boiled in their tanks." So that was the title of the novel, and they wrote alternate chapters...

Jack's talk was like [his poems in] *Mexico City Blues*, basically. Especially when a little drunk, then he'd go into like Celtic periods—Celtic periodic sentences... d'ja Bambi, d'ja Bambi, J amac, J amac—Kerouac. He used to

47

relate to the sort of silent, withdrawn people through their shyness and try to bring them out quite a bit by insulting them, or by characterizing them in Kerouacian novelistic caricature, and they'd see themselves placed in eternity and responding humorously.

...The amazing thing, really, about Jack was that he really rose above...his parents, his own shyness or timidity, and really was like a universal mind when writing, taking it all in...negative capability, Keats— ability to hold a number of simultaneously dissimilar and contradictory ideas in his mind at the same time without breaking down, or without exploding, or without having to choose, but representing them all in different dramatic form.

William Burroughs:

I met Jack up at Columbia. I was looking into going to sea and he told me something about getting papers and all that kind of thing. So we did talk about that, the first time I met him, not about writing. I wasn't at all interested in writing at the time.

Joan and I were older, and we had done some more reading than they had at the time. I didn't think anything special about it. I recommended a number of books. I think it was Spengler and I think, I'm not sure, Korzybski, Céline, various writers that they apparently had not contacted at the time.

I had a small allowance from my parents. I was working in various jobs, bartending, one thing and another. But I wasn't interested in writing. I didn't write anything until I was thirty-five, and that was about six years later, in Mexico. Jack had suggested that I write and I wasn't too interested for a long time. I would say he was much more instrumental in later writing. *Naked Lunch* was his title that he suggested. But that was later. That was after I had written *Junky*. Then I was more interested in writing, of course, having written a book that was published.

Jack was quite young at the time. He'd done an awful lot of writing. He'd written about a million words, he said. I don't know if he'd actually written that much. I had seen some of his writing, which, frankly, I didn't think was all that good at the time. In fact, it wasn't. I remember one short story that he had written at the time. I didn't think it was publishable. In fact it never was published.

Jack was gregarious. He liked to get out and drink and talk. Quite gregarious. He liked to see people. He was always with people.

Among Ginsberg's group of "junkies and geniuses" was a man who was a bit of both, Herbert Huncke. Sometimes he worked as a seaman, but he was street-wise and attractive enough to work as a gay hustler, and when circumstances required, he was a thief.

Herbert Huncke:

I met Bill Burroughs first. At the time that I met Burroughs, I had just returned from a trip aboard an old tanker as a seaman. I'd had someone take care of a small tenant apartment that I was living in down on Henry Street in New York City. This friend worked as a soda jerk at some drugstore up near Columbia, and during the course of the job Bill had gotten into the habit of stopping by in the afternoon and rapping with this fellow. His name was Bob.

One afternoon Bill asked Bob if he knew any place he could maybe unload some morphine Syrettes and a sawed-off shotgun. It might have been a machine gun. And apparently Bob said, "Oh, yes. A friend of mine is just getting back. . . ." And it happened that we were just getting back from our trip aboard this old tanker. Phil, who later became "Sailor" in *Naked Lunch* and hung around with Bill very closely for a long period of time, taught Bill a little about picking pockets in the subway, stuff of that sort. Things that Bill was interested in.

The night that we got back I hadn't even seen Bob, and when he did show up, he said, "Listen, there'll be a friend of mine stopping by in a little while who I want you to meet." And he hadn't any more than said that when there was a knock on the door. I opened the door and there stood Bill Burroughs. It was really quite a surprise. I was absolutely sure that we were going to be involved with federal agents in no time flat. Burroughs gave me this really almost traumatic impression. He was standing there in a Chesterfield overcoat, gray snap-brim hat cocked down over one eye, one hand in a glove and the other glove in his hand, standing there with a very dignified air.

He said, "Good evening."

Bob bounced out of the other room, and he said, "Oh, Bill, come on in. I want you to meet some friends of mine." Phil White, or Sailor, was there, myself, I believe the man that had originally owned the apartment, a man called Bozo, was there also. Phil White shot a couple of people. He killed an old man in a store—a fur store. He was quite a guy.

At any rate Bill came on in and I wasn't at all comfortable with him. I thought we were getting into trouble. The place had for a long period of time been something of a thieves' den, and there was literally an arsenal stashed around the premises, not to mention all the drug paraphernalia lying around. Nevertheless, Bob said, "Don't worry. He's all right. If I tell you he's all right, he's all right." So I said, "All right then. Let him come on in." And he did.

We sat around a kitchen table, and he and Phil began talking. Just how the conversation got around to morphine, I can't recall, but it did get around to the word morphine, and my boy Phil was all ears immediately. He really liked to shoot up junk, and he thought he'd run into a nice touch. As it turned out, he had.

I can't recall what took place that evening, except that Bill had his first shot of morphine. He produced two or three Syrettes and we cooked them up. Bill had a shot and said it was good. I had a fix, agreed with him.

On the strength of that he and Phil became very close partners. I didn't know where Bill was living at the time, but it later turned out that he was on Waverly Place, just down the block from Washington Square.

The next time I saw Burroughs was on a Sunday afternoon, and he was walking along the street with Jack Kerouac, and he introduced us. I was rather surprised to see him with this typical, clean-cut...well, I was and I wasn't. Because I classified them together. They sort of belonged. Kerouac looked like a typical, clean-cut young American college boy. He was as green, obviously, as the day is long. His eyes were flashing around. He was taking in everything and making little comments to Bill, mostly about just the scene in general. You would've thought he was about sixteen or seventeen. I thought of him as a typical Arrow-collar-ad type. They used to have the Arrow-collar ads with the clean-cut young man wearing a tie and collar.

Bill invited us up to his room. He'd gotten ahold of something. I can't recall what it was. It may have been

Herbert Huncke, 1976. Photo by Lawrence Lee.

peyote. He wanted to find out if it had any kick to it. Would I try it? So I thought to myself, "What have I got to lose?" So I took a skin shot, or a muscular shot, not very large.

No sensation at all. Whatever it was, it was a blank insofar as kicks or sensations.

Following that Bill immediately wanted to try it also. Bill had his own way of shooting up, which consisted of him making sure that his sleeve was rolled up as high as he could get it, that there was a bottle of rubbing alcohol nearby, and cotton. He'd dab the cotton into the alcohol and clean off a little spot on his arm, and he'd look at the point on the end of the dropper to make sure that the point was good and sharp. And he'd sort of feel around his arm until he'd located the spot he thought he wanted to use. And he'd inject the needle and squirt it in.

So, he agreed with me. He said he thought it might have given him a bit of a headache, but he agreed there was no worthwhile sensation.

He offered Jack a taste, and Jack was obviously curious, but he decided he'd pass it up, that there was really no reason for him to try it since neither of us had had any sensation. Why should he bother with it? Following that we planned to go out and get a cup of coffee. We were coming down the stairs and Bill and Jack were talking, and Joan was mentioned, who later became Joan Burroughs. She was mentioned as being a college widow. All of which didn't mean anything to me, except that her name was Joan, she had an apartment up near Columbia, Jack implied that she had a crush on Bill, Bill should take advantage of it.

When we got down onto the street we split up. They wanted to go and get coffee, and I had a habit at the time and I knew I was just wasting my time talking to them, because I had already sounded down for money. Bill said he was broke, and Jack didn't have any bread, so I went on about my business.

I went back up to the Forty-second Street area, the area that I knew the best. The area I'd be most apt to accomplish something for myself in the way of finance.

Prior to this particular time I had met Kinsey. Kinsey had sent a very good-looking little college girl over to a table where I was sitting in a cafeteria, and she explained

that there was someone that was very anxious to meet
me, and that he would give me some money if I would
meet him, and that I didn't have to do anything in the
way of personal contact with him. All he wanted to do
was to ask me questions about my sex life.

He had watched me, apparently. On the strength of
that he decided that maybe I had an interesting sex life.

At any rate, I was agreeable about meeting him—a
little hesitant at first because I didn't know just how
freaky he might be, and I had no desire to get involved
with some off-the-wall type that I couldn't stomach, or
something of that sort.

I was curious. Who was this guy who wanted to
know all about my sex life?

So I said, "Well, look. Give me a telephone number
where I can reach him." She did, and I called, and he
convinced me that it might be worth my time to see him.
We got together. I became somewhat of a friend, and he
explained what he was doing and what he wanted to do.
I must admit, it sounded well worth the effort and time.
He also offered to pay me so much for everybody I'd
solicit for him. I became a pimp for Kinsey.

Everybody was living behind four walls. What they
did sexually was just not discussed, no matter where
you'd go. Same things that are going on today and have
been going on since 'way back when.

Kinsey would look for me when he'd come down to
Forty-second Street, or after I'd introduced him to somebody. We got into the habit of going to a place called the
Angle Bar. It was designed in such a way that you could
go in from Eighth Avenue and there was a long bar on
the left. To the right there were a few tables. You'd go
beyond that and there would be an abrupt L-turn, and
you could go right out on Forty-third Street. It was a
good spot for anybody who wanted to snatch a few
bucks off the bar, or whatever.

At the time I am speaking of—back in the forties—
there were really people that lived right there and
worked that street like it was a place of business. A kid
would pick somebody up. He'd go out. He'd come back,
maybe get somebody else. It depended. That's among
the male prostitutes. There were female prostitutes as
well. There were burglars and thieves and muggers,

people of that nature. They let you hang around the bar if you had enough to buy yourself a drink. You could stand at the bar, and before long, somebody would approach you, or you maybe had a john for the night or for the evening.

It was a big place for these guys to meet later at night after they'd been out and maybe made a score. They'd fall in, and it would be playtime for them. They'd get together, go up to somebody's apartment. They'd bring their old ladies along. If they were potheads, there'd usually be pot around. Pot was becoming a big thing at that time. It'd been smoked a lot, but people were still a bit leery of it, even people that had been in contact with it on the streets and had used it. They were still under the impression that it was a dangerous drug.

At that time Forty-second Street was in some ways far worse and far more deadly than it is now.

Somehow or other all of us got into the habit of meeting at the Angle Bar. That would be Jack Kerouac, I met Allen Ginsberg there, first time, and Allen was really a starry-eyed kid then. You can't believe the sort of angelic expression of his face. He was really a child. Bill, of course, was the focal point. He was sort of the head man. They all followed his lead. Whatever he said was the word. Jack had married Edie Parker.

Lucien Carr:

Jack was just—ah, you know, he couldn't be led, and he was recalcitrant, and he was a pig, and he was this that and the other but he was everything in a man that Edie ever thought could exist.

Edie Parker was the best woman Jack ever got involved with, bar none. Jack didn't really have problems with *women,* women had problems with Jack. He didn't have bad luck with Edie. Jack didn't really want to be cornered into a situation where you're building something, because that isn't what he was building. That isn't what he was interested in *doing.* I mean, the idea never came across his mind. If someone said, "Let's get married

54

and move to the suburbs," he'd, like, disappear.

Edie's father was a car dealer, a Buick dealer, and had a big boat on Lake Michigan, and Jack could fool around on that. Money and wealth and all that *did* impress Jack. I'm sure that six months of dabbling, doodling around there amused him...but anything that tended to trap Kerouac, whether it was a woman, or a job, or a jail sentence—it was something he didn't want to get involved with.

Herbert Huncke:

Edie at that time was kind of a cute-looking chick. She had blonde hair, green eyes, and she wore her hair kind of fluffy. She had a nice body, carried herself well.

She would come down with the fellows, usually to sit around and listen to this bullshit. Joan got into the habit and sort of appeared on the scene. Joan, of course, was an entirely different type all the way around. I think Joan Burroughs was one of the most beautiful women I've known. I don't know how to describe her other than to say that she had an inner beauty that was so warm and so outgoing that it sort of swept one off one's feet. I've heard people refer to her as being slightly crazy. I felt a little differently about it, but there were some things that she couldn't've been straightened out on, probably. It would have been easier for her, but she had the conviction of her own belief, whatever it was. She admired Bill beyond words. I mean, there was no way to describe her adulation for Bill. She would have followed him anywhere, I guess. And did.

The place, as I say, became a hangout for our meeting and we hadn't been meeting there very long until Kinsey appeared on the scene. The young man that worked with Kinsey, Wardell Pomeroy, became part of the scene, too.

What they would do is go back to the university in Indiana, and they'd digest what they had acquired in the way of knowledge concerning the subjects they were interested in, and then accumulate a little more money. I don't know how it was funded. Then, the first thing you know, they'd be back in New York, and we'd all be together again. I liked Kinsey. He was a very great man in lots of ways. He had a marvelous sense of humor. He was very likeable, very warm and understanding. So he also became much of the scene.

All during this period Jack would be there occasionally. Once I was uptight for a place to sleep, and he invited me to ride out to Ozone Park, where he was living with his mother. On the way out we enjoyed ourselves immensely, talking and laughing about things. After we got there and the mother took one look at me, Jack's attitude changed almost immediately.

She dominated his life to a terrific extent. She didn't approve of Ginsberg. She didn't approve of anyone that I knew of. I couldn't even tell you what she looked like. She was so evasive and so absorbed in Jack that it was almost impossible to get any kind of a picture of her at all. She might as well not have been there, except for the effect she had on him.

So I made a long trip back to New York. He stayed on there at the house. He was very apologetic.

Lucien Carr:

Jack took me home to meet his family—this must have been the first time I met his mother and his father. So here he comes trooping in with his little friend Lucien, and God knows what he said about his friend Lucien to his parents, right?

So we sit around there, and everyone's sort of uncomfortable, in his mother and his father's living room...and his father said, "Let's go out and get a beer." We go dodging across the park into the nearest bar, where I come up with my quarter to get a beer.

"No," says Old Man Kerouac, "I can buy a millionaire's son a beer—"

How did he figure I was a millionaire? Jack had told him. Until the last time I saw Jack, it used to be one of our greatest jokes.

But my father was a sheepherder in Wyoming. When

the weather got too rough he worked as a bank guard down in Denver.

Herbert Huncke:

Christmas rolled around, and Edie and I found ourselves alone in the apartment. Bill had gone to St. Louis to see his family. Joan had gone out to Tuxedo Park. Edie and I had Christmas dinner, and I was feeling fairly congenial. We ended up in bed together, and absolutely nothing happened. That's the truth. About three o'clock in the morning the door opened, and who walks in but Jack.

It was perfectly all right with Jack. He made no fuss about it. He didn't say anything. I guess he thought it was pointless to make a remark of any kind. And he was right. There was nothing to say. Jack went on about his business. I went to sleep. What happened between the two of them later, I have no idea. But it was after that that I began seeing less and less of everybody there.

The only person that I did keep in fairly close touch with was Allen, when he'd come back from his trips. He was pretty undecided about what he wanted to do— whether he wanted to be a poet, historian, teacher, what-have-you. Some friends of his had loaned him an apartment on York Avenue, and he was living over there. I had been going through a bad stretch and really didn't know where he had moved to, and, purely by accident, I had run into him. He'd gotten a job with the Associated Press people for awhile, and I ran into him one night cutting through Rockefeller Center, and he gave me his address. One night when I was just too beat to continue doing anything—I was just about two steps this side of being dead—I knocked on his door, and he took me in, and I slept for two days and finally came out of the condition I was in.

During that time I met Lucien Carr for the first time. I knew he didn't want to be bothered with me. He'd just come out on parole, and I'm sure the parole officer had laid a heavy story on him, and one thing he had been told not to do, undoubtedly, was to associate with other felons or ex-criminals, so there was no congeniality between us at all. I didn't care much, but it worried him. Apparently he was going through some funny stages. I really didn't know the intimate details of their lives. They were so close, all of them. Allen was in love with the whole bunch, and Allen and Jack slept together occasionally.

I ended up being involved in a big scene and being sent to jail—prison. My first felony. Also, Allen was arrested at that particular time, and he was pretty upset by the whole thing. It terrified him, really. Jack would get nervous if anybody would light up a stick of pot.

Bill had rented a little pad down on Henry Street. I again had no place to stay, and I stayed there. I was arrested while I was staying there. I was using junk again. It was also in this building that Phil borrowed the Beretta and went on his little shooting spree. He very nearly had talked me into going out with him. He had gone out with this gun and didn't accomplish anything, shot one man because he didn't have enough money to satisfy him.

Phil used huge amounts of Tuinols and then would take a little fix on top of it, and he'd be completely out of his head, beyond control. He finally came up to my place and he told me about what had happened, and I said, "Well, you better get rid of that gun as fast as you can." He wanted to give it back to its owner and I didn't feel that it was fair to put the guy under that much pressure without forewarning.

I said, "Are you going to tell him?"

He said, "I'm not going to tell him a fucking thing."

I said, "Well, you better do something else with the gun, then."

So he did. Between the two of us we broke it up and we spread it from one end of Brooklyn to the other. I'd take a piece of it and pitch it over a fence in an empty lot, and another tiny piece of it—the trigger—down the sewer somewhere else, and that's how we got rid of it.

That particular place, on Henry Street, was a place that Jack used to visit occasionally. He liked it. The rear windows looked right up toward the Brooklyn Bridge. You could see the ramps coming over from Brooklyn. At night it was interesting to watch the lights from cars, and Jack would sit up there and gaze out the window, obviously plotting his stories. I frankly never thought that

58

he'd become a writer. He never spoke of it. He was very quiet about his writing.

When *The Town and the City* was published [in 1950]—it's very definitely in my mind, because I was sent away on my first felony the following day—Jack had come by to see Allen, and he was on his way over to visit John Clellon Holmes, and he invited Vicki Russell and Jack Melody and myself.

We all piled in the car and drove over. Melody had a car—a stolen car. We drove over to Holmes' place. Vicki was there also. There was a party going on up at Holmes' place. He and his wife were very nice people. They were living on Lexington Avenue just below Fifty-ninth.

Jack Melody, Vicki, and myself didn't stay very long. We had pulled a so-called caper late in the afternoon, and it turned out to be a pretty disastrous thing, because it was a vengeance deal that I didn't know anything about.

We were finally caught. We robbed a cop's place—an Italian-Sicilian—and apparently there'd been a feud going on between the Melodias—Jack's real name—and the cop. I don't know how much pornographic stuff we got out of there, not to mention guns and fur coats, jewelry, and stuff like that. Just an unlimited amount of everything. All of this I stashed very carefully on York Avenue. Allen was getting leery, and he was getting ready to go away anyway.

Allen didn't know that we were going to stash it, but he knew what was going on. In fact he had been out with us one night and had sat in a car and watched while we did a little routine. I guess it sort of excited him.

Vicki and Jack Melody, who were supposed to be deep in an affair, became argumentative, and we left Holmes' place and started over to Long Island. I rode just so far listening to these two curse each other out, and finally I said, "Look, let me out of the car. I'll go on about my business. I'll see you back·at the apartment in the morning."

I went out, stopped in a couple of bars, had a couple of drinks, ran into somebody that was sort of interesting, and we went to a hotel, the old Grover Cleveland. I awakened about ten o'clock and figured, well, everybody should be stirring around, I'll go on back to the apartment. Also, we had the business of unloading all of this crap, getting rid of it, out of the place. We had planned to see the fence.

When I got back, nobody is there. The door was unlocked, but nothing had been touched. The place looked all right, but there was a funny feeling about it. If I had followed my own hunches, I'd have split. But I didn't.

I sat down, I cooked up, I had a fix. I thought, "Well, maybe I'll straighten up a little bit. I'll look around and see what's there, what isn't." So I did. I went on about my business, trying to figure out just exactly where we stood, and a lot of the good swag was gone.

Nobody called. We didn't have a phone, to begin with. Obviously something was afoot, but just what I didn't know. So I was just in the midst of getting the place swept up a little bit. It was a beautiful spring day

All of a sudden: BAM! BAM! BAM! The door flung open and here is Vicki with her hair standing on end, tears streaming down her face, and Allen sort of groping his way along without his glasses, couldn't see.

I said, "What in hell?"

"We've gotta get out of here, outta here immediately."

I said, "Well, all right. What's the trouble? At least tell me."

I made the mistake of asking questions. My first thought was: my works, my stuff. That I knew I had to have, and I thought, well, anything I can convert into cash quickly, that's portable, let me grab that.

What had happened was that they had driven this friggin' car over to Long Island, and had created some error in turning, or something—traffic violation—just at the time a cruiser is coming down off the ramp into the parkway and had spotted them and had put the siren on. Jack Melody stepped on the gas and made a U-turn right over the center. That was it. The car just couldn't take it, and the next thing you know, SMASH! BAM! into a stanchion.

Allen's glasses went one way . . . he had decided he'd ride over with them while they unloaded this stuff. Their story was, they were going to try a new fence and see if

60

they couldn't get better money than we'd been getting. This was all to be a happy surprise for me.

Anyway, Allen had suggested that maybe they take him along and then drive him over to school. So he had this huge notebook with story after story concerning our activities and so on, the address of this place, and that's how the cops got the address.

In fact, I was all ready to go out the door and I was just calling them to come on, let's get out of here, and five great big beefeaters came down the hall, and that was it.

They didn't have me linked up to that at all until much later, which was part of another story. They got my name on something else. So, I got five years out of that and did almost every day of it. Of course, it was obvious that Allen hadn't done anything, and everyone was more than willing to say that. We all said that poor Allen was a victim of circumstances in this situation.

That's when he met Carl Solomon, at the mental hospital, and then he was an outpatient for a while.

Vicki was sentenced to two and a half to five, suspended. So that was the end of that.

Although Jack had left Columbia in 1942 the University and its fringes provided an arena for his friendships for the rest of the decade.

Allen's acquaintance with Haldon Chase was Jack's round-about connection to a circle of students who came from Denver. Aside from Chase himself, who had pursued his boyhood interest in American Indian culture to Columbia, there was Ed White, who had not yet made up his mind to be an architect, and, as well, young men from Denver who had known Chase and White in Colorado—the footloose Al Hinkle and a handsome young car-thief named Neal Cassady.

Another Easterner connected with the Denver circle was Allan Temko. When he met Jack in the mid-forties, Temko wanted to be a novelist and admired Ernest Hemingway, but considered Joyce a finer model. Later he would encounter Jack in Denver and in San Francisco, where he established his reputation as an architectural critic and historian.

Allan Temko:

Jack was a year ahead of me, and he had already left Columbia when I came. I met him in the West End cafeteria. I was living in the dorms, and I invited him to my room, and we talked. In fact, we became friends. I think at that time he was forbidden to be on campus.

I can't remember who introduced us. It might have been a very wonderful Columbia student named Jack Fitzgerald, who came from Poughkeepsie and who was a writer.

Hal Chase got out of the Army during the war, and I saw him on leave when he was already a civilian. He had been in the ski troops and had come back. And he got into this Dostoevskian scene. It was just like *The Possessed*. Terribly destructive people. And they were the first people I knew who were seriously involved in drugs.

I didn't know about Kerouac, but Burroughs at that time was into drugs seriously, and Kerouac introduced me to Burroughs one night in the West End. It must have been '44. I was on leave.

It was very funny, because Burroughs hated Roosevelt, and he wanted to hire an airplane at some New Jersey airport and fill it with horse shit and pitchfork it out over the White House. He wanted to fly down to Washington, and I was in the Navy. It was very funny, and Burroughs had very good clothes then. But of course, Kerouac was conspicuous for his not dressing the way Ivy League boys dressed. Not that Columbia was ever fashionable the way Yale and Princeton were. Burroughs wore these wonderful Chesterfield coats and bowlers, and he still belonged to the Racquet Club. He had Ginsy there one night. Burroughs was still very much the disreputable member of the Burroughs family of Adding Machine fame—very snobbish, very brilliant, terribly cold.

I knew then he was capable of killing someone. They were all very unattractive in that way. The level of violence was high, and Kerouac liked that, and Ginsberg liked it, but it horrified me. It was very Dostoevski.

Lucien Carr and Burroughs belonged to the real ruling class of this country. I found Burroughs fascinating.

Very reptilian, but brilliant. Carr, whom I didn't meet until after the war, I found loathsome. I had no common ground with this spoiled and destructive boy.

Of course, everything was different because I was in the war and those guys were all out of the war. Not that I was a gung-ho killer, far from it. Maybe they were more correct in their sense of the absurdity of the war, but pacifists like Robert Lowell were far more profound about that.

I felt that these people were very nineteenth century and *Lower Depths*. Very much like St. Petersburg in the under-thing of New York. They were the first people who were talking of Céline, partly because Kerouac read French. I read French, too. In fact, Kerouac spoke a kind of French-Canadian that's really like the English hillbillies in Virginia speak, an English of the seventeenth century. Sometimes Jack and I spoke French, walking on the beach at Far Rockaway and looking out to the Atlantic toward France.

Jack and I lived near one another. My people lived in Richmond Hill, which is part of Queens. He used to come over in the evenings when I was on leave, or after the war. I lived for awhile with my parents before I moved back to New York, and he'd come over, and we'd drink my father's brandy, and I'd walk back with him.

His mother liked me, as compared to most of his other friends. She liked me for the wrong reasons. And she'd get letters to Jack from Ginsy at that time. They were very funny. The return address—because she'd throw away a letter if it came from "Ginsberg"—it'd be something like: "Irving Potts, Stove Street, Oven, New Jersey." The whole joke would be carried through in the address.

It was fun to walk with Kerouac along the railroad line. There was a railroad yard near his house. I think it's all electrified now, but at that time there were locomotives, and they would let off steam. That's when he was at his most winning, because he would yell and holler and whoop when the locomotives chugged. He liked the noise. He liked to write and hear those locomotives chugging and the cars shunting in the yards. He had a good ear—a good, natural ear.

He was very high on Wolfe, and there was then a lot of interest in Scott Fitzgerald and Hemingway as fine writers, versus Wolfe as New York telephone directory writer, putting everything in. We used to talk about that. I didn't think Hemingway was so good then, but one didn't talk to Jack of literature in the same way one talked to Hal Chase, who had a different kind of sensibility. Hal was very precocious, terribly brilliant. He wrote, when we were very young—seventeen years old—an imaginary dialogue between Dostoevski and Nietzsche. Kerouac wasn't capable of that kind of thing. Well—he wouldn't be interested.

Neal Cassady came to Columbia and showed up. The Denver boys [specifically Hal Chase and Ed White] had him around a lot, and he had these idiot girls around. He had one from Denver.

I could never understand the fascination these people held for Kerouac, except that he thought they were America, and they are. He always thought that Neal was Huck Finn and Bob Burford was smart-aleck Tom Sawyer. But Neal isn't Huck Finn. Huck Finn's impulses are always good and constructive. Neal was a terribly treacherous and untrustworthy and destructive person.

There was a born hatred between me and someone like Neal Cassady, because I felt he was just a sponger and useless. I didn't see his charm. He didn't say anything. He just sat around and was just, well, an encumbrance. I didn't ever want to have much to do with him. I thought he was good-looking. I thought he was criminal, in the worst sense. That is, I felt he would perform a criminal ripoff on anyone. I think he had no loyalty to anyone. Kerouac used him for literary material, but I wasn't interested in that.

Lucien Carr:

I think Jack felt at home with Neal. Despite the fact that he admired Neal he felt at home with him. He never felt at home with Allen, he never felt at home with me.

If Jack suddenly were living in Lowell now and nothing had occurred, and we're back in 1942, and Jack has to take a friend home, I wonder which he would take. He surely would not take Allen, because Allen's a "member of the Jewish cabal."

He would *prefer*—I mean, not only to his family, to all his friends that work in the local gas station—I think he would prefer to take Neal. Of Jack's real, dear friends that he made—of those three, anyway—the one he would most like to take home would be Neal. Neal acting well, that is.

Allan Temko:

I liked the way Jack talked of the way people walked in these towns in Massachusetts, slouching with their hands in their pockets. Kerouac used to walk that way. And he had a great sympathy with that culture from which he had sprung, and I always thought it was a pity he didn't do more with it.

He wrote one novel that hardly anyone ever has read, but I like it very much—*The Town and the City*. And Kerouac also was a very good literary friend, and a very generous guy.

Leo died in the spring of 1946. His death was the impetus for Jack to begin a long, serious first novel, and his funeral provided the culminating scene of that book. Leo's body was taken to Nashua to be buried alongside Gerard. The funeral was a big reunion that gave Jack his last look at a full assembly of the New Hampshire uncles, aunts, and cousins who had remained distant figures throughout his childhood. They are only shadows in Jack's novels. The Martin family he created for his first published book portrayed Leo, Gabrielle, and children whose personalities are drawn from traits of Jack, Nin, and Gerard.

In the funeral scene near the end of *The Town and the City* the destinies of most of the Martins are sorted out. The two characters exempted from neat endings are the mother, Marguerite, whose fate as a widow goes almost unconsidered, and Peter, the son most like Jack, who is seen leaving "Galloway" to begin adventures wherever the roads may take him.

When Leo died Nin was serving in the Women's Army Corps, where she would meet and marry a soldier, Paul Blake, and begin a separate life in North Carolina. Gabrielle continued to work as a leather-cutter for the time being, exempting Jack from Leo's deathbed admonition that her welfare should be his son's first concern.

There were other imprecations. During Leo's last months, when his belly was swollen grotesquely and he was wracked with pain, Jack cared for him for many hours or many days while Gabrielle worked at the shoe factory in Brooklyn. Jack was made to understand that his ambition to become a successful writer was a boyish fantasy, that his friends were criminals or worse, that his mother's house was dishonored when he brought home a Jew, such as Ginsberg. Leo died bitterly, determined to call every claim he had upon his son. Perhaps as a result of these last days it is George Martin, the character based upon Leo, who most completely comes to life.

The Town and the City is a fiction, with characters and incidents more imaginary than those of any other Kerouac novel, even the fantastical *Doctor Sax*. At the same time it appears to reveal more than any of the others about Jack's attitudes toward his family and himself as a very young man.

Kerouac's first novel resembles the work of his favorite author, Thomas Wolfe, in the leisureliness of its telling and in its attention to the small details of human life, but the influences are neither embarrassing nor restricting.

Burroughs had told him to read Gide and Céline, and Professor Weaver had sent Jack to Melville and the Gnostics. But Wolfe remained his principal model, perhaps because he suggested a way for the novelist to act as a man, as well as setting out the obligations and possibilities of the form itself. During his first months at Horace Mann, on one of the days when he cut classes altogether, Jack had gone to a movie and seen the German actor Harry Bauer as Handel, kneeling in prayer before he sat down to compose. Jack prayed in this way before he wrote, a ritual he performed for the rest of his life. It was the sort of thing a genius might do. He might, as well, if he were a novelist, array his whole youth in a manuscript of daunting length and scope, and wait for the self-regulating universe to provide the editor who would shape it into a publishable novel.

The Town and the City reached nearly 1,200 pages in manuscript and, like *Look Homeward, Angel,* takes place for much of its length in a house of many rooms. The boarding-house operated by Eugene Gant's mother is populated by the real people of Thomas Wolfe's childhood, and the city is a distant goal that Eugene yearns for. In Kerouac's first novel it is the cramped city apartment where the Martin family meets its doom. The big house in the town, where the early chapters are staged, is large enough to hold nine children, of whom eight survive to figure in the principal action. Five of them, the sons, are aspects of Kerouac himself.

Wolfe said that all serious fiction is autobiographical. *The Town and the City* is autobiographical, too, but Jack had not had time to reach the "middle distance" from which Wolfe claimed to have written. Kerouac was twenty-four years old when he knelt in prayer and rose to begin the book that would vindicate him to Gabrielle as a serious author.

Only Marguerite Martin, the mother, is French-Canadian, and early in the book there is a scene in which she sets out a meal for her sons and watches them eat it, appraising each of them with "the judicious and patient eye of an eternity."

Francis is the twin of Julian, who dies at eleven before the story proper begins. Just as Gerard returned in dreams to comfort Gabrielle, Julian appears to Marguerite. Francis is shy and studious, too tongue-tied to conduct a romance with Mary Gilhooley, the Irish girl from the other side of town. She mocks his seriousness and throws him over for a muscular athlete with a roadster. Marguerite sees Francis as "trickling himself away in a black ennui."

Joe is the restless eldest brother, "lonely in the company of many women and scores of men." He will fight World War II at the side of Paul Hathaway, an impulsive polygamist who marked Jack's first use of Neal in a novel. After the war, Joe will return to New England and settle down on a farm with a girl from town.

Little Mickey Martin spends his time writing novels of rafting adventures on the Merrimack and publishing newspapers about his imaginary racehorses and baseball teams. Charley, the youngest boy, is collared by a gruff policeman for breaking an old man's window with a slingshot. It is Charley who is most affected by his father's eventual failure in business.

It is Peter Martin, the second oldest son, who triumphs as a high school athlete, attends the University of Pennsylvania on scholarship, impulsively renounces athletic stardom to become a merchant seaman, and enrages his dying father and fretting mother by taking a mistress and spending his time in the company of addicts and intellectuals. In the kitchen scene at the beginning he is "rueful, rough, noble and sensual in the eyes of this silent mother," who also can read "his brooding ambition."

The sisters, businesslike Rose and the younger Ruth and Elizabeth, are sketches of Nin at various ages, although Liz also resembles a high school girlfriend of Jack's who longed to become a successful big-band vocalist.

Through the device of the five brothers Jack compresses all of his boyhood into a relatively short span of years, and there are confrontations between Martin sons who are all aspects of his own character.

For example, Francis, who enters Harvard as a commuter student, becomes a cold and analytical nihilist who cites Gide as his prophet and *The Counterfeiters* as his gospel. Peter, who is portrayed as equally bright but immune to cynicism, laughs at his brother's description of having seen "the nightmare in all its clear, full contours."

It is Francis who fails the aptitude test for Officer Candidate School and then rebels against the discipline of boot camp. The long sequence of his psychiatric confinement owes more to Dostoevski than to Wolfe, and ends when Francis spots a Navy psychiatrist with a copy of *The New Republic* tucked under his arm. Their therapy sessions become negotiations that lead to the doctor's collusion in Francis' discharge. Francis never discusses pacifism with the psychiatrist. Instead he simply argues that he cannot take orders, presenting his ability to articulate this view of himself intelligently as a token with which to buy his way out of the war.

Peter leaves Penn to become a merchant seaman. There is no conflict with a complicated coach, simply a declaration: "It's human life I want—the thing itself—not this."

After Peter returns from sea, the novel focuses on the conflict between George, the father, and Peter, with New York City as a backdrop. Writing only months after the events he was describing, Kerouac was forced to establish his circle of

New York friends as actors in the novel, and to play out his disagreements with Leo in a manner that did his father honor without suggesting shame on his own part.

Kerouac grants George Martin several happy months in New York before cancer strikes. George spends much of that time ranging the city, reminiscing about his happy youth in New Hampshire. At the end of a long, rhapsodic passage describing George's progress through the city, Kerouac shifts his attention to Peter, who is observing the complicated sociology of Times Square. Suddenly the young Jewish poet Leon Levinsky [Allen Ginsberg] appears, and begins to deliver news of Kenny Wood [Lucien Carr], the crippled homosexual Waldo Meister [David Kammerer], and Will Dennison [Bill Burroughs]. Judie Smith [Edie Parker] has appeared in the college scenes, but Levinsky, who is explained as a friend of Peter's from Penn, and the others simply materialize. As portrayed, however, they are likelier acquaintances of the dilettantish Francis than the no-nonsense Peter.

Peter's first scene with them is set in a Times Square cafeteria where he and Junkey [Huncke] listen to Levinsky lecture on his theory of "the great molecular comedown," a post-atomic disease of the soul that will reveal the "geeks" dwelling within the character of the unsuspecting populace. Levinsky's "great canvas of disintegration and sheer horror" was drawn directly from an essay by Ginsberg, folded into Kerouac's novel with Allen's consent.

As George comes to know Peter's friends he despises them. Leo's harangues against Jack in his dying months are directed against Francis and Peter in *The Town and the City*. Francis is in New York, too, involved in liberal machinations that appear to be part of the birth pangs of the United Nations, but too proud to acknowledge his father to his friends when they pass on the street. George is suspicious of these friends, connecting them in his mind with a novel he has borrowed from the library, the story of a small-town sissy who ripens into a homosexual politician. "This generation *knows* right and wrong," he says. "They don't *believe* in right and wrong."

The crisis comes when Peter arranges a meeting between his parents and Judie, the mistress of whom they disapprove. Things begin well between Peter's family and his girl, but the police interrupt with the news that Waldo Meister has killed

69

himself by jumping from the window of Kenny Wood's apartment. Can Peter help identify the body? Peter's parents are horrified. "It's just typical of poor people, always afraid of everything," Judie says. "If you get in trouble and you need money to get out of jail, *I'm* the one who can get you out, not *them!*"

By the end of the book Liz, the sister who married a jazz musician, has turned into a bleached blonde bar-girl. A bull-dozer on Okinawa exhumes young Charley's overlooked corpse. Francis drifts into a meaningless affair with a friend's wife. George dies. The comedown is complete.

Jack spent three years writing *The Town and the City,* years in which he also experimented with beginnings for *On the Road,* a novel whose title was firm in his mind before he sat down to write it. Impressed by Neal Cassady's letters, and by their soul-searching conversations together, he had decided to be honest in his next book. Only the names would be changed. But it was 1951 before he was able to write in this way. He filed the letters from Neal, Allen, and his other friends away neatly with notations about what was going on in his own mind when he had received them. Superbly organized from the beginning of his career, he was a most formal curator of his own memories. He intended to make use of them.

On the back of the envelope of a letter from Ginsberg, he scribbled: "My brother, Gerard—My Shadow, Sax—My love, Mary," a succinct forecast of three of his best books, *Visions of Gerard, Doctor Sax* and *Maggie Cassidy.* Even as he finished his huge manuscript of *The Town and the City,* his far larger book-of-many-books was shaping itself in his mind.

By late 1948 Lucien had been freed from prison and had begun to work as a wire-service editor, staying clear of his old friends to meet the terms of his parole. Ginsberg had been expelled from Columbia for a term, and the proximate cause was said to be a maid's discovery of this declaration, written on dust on a window: "Butler has no balls." Bill and Joan Burroughs had repaired to Texas to conduct farming experiments.

Jack's closest literary ally at this period was John Clellon Holmes, then in his very early twenties, who had gone to Columbia after Jack had left and who had tried to write a first novel patterned after Graham Greene, its protagonist a hired killer who discovers he has been hired to kill himself.

Both Kerouac and Holmes wanted conventional publication and acceptance, and found very soon after meeting that they spoke the same language, the technical language of novelists.

Holmes came from a family that had disintegrated during the Depression. He was an outsider in the war, too, and, like Jack, was willing to sacrifice a good deal—even a marriage—in order to pursue his writing.

John Clellon Holmes:

I didn't know Jack at Columbia. Jack had an enormous stake in going to Columbia, initially. It was success for him. It was a possibility for fame, for accomplishment. This is before the war, in the early forties. Then he got serious. He started reading and he really wanted to write, and when he broke his leg and the athletic thing went out the window, then he became very serious about being a writer.

I went to Columbia after the war, because of the G.I. bill, primarily. I was living in New York, I respected the institution, and I felt profoundly ignorant. I wanted to know things, and they had good people there, and it was available.

The thing about Columbia was that it's right in the middle of the city, so that the life out there impinged continually on the academic scene.

Jack went to Columbia, I'm sure, because he was thrilled at the idea of a Canuck kid from a milltown going to New York. And there he met other people as complicated and interesting as himself, which he couldn't find anywhere else. And he discovered what he was really interested in, which wasn't Columbia. It was everything else.

I had never lived in any city of even comparable size up to that point. It was exciting. All of life was on the corner. It wasn't an ugly place. The thing that I think excited me—and I think it excited Jack, too—was that on this one little island you could go anywhere for a dime,

and you could get into different worlds. There was a
tremendous openness about it, not the kind of armed
camp that it is now, I gather. It was exciting,
tremendously exciting.

You were never more than fifteen minutes from
anywhere.

After I finished my G.I. Bill at Columbia and then
the New School, there was another program that you
could do then if you were self-employed. You could get
something like fifty bucks a month. I was self-employed
as a writer. I was doing ghost-writing jobs and trying to
publish poetry. Mainly I was interested in, where's it all
going? I was avid for life.

When I met Jack and Allen and the others they
seemed clearly the most interesting people I had met in
the four years since the war. None of my crowd were
fired at in anger. Jack was on a ship where there were
torpedoes and stuff, but no, none of us.

In my particular case the war was certainly off to the
side in that I never left the country and I never had sea
duty. But I did work for longer than I care to remember
with the wreckage, and this had an effect on me.

The war in Europe was still going on, but the war in
the Pacific was really gearing up, so we got people back
in St. Albans, Long Island, which is where I was working
in a huge hospital out there, from the Pacific with their
battle dressings still on. This isn't really being in the war,
but it's seeing the result of it. In a sense it would have
been better to have been in it, where you have flesh-fear.
All I saw was the scraps.

The veterans, the guys—the Mailers and so forth,
who were actually in combat—came back with a much
more hardened attitude toward things. There was a way
to feel about combat. There was a way to understand
that kind of experience. It's difficult for me to say this,
but I think it's true, that there was a way to go through
combat for tyro writers. It had already been worked out
by Hemingway and all the rest.

But the thing that happened to Jack and the thing
that happened to me and the thing that happened to
Allen to some degree, too, was that we didn't want to be
involved in it to begin with. I guess nobody did, really,
but we were caught up in it and sucked up in it. But
because we were not in fear of our lives moment to

moment we could notice the enormous changes that this experience was going to make in people, and it was making in us, and it was making particularly in people our age.

Up in Spanish Harlem on July 4, 1948 Allen was giving a party. It was terribly hot, and my then-wife was out of town. I went up there with Alan Harrington, who had met them—or met Jack, anyway—a week or two before at somebody else's party.

John Clellon Holmes, 1976. Photo by Lawrence Lee.

So up we went, and there they were. I cottoned to them immediately, and we became friends terribly quickly, particularly with Jack. There was something about Jack. I mean, I love Allen and loved him then, or he fascinated me, but there was something about Jack that I sensed immediately. He must have felt something similar, because we became friends very, very rapidly.

I wrote a novel before *Go*. I was working on it then, and I finished it within about eight months after I met Jack. It was never published; it was a terrible novel.

Since I was four years younger than Jack, he had read more than I had. Also, he had a formal education. I didn't. I was twenty-two and he was twenty-six. Think about that for a minute. And Burroughs was thirty. That seemed like an absolute grayed image.

Jack and I shared certain things. We discovered certain things together. We read Melville together. We read Blake together because of Allen's influence. I turned Jack on to Lawrence. Lawrence always had been a big thing with me. He'd read Lawrence, I think, a little bit, but he hadn't read him seriously.

He turned me on to Céline, whom I had not read. I had read Wolfe. I didn't want to go back and read him, although Jack was still very enthusiastic about Wolfe. Dostoevski was where we intersected again. I had read Dostoevski before and was already very influenced by him. Jack had a tremendously free and easy feeling about Dostoevski. He treated it like reality. So we would talk about characters as if they were real. We'd spend whole nights saying, "Kirilov wouldn't say that, he'd say *this*," and we'd invent whole conversations and scenes. Novelistically, I think Dostoevski was where we really intersected. We used to laugh and giggle about Dostoevski.

Jack was living with his mother out in Ozone Park. He'd spend most of his time out there, and then he'd come roaring into New York to party, to get laid, drink, and everything. At that particular period he would most often stay at my place because he had to stay some-where, and he'd be around for two or three days, maybe three or four, and then he'd disappear again.

I went out there to Ozone Park. It was a very, very formalized situation. Mémêre was the other side of Jack wrought to its uttermost. She was very precise and very fastidious and hated disorder, but was herself very irrational.

Every time Jack limped back after three or four days in New York, she would give him a hard time. She was worried about him. He was her baby boy. I used to go out there in the afternoon sometimes. It was pin-neat. Everything was in its place.

Jack had his little room, and he liked it that way. Among his friends of that period, I think she thought I was okay, because I was blond, I was a WASP, and I was polite. I was straight, anyway. I mean, she didn't demand a tie or anything like that, but I've always been respectful of my elders.

When I visited Jack, we talked, we didn't drink. I wasn't constantly trying to draw him out to the bars or back into the city, so she figured I wasn't a pernicious influence. I acted toward Mémère the way Jack acted toward my mother.

Jack with older women, with parents, was incredibly proper and straight and deferential. My mother, to this day, will break into tears when she thinks about Jack, because Jack was simply so nice to her. He wasn't putting her on. That's what you did with mothers.

Everybody was attracted to Jack. You couldn't not be in those days.

My first wife, Marian, loved Jack. She also recognized him as a potential danger to the tranquility of the house, because he would blow in and everything was going to be in an uproar for who knows how long. Jack never was like Neal. He didn't take things over, didn't con, but it meant—*ooh-la-la*, it meant the phone would ring, and people would come over, and beer would be gotten out. She went along with it, but she saw that his effect on me was a danger to her. It was mainly her war with me, not him, however.

It was my feeling that you had to have as much experience as you could get. But I hadn't decided on what the novel was going to be like—what any novel was going to be like. What the fate of the novel was going to be. I was attracted to this experience because there was no way to understand it except by going through it. Of course, it attracted me because it was open, it was free, anything might happen, and there were fabulous people, interesting people, talking about real things, it seemed to me. That's the way I thought about it. It never occurred to me to write a book about it until I was up to my eyeballs in it.

I had the idea for my first novel and started it before all this started to happen. The only things in that novel that have any reality at all are the things at the end when I was starting to get involved with this, which I sort of tacked on, and perhaps that's why it didn't work.

When that novel didn't score, and it almost did, Macmillan almost took it, I went through one of those things that writers do, saying, "What's wrong?" And I decided that I had not been writing about anything that I knew about. So then I literally, very nakedly, went back and conceived a novel, which turned out to be *Go*, which was simply out of things that had actually happened. What I was doing really, of course, was learning how to write.

By this time Jack was struggling to write *On the Road.* I saw all of the journals that he wrote in and around *The Town and the City.* He talked to me about *The Sea Is My Brother*, about self-ultimate poetry, and so forth. But he was dead against it then. He didn't show it to me.

When I first met Jack I'd never read a word he wrote. We became friends not on the basis of that at all. He hadn't even typed up all of *The Town and the City* then, and I read it all, and of course it knocked me out. And suddenly I saw that this man that I liked terribly well anyway had something else—that he was a tremendously gifted and unique human being. All through the getting *The Town and the City* published, in the next couple of years while it was being typed and handed around from person to person, he was thinking about the next book and talking about the next book, which he always called *On the Road*.

Also, during that period, he was trying to write it. First he tried to write it the way he'd written *The Town and the City.* He had phalanxes of families and characters. I remember it vividly, because it was so good. *On the Road* started in New York with a rich family, a poor family, all kinds of crazy things. The opening scene was in a penthouse. The mother was based on my mother, whom Jack knew quite well by then. Then there was a whole phalanx of younger children. And then there was the character who was to be the major character—he then called him Ray Smith. This was to be the moment when he decided to reject all this and go out on the road. And the scene itself—it couldn't have been more than 5,000 words long—was enormously funny and real and good, but in the style of *The Town and the City*. He rejected it. He didn't feel right about it.

He wrote seven, maybe ten other beginnings to the book, and they all didn't seem right to him. This went on for eighteen months at least.

This was about 1949. Then he became more and more hung up by his inability to write the damn thing. He couldn't find the entry into it. And he wrote that whole thing which is in *Visions of Cody*, Neal's youth, he wrote that on pot. For a month he sat out there in Ozone Park, every night. He got high on pot and wrote that stuff. He would then bring it in to me, or perhaps to Allen, too. He would wait until his mother went to bed, and he had a little tiny room with a desk in it—sort of an L, a dormer. He'd close the door. As always, Jack's desks were incredibly neat, everything completely put together. He'd blast, get high, and then he'd write all night. And the reason why those sentences are so long and exfoliating and so incredible is because of pot, it seems to me. And he loved that stuff, but he still knew it wasn't the way in. That's when he decided, in '51—by then he'd married again and was living in Chelsea—he literally said, "Fuck it! I'm just going to sit down and tell the truth." And that's what he did.

I think Jack had to have *The Town and the City* published and had to go through the bad times of the editing of the book—the book was cut by a third—and get sick of it. Get sick of the scene, but also take a look at what he really wanted to do. I think if it hadn't been published, he would've become cranky and hung up on it. This way he was freed from it and he could look at it and say, as he used to say, "It's alive."

Jack was very openhanded about everything, and he particularly wanted people to read *The Town and the City*. He didn't have any connections. He didn't have any editor. He didn't know anybody in the racket.

Ed Stringham read the whole book and was impressed by it, as everybody was. Stringham gave it to David Diamond. Diamond gave it to Alfred Kazin. Kazin gave it to Robert Giroux.

Stringham, who worked for *The New Yorker,* was a friend of all of ours. David Diamond was this composer who was an old friend of Stringham and of Kazin. I think that Stringham gave it to Diamond because he knew that Diamond knew Kazin. That's the way it worked in those days.

The Town and the City, however, was turned down by Macmillan. Now whether Kazin sent it to Macmillan or not, I don't know, but the editor who turned it down became a very good friend of Jack's. He's now dead and I've forgotten his name. He loved the book, but somehow they didn't feel it would work.

Then it went to Harcourt, Brace because Kazin was, I believe, an old Columbia school buddy of Giroux's. They accepted it in the spring of '49.

Giroux loved it, but Giroux also wanted to cut it. Jack was thrilled as a young man with his first novel is thrilled, to be treated as if he's done something. So Jack agreed. They worked on it for some months together, and Giroux cut an awful lot of stuff out of it. Some of the stuff wasn't that important, but in a sense, the kind of richness of the book was reduced by the cuts.

When I first read the book in the notebooks, before he had even typed it, it ended with the family all being together. Whether it was an artistic instinct, which he had enormously, or whether it was bitterness, I don't know what made him add that last thing to it, that almost Dos Passos-like section of Peter going off on the road. Perhaps also there was a third possibility, that by then he realized that the next thing he wanted to do was the road experience.

Jack in those years was literally of two minds. When I first met him he wanted to get a farm in New Hampshire. He didn't want to live in the city. He didn't want to go on the road. He was looking for some girl to marry and get a farm somewhere up in New Hampshire, raise a family. Thanksgivings. Christmases. All of that.

And yet he was drawn, of course, in the other direction. More powerfully, as it turned out. But at that point these two things were completely clashing in him.

His father's admonition to take care of his mother and be a good boy was very, very strong in him then. And yet his pole toward chaos, toward the road, toward the West, was equally strong, indeed. Stronger, as it turned out. The adding of the end of *The Town and the City* is tremendously important for an understanding of him, because at the last minute, almost—that is, in the last six months, once the book had been taken, he added this.

He looked upon this book, even when he made a new ending, as a self-contained thing, a fiction. He used to call it a fiction. He never called the later books fictions. They were part of a saga. He was also motivated by wanting to make a novel. The only kind of novel he knew about then, or any of us knew about, was a well-made one. I don't think that he was preparing for the future in his rewrites and cuts of *The Town and the City*. I think he felt—I *know* he felt the impulsion of the material that was coming up, which was the road experience. And he'd been having the road experience all during the writing of *The Town and the City*.

In the months after the editing process was through Jack was very defensive about the editing, with his buddies who knew the book, anyway. I said, "Oh, God damn it, you didn't cut that out!" And he said, "No, Giroux knows." Jack was of two minds all the time. He wanted to get published. He was flattered and pleased and relieved by the fact that Giroux thought he was a marvelous, young new writer. So even against his better instincts—I choose to believe—he accepted all kinds of cuts in that book that I think he personally felt were wrong. He was sorry to lose whole sections, but still, he was feeling very, very upbeat.

He was waiting for publication the way you do, the first book. God, you feel you've crossed over. You've suddenly gotten to someplace. He was feeling full of beans about the next book. He was trying to be responsible, the way everybody does. He was very close to Giroux. He tended to idolize Giroux in the old sort of Fitzgerald-Hemingway-Perkins kind of thing. "I've now found my father," in effect, "the guy who will get me through all of this madness."

Giroux was part of another brilliant class at Columbia, which featured Thomas Merton and three or four other people. He had a background rather similar to Jack's. He was a lapsed Catholic, anyway. I think he was from New Jersey.

They got on terribly well together. Giroux felt that

he'd discovered somebody in Jack—professionally. But also, there was more to it than that. I think he liked Jack—maybe even more than liked Jack. And Jack, who was a person of enthusiasm—that is, Jack wasn't skeptical about anything—he didn't say, well, the good and the bad—it was all good or all bad, and it could change tomorrow. So that when Jack, that summer, moved out to Denver, Giroux came out and they hitchhiked together. This is one of the most comic things. And Giroux, manfully, went through it. But Jack was always after a soul kind of relationship with everybody. Giroux's fascination with Jack was partly because Jack seemed open to everything.

Giroux was a good eight inches taller than Jack and a very manly-looking man, as he must still be, but these were the months between acceptance and publication, when Jack felt, "Christ, I've got it made. All I gotta do is write." Which is all he wanted to do anyway.

Jack was taken up for a season in New York by the literary establishment. He spent evenings with Carl Sandburg and he went to the opera. He literally went out and rented a tuxedo, which he wore under his old camelhair coat. So Jack was flying around in that milieu for a while.

The book wasn't even published. Most of these people had never read a word he'd written, but some-body had told them, "Here's a new young star."

It was all very ironical for all of us. We adored Jack and adored his book. I argued with him a little about the cuts. I didn't begrudge him his sort of Balzacian entrance into high society, which I thought was good for him, but he soon became disillusioned by it.

That was his first taste of the difference between the image and the reality. People treated him like Thomas Wolfe, but he never felt like that. He was always Jack Kerouac with a sweaty jock.

Then, of course, publication. This didn't really crush him, because the book was well-reviewed. It sold pretty good for a first novel. I mean, it limped along, but it didn't do badly. But by this time he was involved in the problems of *On the Road*.

He really thought the way anybody would in his position. He thought he'd broken through. "Now all I gotta do is go on writing books." And then when he finally got to write that version of *On the Road* and Giroux rejected it—Giroux said no—Jack never submitted it to anybody else.

He gave it to me and I gave it to my then-agent, MCA, and they couldn't hustle it anywhere, either. But this flattened Jack out, and he had to go back into himself, which was the best thing for him. Already he was starting to write *Visions of Cody,* and all the other books followed within the desolation of his life.

The version of *On the Road* that John Clellon Holmes handed on to his literary agent was something totally new, a book that read far more like Kerouac's notebook pages and journals than like the reworked prose of *The Town and the City*.

It reached back to 1946 and 1947, to his first meetings with Neal Cassady and to their first long rides together through "the American night."

3 THE ROAD

"What's your road, man?—holyboy road, madman road, rainbow road, guppy road, any road. It's an anywhere road for anybody anyhow."

—DEAN MORIARTY in *On the Road*

< Jack Kerouac, Denver, 1950. Photo courtesy of Justin Brierly.

Jack had been at work on *The Town and the City* for eight months when Neal Cassady burst onto the New York scene in December, 1946, his teen-aged bride, Luanne, in tow.

Hal Chase, Allen's roommate from Denver, had described Neal to Ginsberg and the others as a self-aware representative of the American underclass, a reform-school punk with an eye for poetry. From Hal's letters and from conversations during Chase's summer vacations, Neal had decided that Manhattan was exactly the place for him, a city of poets. In much the same way, Jack yearned to head west to the frontier that he imagined remained there. This is the basic equation of the friendship between Jack and Neal that turned Kerouac in the direction of his best work.

There was an instantaneous understanding between the two men, who, in photographs taken in the early fifties, resembled each other so closely that it is difficult to tell which is Jack, which is Neal.

Neal was four years younger than Jack, born to a wandering family that the Depression would scatter. He had few warm memories of that family. His half-brothers by his mother's first marriage were a good deal older, and they routinely beat Neal's father bloody whenever he came home drunk. Neal recalled his brother, Jimmy, as a bully, and his younger sister only as a dim memory. When Neal was six his parents separated and his half-sisters were sent to orphanages. Each summer, Neal was left to the care of his father.

85

Neal Cassady, Sr., was "the barber" to his fellow denizens of Larimer Street, Denver's skid row, but, aside from manning a third chair at a friend's shop on busy Saturdays, he really followed neither that trade nor any other. Instead he drank.

After the separation Neal's mother stayed on in Denver, and Neal returned to her occasionally until her death when he was ten, but his loyalty was with his father, who offered a world of saloons, flophouses, and mission meals purchased with a hymn. Neal grew up canny and street-wise, turning his remarkable mind to the immediate tasks of survival for himself and his father.

Neal reached out for whatever he wanted, whether it was a girl or a car. He was unburdened by doubts about motive or method. He bragged that he had his first girl when he was nine and stole his first car when he was fourteen. It was the cars that got him into trouble. In a typical incident Neal "borrowed" his boss' car and, when it broke down, hailed a policeman for help. The car had been reported stolen and Neal's boss pressed charges.

In Neal's conversation and in Jack's fiction Cassady spent five years of his youth and young manhood in jail, but this is an exaggeration. The five years beginning in 1940, when Neal was fourteen, were checkered with convictions and reformatory terms, including one successful escape, but the total time served was less than a year.

When he was sixteen Neal met the man who would supply the roundabout link to Jack Kerouac and his friends. Justin Brierly was inspecting one of his rent-houses in Denver when he encountered Neal in a hallway.

Cassady regarded him as an intruder. "How did you get in here?" he asked. "This is my house."

"I'm sorry," Brierly said, holding up the key. "This is my house."

Brierly, then in his mid-thirties, was a handsome attorney who sat on the school board and was active in Denver art and music circles. He was involved in formal efforts to aid truant boys and he served Columbia University, his *alma mater*, by screening local applicants for admission. This last role was his connection to Hal Chase, Ginsberg's friend.

Neal was naked at the time of their surprise encounter, and

Brierly cannot but have been struck by Cassady's piercing blue eyes, his chiseled features and his hard, well-muscled body. After a few minutes of talk he also was impressed with Neal's energy and intelligence.

By 1944, when he was sentenced to ten months in the Colorado State Reformatory at Buena Vista, Neal had come to rely on Brierly for a variety of favors. He wrote asking the lawyer to cover an unpaid bill at the bar where Neal's brother Jack had worked before joining the Army, and he chided Brierly for failing to cadge permission from the warden for Neal to visit a medical specialist in Denver, a trip that would have amounted to a leave.

In the dense block of rules and questions printed at the top of the prison stationery, Neal explained his relationship with Justin by the word "friend."

Neal's friendships and sexual relationships held a quality of transaction: something Cassady wanted in exchange for something the others needed, hard-pressed though they might be to give it a name. For Kerouac and Ginsberg—although not for Burroughs, who remained unimpressed—Neal provided an example of instinct in action. In exchange, Neal wanted from them instruction in how to express his feelings. For Neal, in this instance, the transaction was incomplete. Aside from a few fragments of autobiography and his voluminous letters, he did not become the writer he said he wanted to be.

But Jack found in Neal the principal character for the novel that his closing scene of *The Town and the City* pointed toward, the road book, and Neal also gave Jack the method of telling that story. As Kerouac once put it, "The discovery of a style of my own based on spontaneous get-with-it came after reading the marvelous free-narrative letters of Neal Cassady, a great writer who happens also to be the Dean Moriarty of *On the Road.*"

When Kerouac and Cassady became friends late in 1946 and early in 1947, Jack was working on the idealized version of his boyhood which fills the early pages of *The Town and the City,* pages Neal read over Jack's shoulder as he typed. When he began his own writing exercises with Jack as tutor Neal set down his boyhood in letters meant to please Kerouac, and in those written with the help of marijuana Neal abandoned the etiquette of the "friendly letter" as taught at Denver's East High School, piling impression upon impression, all of them tumbling off the page with the clatter of life itself.

A few nights after Neal arrived in New York he seduced a trembling Allen Ginsberg after an evening wandering across New York with Kerouac and other company, and the two pledged undying love. However authentic that love was—and Neal's letters to Allen indicate that it was genuine—Cassady's pansexuality differed from Allen's confirmed, if uncomfortable, homosexuality, a difference that led to a good deal of pain for Allen in the years ahead.

At one point when Ginsberg was imploring Neal to experiment with a monogamous, gay life together Neal patiently explained that his feelings for Allen transcended physical sex, and that the ideal situation would be one in which the two of them lived together with a woman whom they both could love.

Because Ginsberg, Burroughs, Huncke and others in the circle are homosexuals, it has become fashionable to assume that Jack and Neal were gay men too repressed to act out their love for each other openly, a theory ratified by the fact that both men did, on occasion, sleep with other men. There is no evidence, documentary or otherwise, to support the notion. However, it would be difficult to imagine two human beings, sex and sexuality quite aside, more intensely interested in the contents of each other's minds than Jack Kerouac and Neal Cassady.

Throughout the late forties, as *The Town and the City* accumulated page by page, startling Allen and the others with its bulk and the precision of its recollections, Neal gave Jack a focus for his impulse to stand up from the typewriter, kiss Mémêre goodbye, and go on the road.

From a distance of two thousand miles, Larimer Street, a dismal, red-brick dead-end, glowed for Jack with the leftover magic of the West and the roads that led in that direction. In the summer of 1947, six months after he met Cassady, Jack went west for the first time, to Denver. Neal was involved in a bisexual quadrangle that summer and had little time for Kerouac, but the trip gave Jack a chance to see the scenes of Neal's childhood and young manhood and, the following winter, to try on Cassady's prose style for a possible fit, writing about the easy society of the poolhalls in a narrative which was a discarded beginning to *On the Road.*

On the Road, the book which finally brought Jack fame and a degree of material success, existed in his mind and under that title for four years before its composition and for ten years before its publication. It was not until 1951, as John Clellon Holmes has described, that Jack sat down and simply wrote the book, as Neal would have written one of his long letters. The book's center, its energy, is Neal himself: Neal driving, Neal stealing cars, Neal talking his way out of a tight corner, Neal and his women. (Neal and his men were left out.)

Thus, the book is a prolonged meditation on the subject of Neal Cassady and, even at that, could not contain all that Jack wanted to write about this remarkable figure. For example, some of the material about Cassady which Jack wrote during his attempts to begin *On the Road* during the 1940's became the opening of *Visions of Cody,* written as *Visions of Neal.* The latter book was completed with rhapsodic variations on a documentary record of the two men's time together in 1952 with Neal's last wife, Carolyn, a time when the Cassadys were more or less settled in the San Francisco Bay Area. From that point on Jack traveled alone, alternating between compulsive wandering and a return to the home—Mémêre's, Nin's, the Cassady's—where he wrote the bulk of his legend.

On the Road is the portrait of a man racing to make up for any and all lost time, a portrait of Neal. It gives the impression of a single journey that sweeps back and forth across America. In truth it was several journeys, consolidated at the behest of the book's editors, who, noting the absence of solid motivation for the trips in the first place—Jack's accurate recollection provided fiction stranger than fiction was expected to be—insisted upon compression.

On the Road opens with Neal's first visit to New York in 1946, follows Jack to Denver in 1947 and on to solo adventures in California, but the book is at its best when Neal is on stage and the two are on the road together.

Their first trip took them from the East Coast to San Francisco by way of the Burroughs household in New Orleans in early 1949. Later that year, there was a trip from San Francisco to New York and, the final episode of *On the Road,* a journey from New York to Mexico in 1950. The motivation for the trips which *On the Road*'s editors had sought was, in fact, the complicated sex-life of the book's principal character, Dean Moriarty—Neal. It is present, of course, between the lines of that novel, but Jack's record of the time did little to convey directly the passions involved, perhaps because they were unfathomable to the principal actors in the story at the time.

Instead Jack centered on accurate description of Neal's world, and Kerouac's summer alone in Denver in 1948 offered him a chance to range Larimer Street and reconstruct the world of the flophouses and poolhalls where Cassady had grown up.

In Jack's homemade mythography Neal's poolhall cronies took on the quality of the hero's companions in an ancient epic. One such companion was "Tommy Snark" of *On the Road*, "Tom Watson" of *Visions of Cody*, a slump-shouldered youth with a soft voice, large, hurt-looking eyes and a nearly unbeatable pool hustling style. He has remained in Denver for the rest of his life, pursuing his skills with a cue, at cards, and at the track. His real name is Jim Holmes.

Jim Holmes:

I knew Neal very, very well, and for years before the other people involved knew him. I felt that there was a little feeling of, oh, perhaps jealousy or some sort of hostility between Jack and I when we first met in relation to the amount of time that Neal was going to spend between the two of us. Not that I really cared, but somehow I think he did, and so we never went out of our way to be around each other very often.

I'm not a very big person, and so I have to compete in things of skill. I played table-tennis before I played pool. As soon as I got good at one thing I would start on something else, and so at the end of my table-tennis playing, I started playing pool, and I was very good at playing pool. I thought I was the best pool player in Denver, but I imagine that was a matter of opinion.

Neal used to come in and watch me play. Finally he approached me and said, "Well, come on and let's get something to eat," and I went down and I thought he didn't have any money, which I found out later was usually the case, and so I bought him something to eat.

The man was very, very energetic and very personable and he would—I don't think intentionally—but he would actually flatter you, your ego, in such a way that he would almost immediately be liked. Like when I bought him the meal, you would think it was the greatest thing that ever happened in the world. Of course, that makes you feel good, and so almost immediately we became friends.

Regardless of what you did or who you were, Neal approached everyone over the years the same way. For example, if you were a young girl and he was interested in you and you were going to college, immediately: why that's the greatest thing that ever happened. You know, "You really are going to college?" and all that sort of thing. I don't think it was a put-on. It was a technique, however. But it wasn't a con. He really respected the individual.

And it would be such little trivial things. If you had a record player at home, well, "Would you take me over to your house to listen to your records? I don't have a record player. I haven't had one in years. I know I would just love to hear so-and-so." And he really would want to hear so-and-so.

But at the same time, the people that he's talking to, he really puts them on, too. It was just his way of doing things. I think that this was a natural gift, so to speak.

The man was very energetic, he was very handsome—had a strong body, before he dissipated it—and he could go for days without sleeping or resting or anything. And wanted to. And didn't need drugs or anything to do it. What he wanted to do was just be active and move constantly, and the only time that he lived that I know of, except on rare occasions, was right now.

Tomorrow meant nothing. I mean tomorrow like tomorrow, Wednesday or Thursday, would mean some-thing, but tomorrow like two weeks from now didn't mean anything to him. He never planned his life in terms of goals, like a five-year goal or something, or even a two-week goal. He might in terms of next Sunday, but never any future dates like most people do. He lived right now, right at the moment. And he hardly ever lived in the past unless he was relating an incident that had happened to him that applied to what was taking place now. And it was just a natural gift.

The man was fantastic! You couldn't hardly help but love the man, and I mean that literally. Jack idolized Neal. In fact, almost everybody did. Except my grandmother, of course.

Neal came to live with us and he had been in jail for stealing an automobile or something, joyriding, and he had a crew-cut haircut. Well, back in my grandmother's generation short hair was bad, where in this generation long hair is bad. And so she said, "We can't have this boy coming in here with short hair. What will the neighbors think?" And so I said, "Well, we'll just have to let the neighbors take care of their own problems." And so Neal moved in, and somehow or other they didn't get along too well. It was never anything unpleasant or anything, but there always was this conflict that maybe he was going to lead me astray or something.

Neal could talk forever. Not that he wasn't a good listener as well. And he could paint pictures with words. Kerouac, in my opinion, was as much of a reporter as he was a writer. He would take a situation as it happened and report it as accurately as possible, even using the same words, if possible, and then he assumed, of course, that over a given period of time that the motives would come out naturally, as they do when you report. Kerouac was pretty accurate. It might not have taken place in the same order, in sequence, but that's about what happened. It was a little exaggerated and flowered, of course, but that's about the way it happened.

Neal had problems, of course, and he was pretty sad. That might be why he was so talkative and concentrated so much on now, because he had a very strong death wish. He didn't really want to commit suicide, but he felt that he was going to, and he kind of hoped it would be in an automobile.

One time, for example, we were in California and I think we were driving toward his home. And there was always something going wrong with his car, which I think was a kind of omen. The lights went out, and he said, "Well, we'll just follow this car," the car up in front of us. I said, "Well, fine." And so we followed the car and started going out with no lights—it's about one o'clock at night—and he starts going about sixty miles an hour and half hoping that he would run into another vehicle. I know what he has in his mind, and I didn't like that, of course. So I told him to stop and let me out. If he was going to kill himself, I didn't want any part of it.

He wouldn't, and so I thought, "The best thing I can do is jump out." I knew that would be very dangerous, but I figured the worst I could do was break an arm, or something. So I opened the door and started to jump, and just about the time that I was crouched and ready to go, he said, "Wait, wait..." So I shut the door and we went over to the side of the road and talked for a few minutes. I said, "I'd like to walk into town." And he said, "I really will wait for another car and follow up."

I remember another time that he thought that since he was going to kill himself anyway that somebody should make a profit out of it. And I thought, "Well, this is kind of ridiculous." But I wanted to see what he would do. He said, "Why don't we go down to the insurance company and write out a policy—a double-indemnity policy—and then I can borrow Bob Speak's car, and then when I take his car and run into this other vehicle, you can all make some money." So I went along with him and we went up there and talked to the insurance man, but I don't believe we ever put any money down. But then he went and talked to Bob Speak, this other charac-ter, and Bob wouldn't let him use his car, so this idea passed.

His death, as it turned out, may very well have been on purpose. I don't know.

I actually lived either with Neal in the same room or within a block of Neal for maybe three or four years. We were very, very close.

He would describe things that went on with his father or an incident or something that took place, but he would never get down to basic things like love and that sort of thing. I'm sure he loved his father in a way, but he could never live with him or anything. It was somebody that he would like to see about every year or so, just to see how he was getting along.

And Neal did write. I read, I don't know if it was two or three chapters of a book that he'd started. As a matter of fact, it was very humorous. He had never gotten past the house that he lived in in about three

chapters, and every other word of this house had some
sort of a sexual meaning. When the house would creak in
a certain way it would remind him of a woman. He got
about three chapters of this humorous house and
nothing's happened except all these things in this house
are just simply a woman to him, really. The house, in his
imagination, does everything that a woman would do.

His whole life revolved around sex. It may not have
been sex in the physical sense all the time, but there was
a great deal of that. A lot of it had to do with prestige.
We were all young people, and young men, sex to them
is a sort of plaything. Before you get serious, of course.
He would do such things as date two women and have
them both at different hotel rooms the same night, that
sort of thing. And try to see if he couldn't satisfy both of
them and keep running back and forth without either girl
knowing that he had the other one. More than anything
else sex was a game for him, and also it was proof of
manhood, I guess. And so there was an awful lot of sex.

I think that one of the reasons that he had to be so
active and to do things—talk so much and be with people
all the time and have sex all the time—was to keep his
mind occupied because of this death wish that he had.
He didn't want to think about dying, and that was in the
back of his mind all the time. Many of these people,
though, I guess didn't know it.

Neal never settled down. Now he might look like it.
He worked here in Denver at various jobs and stuff, but
it was just something that he did. Even if you're not
settled down—suppose you're on the road all the time
like a salesman, but if your mind is settled down and at
home and you're thinking about the wife and the children
and that sort of thing, you're much more settled down
than a guy that's there at home, working, and his mind is
off somewhere else all the time. Neal was never settled in
that sense. His mind was always somewhere. His mind
was always here, now, but I mean he wasn't home very
often, and when he wasn't home, he wasn't thinking of
home, he was thinking about whatever it was he was
doing at the time.

Jack would have liked to have lived the life of Neal,
and in a sense he did. He imitated Neal. It's awful hard
to explain Neal Cassady because you just don't run into
people like that. You just never see them, somebody who

is willing to give you their undivided attention for hours at a time. How many people do you ever know that will do that? For nothing?

It wasn't a con insofar as I would go through a certain amount of lying and pretext to get you to play me a game of pool. It wasn't that sort of thing at all. Neal didn't care whether he won the pool game or he lost it. It was the fact that he went through this process and played pool.

Neal was the kind of guy who could do more with, say, two to fifty dollars than any man I ever knew. He could make it last longer, go farther with it and so on, but if he got over fifty dollars, say he had five hundred, he would get rid of four hundred and fifty dollars so quickly you couldn't believe it—until he got down to the fifty. And then that fifty dollars, it would last longer than you could believe, too.

He had a theory that the third favorite would come in at the track every day. And the third favorite did come in almost every day. So he would go out to the track and play the third favorite every day, and it would come in, and then he would continue to play till it would come in the next time. And then there would be a period of three days during the year, of course, when it wouldn't come in at all, and he would lose all the money he made—plus.

Now you could do it if you qualified it and you had a lot of patience and you took, say, the four best trainers and the four best jockeys, and when you had the best trainer and the best jockey on the third favorite and played him, you would come out at the end of the year with a slight profit. But Neal just simply played the third favorite, regardless.

If it was less than fifty dollars, he would never lose it, but anything over fifty dollars, he had to lose. We went out to the track and he's sittin' there, and he said, "Can you imagine that this must be one of the most wonderful things that ever happened to me? Here we are. Just think about you and I [sic] being here, and we're experiencing this." I thought, "Hell, are we experiencing it now?" And he said, "It's been almost two and a half days and the third favorite hasn't come in yet. Isn't that wonderful?" And I thought, "Yeah, it's a little unusual, but I wouldn't put it into the wonderful class."

But to him it was living an event. Even though it was

a trivial event, he was living it. It had happened. The money didn't make any difference. The fact that he'd been losing for three days didn't make any difference.

And so my whole point is, even though it looked like he was doing all this conning, that wasn't his motive. He wasn't interested in conning people. He was interested in the thing happening. He was a natural Buddhist, if that makes him a Buddhist, because that's the way he was— perfect.

Neal's high school friends included both the rich and the poor of Denver, and one of the other boys who arranged for Neal to stay with his own family during the early 1940's was Bill Tomson, who stayed in Denver to build a successful retail lumber business.

Bill Tomson:

I met Neal through some friends at East High School, and he later lived with me for about three months in my parents' home. Then our relationship was a fairly strong one. I was the youngest of the group. Neal was four years older than I am.

I remember reading in one of Jack's stories something about Jimmie Holmes' gang or something like that. I think that's either a misconception on his part or a literary thing, because there wasn't any gang, either in the literal or any other sense in terms of working together towards some common end. It was rather a loose relationship of close friends and that was about it. The friends involved Jimmie and Al Hinkle and Neal and myself, and we all had friends other than that, outside that situation basically based on the pool game and movies and cars. Also, we were all at that time reading the philosophers—Nietzsche and Schopenhauer and so forth.

I think Neal probably picked up his intellectual interests from Justin Brierly. I think Neal searched for a father kind of relationship and security in almost everyone he met, and Justin was a rather pedantic, but whimsical, bright teacher who took a tremendous interest in Neal. Neal had gone to East High School prior to going to Buena Vista Reformatory and met Justin at that time. When he got out Justin took quite an interest in him. He wanted to try and get Neal some sort of academic structure.

I thought that in part Neal used homosexual relationships to gain favor and to continue a relationship that was otherwise beneficial to him. I don't think that it was as casual a thing for Neal as some people might think. I think he viewed it totally differently and didn't take the same things from it as he did with girls.

I think Jack was probably just totally amazed in the beginning with Neal's energy. Neal was an extremely hyper person—very, very hyper, very energetic. He was exceedingly persistent for things that he wanted to do in the short run, just very persistent. He came to New York probably feeling a little bit uneasy to meet all of Hal Chase's friends. I think he used that energy to bolster any feelings of insecurity, to show that he could meet head-on these people at Columbia.

Neal was seriously affected by Jack. I remember getting a letter from Neal when he first went to New York, and he was calling me "younger brother" and Jack the older brother. So Neal looked up to Jack for his tenacity and for his intellectual competence, as well as finding companionship in Jack's energy.

I think that all of us were pretty much malcontent in the sense of looking at society. Not alienation, exactly. It just seemed to me at that point in life you're ravenous, going around eating big gulps of other people's ideas and then trying to compare that with a fairly youthful idea of reality. And bang! All of a sudden you're acting differently, doing things differently than other people on the street—and thinking. I don't think that people were considering starting movements. I think that it was part of the intense life, that kind of compassion and intellectualization that was the "historical" thing. It was the energy of that moment. I don't think there was a great deal of looking into the future.

When Neal went to New York late in 1946 he took along his fifteen-year-old wife Luanne, and his close friendships with Jack and Allen—a sexual relationship in Allen's case—were deferred until she returned to Denver two months later.

Luanne, a blonde with masses of curls and a movie starlet's good looks, appeared as a "child bride" to such members of Jack's set as John Clellon Holmes. Near the beginning of *On the Road,* in which she is "Marylou," Jack sketches her as "a sweet little girl...awfully dumb and capable of doing horrible things."

Later in that book Marylou and Dean quarrel, and Sal Paradise, the Kerouac figure, remembers something that his "aunt" (Mémêre) once told him, that "the world would never find peace until men fell at their women's feet and asked for forgiveness."

Dean Moriarty replies that he knows this, and Paradise tells him, "The truth of the matter is we don't understand our women; we blame on them and it's all our fault."

Throughout the course of their friendship Jack and Neal shared several of the same women as lovers, including two of Neal's wives. The pattern was usually the same. Neal would build up Jack in the eyes of the woman concerned, signal his consent to Jack, maneuver the two of them together and retire from the scene. Luanne was among the first of the women with whom this happened.

By the time that Jack wrote his description of Luanne as "awfully dumb" he had gone through a brief but intense affair with her, late in 1949. While Jack might accurately have portrayed Luanne as inexperienced (she was, after all, only a teenager) he had ample evidence against her stupidity.

Even as a confused teenager, Luanne was a complex individual. She idolized Neal and wanted desperately to share his life, but she, like Carolyn, came to recognize the difficulties implicit in maintaining that liaison, and resolved to make the best of it. Luanne and Neal had grown up in similarly difficult circumstances and were each set adrift early on; perhaps, combined with their early experiences together, this helped her understand Neal better than anyone else.

Luanne Henderson:

Hal Chase and Justin Brierly and Neal were all very close

98

before I met Neal. I was fourteen. He was nineteen. We were married when I was fifteen.

Neal was living with a girl named Jeanie when I met him. He stayed at her house with her and her mother and her grandmother. That was really a weird one. The grandmother was an alcoholic, as well as the mother, and she must have been about in her seventies then. The mother was about in her fifties and Jeanie was a little younger than I was, because she was behind me in school. And somehow or other, I don't know how, she and Neal had become acquainted, but he was without money, not living anywhere, and Jeanie took him in. And he promptly took over all three of them, taking turns with the grandmother and the mother.

I was sitting in Walgreen's Drugstore and Neal and Jeanie came in, and he walked up to me and turned around to Jeanie and said, "That's the girl I'm going to marry." We'd never met or anything, but he didn't know Jeanie knew me. This was right by the pool hall, the pool hall where all the boys used to hang out.

Denver was really a very small town then. It was large in area, but you knew everybody in town and after dark it was all young people that were out. So Neal sent Jeanie over to get acquainted, and she finally told him that she knew me, so he sent her over to ask me if I would like to go to a party. And so I gave Jeanie my phone number and she called, and I talked to Neal and he said he was trying to fix me up with a date. He got me a date with Dickie Reed, who I'd known for years. He was like a brother to me, but I went ahead and said yes, because I was interested in Neal. And it started that night.

He passed me a note when we went to a bowling alley and said, "I'll call you in the morning." And I was thrilled. Oh, God, my heart was pounding. At fifteen you can get pretty emotional about little notes and such as that. And we just went from there. I saw him every day.

I knew Neal was staying with Jeanie, 'cause I used to go over to the house with him, but I didn't realize that she was as involved with him, because, especially at that time, I was very sensitive to being accused of being a man-stealer. And when Jeanie broke down in tears in front of me I really got uptight about it. But Neal hadn't told me and it made me realize that Jeanie really did care a great deal for him.

It was all so damned serious. The night that we got married, I'm standing on the streetcorner across the street from the drugstore and Neal's having a big meeting with Jeanie over in front of Walgreen's. Bill Tomson's trying to make me. It was just a ridiculous scene.

My mother was aware of us getting married because I had trouble with my stepfather before this had happened, when Neal and I were going together. My stepfather had given my mother an ultimatum: it's either her or me. He was getting interested in me and it was becoming a problem, for him as well as me. I was supposed to go live with my brother, an older brother. That never mattered because I went ahead and got married.

Neal and I got married August 1, 1945. I had been seeing him off and on and in between, while he was living with Jeanie. There was a cabin up in the mountains that someone in Jeanie's family owned. One night Neal was working—and by this time he and I were getting quite close and were talking about marriage—and I had to wait until he got off work, which was about eleven o'clock. There were two other couples waiting with us. I was alone. We decided to take a ride up and show these two guys that were with my girlfriends the cabin, since they'd never been there. There was a secret way you got in, underneath the boards, under the windows. It was a magnificent cabin. Old roller pianos, trunks of old clothes from the eighteen-hundreds. We were all dressing up. Everyone was playing house.

So we spent the evening there for about an hour, and the police broke in on us. It seems that there had been a tough-looking blonde going up the road in a '38 Ford coupe—me. We had to pass one house getting up to the cabin. They were saying that dope had been hidden in the house. I mean heavy—heroin or something. I was so unaware of anything at that time. Pot and pills, but not heroin. Anyway, I was the only blonde in the crowd. We were all taken in. And being totally ignorant as to how police work, they scared the hell out of the other kids. I refused to tell who I was for three days and sat there languishing, playing my dramatic role. I'd seen too many movies of Humphrey Bogart. I wasn't going to talk. Until

Luanne Henderson Cassady, 1945. Photo courtesy of Carolyn Cassady.

they started talking about fourteen years in jail.

We were in there with another girl who had murdered her baby. She was eighteen years old. She waltzed up and said, "What are you in for?" And, really, none of us knew. So my girlfriend asked her, "What are you in for?" And she said, "Murder." She'd seen too many movies, too, but she made a very dramatic point out of murder and it scared the hell out of everybody.

My friends were all let loose because they told their parents' names. Neal wasn't with us. We were supposed to have picked him up at eleven o'clock. But I had to stay for three days, and Neal was going crazy trying to find out where I was. When they finally released me after I told them my mother's name, Neal met me when my mother came to get me and he said, "That's the end of that. We're getting married." I had to go to court, and they finally just charged everybody with malicious mischief.

This was in the summer when all this occurred, because we were married the first day of August. I had to go to court that morning and pay a thirty-five dollar fine for the break-in, and then we went and got married that evening with Jimmie Holmes as an attendant.

But in any case, Jeanie was very, very jealous, very possessive of Neal. Since she'd been supporting him, she considered that she was doing the whole bit for him. He was trying to see her without my knowing it, and of course I knew it. We were going through a very bad scene when he was running with Jeanie and any other girl that happened to be walking by while I was working all the time. And finally I gave him an ultimatum and I told him, "Let's just forget the whole scene, or else do it. One way or the other." And so he said, "Okay, but we've got to get my clothes out." Neal's books were very important, and that's what he wanted mostly. So we went to Jeanie's together and asked her for his clothes and books, and she said no way. He was going to have to come back home, and that was all there was to it.

So we left her at this apartment of Al Hinkle's girlfriend and went over to her house, and Neal climbed up on the roof and went in and got his things and threw them down to me in the alley and we both went running out of town.

We hitchhiked to Nebraska, where Neal got a job as a dishwasher and I got a job as a maid. I was working for this blind lawyer and I got one room for both of us, but no board. Twelve dollars a month. I got one day off a week. I had to be up at five in the morning and have the house downstairs cleaned before the family got up, and I didn't finish until after dinner, which was about seven o'clock at night. Of course, I used to sneak food down to Neal before he got the dishwashing job. We didn't have penny one.

I had an aunt living in Sidney, Nebraska, that we stayed with the first couple of days we were there, but this lawyer and his wife were no relation whatsoever. She was really a bitch. She worked me like I was some kind of horse. I was just fifteen and I didn't know that much about heavy housecleaning, and I'd have to do things over three and four times, cleaning blinds and scrubbing toilets. And at night Neal would read Shakespeare and Proust.

I think at that time Neal was just trying to consume anything and everything. He was into Proust for quite a while, but he was just jumping from one thing to another. He was trying to get everything that he could. He was eating up books and trying to teach me at the same time. We would read for hours and hours and hours at night, and if I didn't understand something, he was very patient with me. He was good. He would take the time to explain and get into it a little deeper, and the thoughts behind it.

Neal was something to behold. I've never met anyone like him yet to this day. I doubt if I ever will. Neal was a very, very unique individual. Of course, he cheated himself, but I feel that he was cheated terribly, not only by life but by those who were around him. I think people got into a very bad habit of taking from Neal. I don't mean that there wasn't love or anything of that sort, but Neal, when we first met, had a tremendous amount of ambition, which was why we went to New York.

When we left Nebraska Neal came home to find me on the front porch in the middle of a big blizzard. She was making me scrub the porch on my hands and knees, and I was turning blue. Neal came home and he took one look and he said, "That's it," and he jerked me up and said, "We'll pack, and then we're going." Later that night I went upstairs and stole three hundred dollars that I knew they kept in a box, and he went out and stole my uncle's car, which I know Neal would never have risked otherwise. He had been in Cañon City [reformatory] before that, and he was just literally terrified of jail. I mean, he was really terribly paranoid at that time. A policeman would just send him into a fit.

We left Sidney, Nebraska that night. He had to drive on the passenger side with a handkerchief tied over his eyes and me looking out that window for the police, because all of the windows were totally iced. You couldn't see a damned thing. He finally changed and got over on the passenger side because he was more sheltered. He was driving with one hand and one foot on the gas. I don't know how in the hell we made it, 'cause those roads were like ice that night. We did slide off the road a couple of times.

So we made it, and the car conked out when we got as far as North Platte, which wasn't too damned far. At first Neal had it in the back of his head to go to his friend Ed Uhl's ranch and try to get some money. But then during the night when we were driving, he said, "The hell with it. We're going to New York." Ed White, Hal Chase, all of them were back there then. I don't think he was too much in correspondence with them, but he'd been close with them before they had gone.

I knew very little about Ed White. I didn't meet him until we got to New York. Ed was always very, very kind to me. I was much younger than most of them. To me, they were all a great deal older and more experienced and mature and sophisticated. I always felt like that.

It was always kind of hoped or assumed that Neal would eventually get to New York, because it was his big dream, getting to New York and wanting to go to Columbia. At that time I don't think that Neal was aware of Jack, because Allen was primarily close to Neal on that first trip. We were involved with Jack and saw him often, but not nearly as close as Allen and Neal were.

When we got to New York we went to Columbia right away and got ahold of Hal, and he introduced us to Allen and Allen's cousin, a red-headed student who lived over in Spanish Harlem and was kind enough to let us stay with him over at his place. It was a large, cold-water type flat. So Neal and I stayed with him.

I got a job at a bakery and got caught stealing the first day I worked there. Fainted because of the whole scene and everything. I'd never been involved in anything like that and I wouldn't admit that I'd taken the money, and the way I did it was so stupid, it's no wonder I got caught. I deserved it. But I fainted, and the manager of the store was nice enough that she didn't do anything about it. She put me on a bus. Neal was waiting for me up at Columbia and I didn't have any money—or a job, then. First day, which was a disaster. It put me through a bad month or so. I really went into a depression.

Neal and I had gotten an apartment over on 113th, not too far from Columbia. Neal wanted to go to Columbia. He wanted to write. He had already attempted writing when we were still in Denver, when I was working and he was either running around or sitting at the typewriter, one of the two. But he had definite dreams and motivation, then especially, that he knew what he wanted and was going to do it. And then after we went to New York, and it seemed like especially after Neal and Jack got very close, he was involved more with Jack's writing or getting more interested in their aspirations. And the fact that they were writing about him, of course, was a lift for him, that they found him interesting enough at that point.

But that thing at the bakery really sent me into a tailspin. We moved to New Jersey, we spent Christmas over there. We went to Bayonne and got a room. Neal was working at the parking lot next door to the New Yorker Hotel, and finally things had settled into a beautiful routine as far as what I thought I had always wanted, with Neal coming home from work every night. It really was, it was beautiful.

We had one little room with kitchen privileges. I can still remember Neal laughing. I went to the store—we had no money—and I got paper drapes and a phony rose. I really was fixing that room up. I hemmed these silly drapes. And I cooked Neal the first meal that I'd ever cooked for him. I cooked spaghetti. I'd watched my mother cook spaghetti, and who couldn't cook spaghetti?

No one bothered to tell me that you boil the water before you put the spaghetti in, right? In it went, and it came out just one big lump. I had to slice it to put it on the plate for Neal, but he ate it, every damned bite of it. He ate it. Both of us did. Of course, in those days we would have eaten most anything, I think.

We were getting along just beautiful, everything was going fine, and, without planning it or forming it in my mind, or anything else, Neal came home one night from work and it just came out of me. This is something that I've tried to sort out in my mind, the reasons behind it, a thousand times, and still never really can come up with any satisfactory answer. A thousand excuses. But I told him that the police had been there that day, knowing Neal's fear of them, and put myself through a complete, endless torture.

He went into a complete panic, and I had to start throwing everything in the trunk, which was one of the few things that we had that we were dragging around with us, a huge trunk and the suitcases. And Neal left me to bring all the things and meet him in Jersey City. I had to struggle with these things down to the bus stop and get them on the bus, two suitcases and this trunk, and we went on the road around New York City and New Jersey. We were sleeping in parked cars for about three weeks.

I wound up taking a bus back to Denver. Neal stayed in New York. I slept in a bus station for two nights and I finally called my mother.

By early 1947, when Luanne left Neal behind in New York, Jack had spent more than a year on composition of *The Town and the City*, alternating bouts of work on the book at his mother's flat in Queens with excursions into the city to reconnoiter the Forty-second Street scene with Huncke and his friends.

Although Jack was wary of Burroughs' morphine and, to a lesser extent, of the general experimenting with marijuana, he found benzedrine useful as his Wolfean manuscript reached, and then surpassed, a thousand pages. One of his first pieces of writerly advice to Cassady was to "write with the zeal of a benny addict."

Late in 1946 Kerouac had been stricken with thrombophlebitis, a blood-clotting disorder, which in Jack's case was confined to his legs. They became enormously swollen and tender during an attack. His general discharge from the Navy qualified him, barely, for veterans' benefits, and he had been in the V.A. Hospital in Queens undergoing treatment for the ailment just before Neal and Luanne arrived in New York. The affliction was painful and persistent, and it brought the threat of clots that could reach his brain or his heart and kill him. It was a reminder of mortality that cast its shadow over the novel that he was writing, and made him hungrier than ever to see the world beyond New England and New York.

During Neal's nine weeks of flight from Luanne's phantom policemen, Cassady sometimes took refuge with Jack and Mémère in Ozone Park, and it was during these visits that his friendship with Kerouac was cemented. The conversations between them grew into the exchange of letters that provided Jack with the seed for *On the Road*. Late in February Neal returned to Denver and to Luanne.

Allen promised Neal that he would join him there when the spring semester ended. Burroughs and Joan Vollmer, now married, had moved to Texas with Joan's daughter by her first marriage, and Allen began making plans for a big summer reunion on Bill's farm.

Luanne Henderson:

Neal showed up in Denver on the first of March, 1947, my birthday, and we moved to a hotel together. I had moved to a hotel earlier, for about three days, and my stepfather tried to get me to come home. I wouldn't and he had taken me to a juvenile judge, since I was under age. And she just talked to me for about an hour, and she told my mother and father, "She's a married woman and, as far as I can tell, she's a perfectly capable and responsible young woman. And if I find either one of you bothering her again..." It really did something for me to know, 'cause I expected to be in all kinds of trouble. I'd had no idea that marital status meant something, even at sixteen. I wasn't asking them for anything. But during this thing I had moved back home 'cause I was scared to death that I was going to go to juvenile home or something, and that's when Neal showed up. So we immediately moved to a hotel, and after that we got a boarding room in a private home.

That's when Neal went to work. I can't remember now what the hell he was doing. He was wearing coveralls and he was going out of town working. It was some kind of job. Neal was very proud of it, even after it was over.

Throughout the spring of 1947 Neal maintained his correspondence with Jack, including a long, story-like letter in which he described his seduction of a girl on the bus on the way back to Denver that February.

As promised, Allen arrived in Denver that summer, got a job as a stock-boy in a department store, and arranged his life to accommodate Neal's busy shuttle between his job and Luanne. Allen and Neal's lovemaking continued, and so did a series of conversations in which they relentlessly analyzed their thoughts and actions in an attempt at total mutual self-knowledge. Ginsberg laboriously recorded the progress of their relationship in his journal, and he worked on a series of poems he called "The Denver Doldrums."

Early that summer sitting in Mémêre's apartment in Queens, Jack consulted a map and traced the red line of Route 6 westward, not knowing that this old highway had fallen into disuse. He hitched upstate to the point where Route 6 would take him west and stood in the rain for several hours before buying a bus ticket for Chicago. He was on the road at last, with Denver as his first destination and beyond that San Francisco, where his old Horace Mann friend, Henri Cru, offered the prospect of a merchant marine job.

But by the time that Jack reached Colorado Neal had met and begun an affair with Carolyn Robinson, a graduate student in fine arts at the University of Denver. Like Luanne, Carolyn was a striking platinum blonde, but she was two years older than Neal, and in her own way determined to take life on her own terms. She had received her undergraduate degree from Bennington and was planning a career as a Hollywood costume and set designer. Involved in a busy quadrangle with his wife, Luanne, his lover, Allen, and his girlfriend, Carolyn, Neal had little time for Jack when he arrived. (Nor was Neal welcome among all of Jack's Columbia friends.) Kerouac accepted the hospitality of Ed White, the Columbia architecture student. Allan Temko was a guest in the same apartment, where he worked on short stories and sought to maintain order during the frantic visits by Cassady and his entourage.

In *On the Road,* where she is dark-haired "Camille," Carolyn is as hazily depicted as many of the other women in Jack's writing. Bill Tomson had dated her for several months before introducing her to Neal and losing her to him. In the novel that meeting is portrayed as happening in the space of a single evening in which Tomson, "Roy Johnson," picks up Carolyn and takes her to a hotel room in the company of the poolhall gang. Among them is Neal, who signals with four fingers that he will return to her at four o'clock in the morning. The truth was different.

Bill Tomson:

I went into the service under age and started at the University of Denver as a freshman and met Carolyn, who at that time was a graduate student in art. We had a few dates and talked and so on, and I introduced her to Neal, and they—in a relatively short period of time— became very close. I thought it was a mistake for about two or three weeks, in the sense of, "God damn it, I've lost this blonde."

Neal met her in the Colburn Hotel, where she was living at that time.

Carolyn Cassady:

The way Jack wrote about my meeting Neal in *On the Road* was wrong and seamy. I took offense because he said something about how "Roy Johnson" had picked me up in a bar and taken me to a hotel. I lived in the hotel already, and I'd known Bill on the campus for quite awhile. He'd tell me all these wild stories and great escapades that he and this other guy, Neal Cassady, had done, only he took most of the credit for himself. But I still was beginning to think this Cassady guy was pretty fantastic.

One Saturday afternoon I was in my room in this stuffy residence hotel, and Bill called from downstairs and asked if he could come up for a minute. I was all

Carolyn Cassady, 1947. Photo courtesy of Carolyn Cassady.

disheveled, and I opened the door and here he is with this other guy, and came stomping in and introduced him as Neal.

I thought Neal was at Columbia, a student, with Jack and Allen, because Bill had told me about them. So here he was in Denver, and I guess during the course of our conversation he said he'd come home for the break, or something like that. Anyway, Bill had told Neal that he had this girl with this fabulous collection of Lester Young records, who was Neal's current passion. And of course, I'd never heard of Lester Young, much less had any records. This was to get him up there, I think. Just to be sure to get him there. He'd been telling me so much about him, I guess he wanted to produce him.

He hung around and we talked for awhile, and then Neal asked us to go with him to pick up his things. Of course, everything was very confusing because of all these stories; none of anything was true that they were saying. So I was sort of mystified and of course I'd never met anybody like Neal anyhow. But we went with him to this house where two nurses lived that he'd been living with or staying with before he went to New York. And he'd brought his stuff back there. So we went and he packed up everything and went downtown with him to a cheap hotel and went upstairs to this room. I'm just following along. And the room was all torn up, and obviously some woman was staying there. It was a single room and nothing but female things around. So he left his suitcases and we went back downstairs and down on some main drag.

There was a little hamburger joint, just a counter and a couple of little tables, so he said, "Wait a minute," and Bill and I waited outside on the sidewalk and he went in. There was this really young girl behind the counter, and they were having this heated discussion. And I kept saying to Bill, "Who's that? Who's that?" And as usual he kept trying to dodge, and finally he said, "That's his wife." I said, "Wife?" I had already been getting interested, and Neal had been making all sorts of subtle passes, so that was a blow. I thought, "Oh, well. That's that."

Then we went to a record store. He wanted to go hear some music, and in those days you could get a pile of records and take them in a booth and play them. So

111

he didn't get Lester Young or Charlie Parker or all those
things he liked. He got a whole bunch of Stan Kenton,
Duke Ellington. Our song is Benny Goodman's "Sing,
Sing, Sing." He played that and played that, and jumped
around and did his act in the booth at the record store.

So then he said, why didn't we get together for
dinner? He had to go back to the hotel or something, I
can't remember all the excuses. Anyway, Bill and I went
to where we were all supposed to meet and sat and sat
and sat and nobody showed up. So we ate, and then Al
Hinkle and his girl, Lois—and I guess that's the first time
I met Al—came in and said that Luanne and Neal
couldn't make it and that they had already eaten, but that
everybody was going to come up to my room for a party
to welcome Neal back.

And I thought, "Why my room? All these people live
in Denver and don't have any homes? How come
everybody has to come to my room?" And I was having
this feud with this Filipino elevator boy at the hotel, and
so I was real nervous about this, but Bill said he'd
monitor and it would be fine. And Al explained that since
Neal and Luanne had just seen each other for the first
time after a long time that you know what they'd done
instead of coming to dinner. So, okay. They came up.

When they came up there, I met Luanne. I guess she
was trying to look older, so she had her hair all pulled
back. She and I were sitting on the floor and Al and Bill
and Neal were going over old times and old things, and I
still didn't know. I thought Neal had come back from
Columbia, that he'd been a student there and he'd come
for a break. Neal didn't deny it. He just dodged it.
Luanne's sitting there on the floor telling me about how
wonderful their marriage is, and she's going on and on
with how in love they are and how great he is and she
shows me this diamond solitaire ring. I still don't know
where that came from. I didn't know where he'd gotten
it, but then I didn't know anything about him.

Then she said that there was one thing he couldn't
stand, and that was to have his pants rumpled, that he
was very proud of his creases. And he had on this pin-
striped suit. So she said, "Here, I'll show you." She jumps
up and goes and plops in his lap. He was sitting in an
easy chair, and he just threw her on the floor and she

came bouncing back saying, "See?" So she was gushing away all this time and he was being really just dramatically gloomy all the time and I kept looking at this gloomy guy and listening to this gushing girl and trying to figure it out.

And Al is trying to make it a party for a homecoming and all this. It was strange. Neal got up and stalked around and looked out the window and looked irritated and anxious. When it got to be midnight I indicated to Bill it was time to go, because of this stuffy hotel. So they did. But as Neal went out the door he turned around— they were all going down the hall—and held up two fingers. Two for two A.M. I didn't know that's what he meant, but I didn't have anything to go on, so I didn't know what he was talking about.

Bill hung around for a while and it took me a long time to get him out, because now I guess he was beginning to get jealous. We had had absolutely no romantic inclinations. Or I hadn't. But I guessed now he was going to start that, so I did not want him around.

It was about one when he left. I had a bed that folded up in a closet door, but when it did fold down it took up the whole living room. So at two o'clock there's this knock on the door. I was just about to get into bed. I had my pajamas on.

I opened the door, and there's Neal with his suitcase. Of course, I had to let him in, and then sat and argued with him and he made everything I said sound ridiculous. Why was there any problem? He said that he and Luanne had been having all this trouble, and that they had been separated for months and he'd come back and tried to make it up, but it wasn't going to work. The same old story. It didn't fit with what she'd been doing all evening, gushing away about their marriage, so I was even more confused.

I tried to get rid of him. And well, for one thing, as I said, I'd been having this big thing with this Filipino elevator guy who was apparently the watchdog of all the morals of the hotel, and most of the people in the hotel were retired and very sedate. I was the only single girl and the only under-fifty resident.

I'd already had a boyfriend previously, who had come up in the elevator quite a bit until this elevator guy had turned me in, and I'd had a little chat with the management. They said that they really didn't like anybody staying overnight, so it was very touchy.

So anyway, the point is, I'm teetering. I said to Neal, "My God! How did you get up here?" And he said he'd come in and the night clerk was dozing and the elevator was closed, and he just went up the stairs and nobody saw him. I said, "Well, that's good, but now you can't go out." I couldn't risk his leaving, either. So that was handy for him.

Then I couldn't get him to sleep on the couch. He said, "Well, now, look at that great big bed, half of it going to waste. It doesn't make sense." He made everything seem so dumb that I was saying. So I said, "Well, all right. Over there." I didn't sleep a wink, but he instantly passed out, so it worked out all right.

Then in the morning he couldn't leave right away. We had to wait for a reasonable time for him to go out. We sat there and strung little tiny glass beads on a wire. I still see him sitting there doing this intricate little thing. I was making a set for a model theater, a miniature set, so he was helping me and being terribly charming.

Some time during the morning the phone rang, and it was Bill. For some reason he asked me to come downstairs. Well, I didn't want him to see Neal either, so I did go downstairs. He fiddled around not talking about much of anything, but what he was doing was that Luanne had already come up the stairs, and the minute I got in the elevator, she shot in the room.

Pretty soon Bill said, "Let's go upstairs," and there she was, talking to Neal. I talked to her and she was crying and carrying on and said that their marriage was no good and how mean Neal was. Then she said something about they'd both been in New York, and I was even more confused. But she lied as much as he did, so that it was really hard to figure out.

It was obvious that they were not going to go on with this marriage. And she convinced me that she never wanted to see him again. So I really thought they were through, which, of course, turned out to be pretty funny, especially in *On the Road*, when Jack knew that Neal was running from one to the other of us. Because I believed Neal completely, from that day forth. It was a couple of years later before I found out anything. So she had a good cry, and she left with Bill.

Then it was every day after that, a big, heavy, moving trip, and I'm believing every word. I asked him if he was going back to Columbia, and he said he couldn't afford to and that he would just stay in Denver and get a job.

I moved out of that hotel, and I think Jack had gotten to Denver about the time I was moving. I was there when Allen arrived in July, 1947, because Allen stayed in the hotel room for awhile. He wrote some of "Denver Doldrums" in that room while I was at school.

When Allen came out to see Neal, Neal brought him up to my room. I see now that Allen was interested in Neal more than just intellectually, because Allen got me to draw a nude picture of Neal. They both made it sound objective, impersonal and artistic. They could always do it so I'd sound like an idiot making any of the usual objections. I was embarrassed the whole time, Neal standing there in the altogether, posing just like some Greek statue, with Allen sitting over at the window watching this whole procedure.

I don't know if they were having a heavy affair at that time. Neal was rejecting him somewhat. Jack wasn't really in on all this all the time, but he used to come out to the campus when I was rehearsing plays. I decided to do some acting there, because I was too self-conscious to do it at Bennington. Of all things, one play was *The Blue Bird*, and I was "Light." This thing was fantasy, you know, so who cared? When Jack was there he'd sit and wait for the rehearsals to end, and then ride home with me on the streetcar. I don't know why he was there by himself. I just thought of him as a friend of Neal's. That was my only interest in him. One time Neal and Jack and I all went out to a tavern. Jack and I danced together, and he said, "Too bad Neal saw you first."

Neal and I moved to a room in a rooming house, and Allen would come there sometimes. He really was great. He helped me with my school work. I had to do an oral report once, which I loathe. Allen just told me all this wonderful stuff, and kind of edited the notes and all. So when I gave this talk, there was this absolute silence, and I thought, "Oh, God, what have I done?" Everybody was

115

dumbfounded, and the department head acted as though it was just the greatest thing that had ever happened, so good old Allen was really nice and helpful.

Neal was very intellectual and talked clearly and sounded like he knew a lot, and certainly Jack and Allen didn't seem to top him that way. He had all of us going at once, and he was able to keep all these balls in the air. He got a job as a jitney driver, and we lived together in this rooming house with a community kitchen.

And then Neal and I rode up to Central City* on a bus. It was going to be this great weekend. I'd never been to the operas up there, but I knew a lot of people from the university that had. So we got off the bus and Neal said he was going to go do something down the street and be right back, and he disappeared. He just vanished. On the way up on the bus he had been real quiet and moody, so he made up some sad story of how torn up he was about something that he couldn't explain, enough of a story that satisfied me, so here I am patting him and telling him it's all right and how sorry I am and all that. That was the first time he'd ever disappointed me. Only the beginning.

Of course, he was torn up about something about Luanne, as usual. I suppose now he realized he'd gotten in too deeply with me. He'd done a super con job, and I'd bought every bit of it, and so he was getting a little panicky that he was really tied up. It was getting tougher and tougher to discourage me, so maybe he was trying to show me that he wasn't all that great, but I was so convinced already I couldn't see it, and I'd forgive him everything. The poor guy.

But then Allen was going to go to Burroughs' ranch, and Neal told me some story about his relationship with Allen and how he felt this obligation to try and be gay. I didn't like it, but I could accept it, so I said, "If that's the way it is, I don't want you, if you don't want me. It's as simple as that. If you want Allen or something else, then go to it."

---

*A mining town whose opera house had been restored for summer performances. Brierly was among the organizers of the season.

So I took all my belongings to another teacher's house for my last night in Denver, because I was going to drive to Los Angeles with some friends the next day. I came by in the morning to say one more goodbye to Neal, and I walk in the room and here is Neal in the middle and Luanne and Allen on either side of him in *our* bed...the three of them. And, of course, I thought Luanne was long gone.

I was twenty-four; she was seventeen. I felt really sorry for her, but I had no doubts that there was nothing more between them. So it was a terrific shock to see the three of them. I had been pretty sheltered. In college, *Lady Chatterley's Lover* was out of the library all the time, but that's about the extent of it. And I just gasped and went out again, thinking it was all over between me and Neal.

Luanne Henderson:

When Allen came from New York that summer of 1947 he literally broke my heart, because he got Neal to go down to Burroughs' place in Texas with him.

Neal and I had a very dramatic scene on the grass at the Capitol Building. Neal was telling me goodbye, and I was crying and telling him that I couldn't live without him. It was just a young girl pouring her heart out. I really and truly thought I would die. At that point I had no visions of any life at all with Neal gone.

He started to leave and I grabbed him around the legs, and he tried to get up, and I was saying, "Please don't leave me, Neal. Don't leave me." And he kind of gave me a little shove and I just fell down, and I stayed there, I was crying so hard. I thought he was gone.

All of a sudden I felt his arms around my shoulders and he said, "I don't ever want to see you begging or crying like that for a man again." He said, "Come on. Let's go."

So we went over to the rooming house, and the three of us spent the night together, and Neal talked to me most of the night, and I was able to accept it. He explained his part with Allen and where he was headed, and that it didn't mean that we were separated or anything else. Anyway, I had finally gotten to the point where I had accepted it, and by this time Allen came home and the three of us were just balling around.

It was about four o'clock in the morning when Allen came home, so it couldn't have been more than a couple of hours elapses and in waltzes Carolyn. I was aware of Carolyn. Of course, I'd met her. She was going with Bill Tomson. But this was shortly after Neal met Carolyn at that point, and I was really unaware that Carolyn and Neal had gotten that involved. But she walked in and caught me in bed with Neal, and she just went insane.

I couldn't understand how she could be the injured party when I was his wife. I just wasn't aware that it had gone as far as it had.

Like the time early that summer that Neal was out all night long. Bill Tomson very kindly came up to our hotel room and told me where he was—Carolyn's room at the Hotel Colburn. Bill was madly in love with Carolyn and was going through just the tortures of hell with Neal there in her hotel room.

"You've got to go up and get him out of there." Bill felt that there was no chance against Neal whatsoever, and that if Neal was allowed to be there much longer, Bill knew that he was a loser. So he was using me to get Neal out of Carolyn's apartment. Which I wanted him out [of], anyway. Regardless of whether I had learned to accept these escapades, it didn't mean I enjoyed them. Neal became very, very discreet after that.

That's why I was a little shocked when Carolyn came to the apartment that morning before Allen and Neal left, and when she saw Neal in bed with me she was livid. She blew it.

Neal was, of course, jumping up and down, trying to explain to her. He had three of us. He had Allen, me, and Carolyn, all of us in the room and [was] trying to placate all three of us.

Allen wanting him to go to Texas. Me, of course, wanting him to stay there. Carolyn was on her way to San Francisco then. He was being pulled in quite a few directions emotionally, and trying to please all of us. So he finally left with Allen the next day, and that was the end of an era. I grew up.

118

Jack had quickly excused himself from the complicated situation in Denver, moving on to San Francisco, where his old friend Henri Cru and his girlfriend lived across the Golden Gate Bridge in the makeshift village of Marin City. The town had been built during the war when the nearby fishing village of Sausalito was the site of a shipyard. By 1947 the town was the staging center for construction workers headed out to rebuild Japan.

There was no seaman's job, but Cru helped Jack hire on at the construction workers' barracks as a night guard. He wore a uniform and—uncomfortably—carried a gun. He was no more at ease posing as authority than he had been in saluting authority as a Navy recruit, and he barely escaped being fired for failing to control the wild parties each contingent of workers staged on the eve of sailing.

Just as Jack had found Neal engrossed in his affairs with Carolyn, Allen, and Luanne, Henri Cru was quarrelling constantly with his girlfriend. Cru alternated between miserliness and extravagant binges, and he drew Jack into an enthusiastic scheme to sell a screenplay treatment to his girlfriend's Hollywood cousin. Cru and his girlfriend flew to Los Angeles with a scenario Jack helped to write, but, aside from a round of parties in Hollywood, the plan came to nothing.

Neal and Allen parted after several weeks together on Burroughs' farm in Texas. Huncke was there that summer, in an uncharacteristic setting, and Joan's son by Bill was born there. Allen, who had made his first journeys as a seaman in the coastwise trade, took a ship from Houston to Africa, where he experienced and wrote the "Dakar Doldrums."

As October neared Jack felt his autumnal urge to head home. He set out for New York by way of Los Angeles. Despite Jack's eventual reputation as the patron saint of hitchhikers his travels often involved buses and trains, as he says plainly in *On the Road*. The last leg of his first trip to Los Angeles was made by bus, and on that bus he met a young Mexican-American woman named Bea Franco, whose family were migrant farmworkers in California's Central Valley.

Jack followed her there, and spent two weeks living with her in a tent as they followed the crops. In Selma, California, he picked cotton himself, because he needed the money. Kerouac and "the Mexican girl," as he wrote of her in *On the Road*, promised to live together when Bea could reach New York, but she never did.

A few days later, flat broke, Jack was back in Ozone Park. He had just missed Neal, who had returned to New York with Burroughs, and had managed to talk Mémère into letting him stay in Jack's room for a couple of days. Since the night that Carolyn had discovered Neal in bed with Allen and Luanne, Neal had conducted his pursuit of Carolyn by mail. Carolyn had moved on to San Francisco.

Carolyn Cassady:

He wrote and said he wanted to come and marry me. I think in one of his letters he said I wrote him eighteen times a week. It wasn't quite that much. But once he'd written me one of his famous letters . . . apologetic, endearing, horrified at how his behavior had *looked* . . . I bought that, too. I believed him again.

He was writing me how he was unhappy, and so forth. And when I went to San Francisco I had a permanent address, and he wrote all the time, like every day. I wish I'd saved those letters. They're the love letters of the century—any century.

So he got on a Greyhound bus, and he had this enormous collection of records that some singer in New York had given him—two or three big cardboard boxes full of records. He rode on the bus in that suit, very careful, every time he sat down, he told me he would pull the jacket down under him so it wouldn't get wrinkled. All the way across the country without creasing his pants or his jacket.

Neal got off the bus and I met him outside the store where I worked, and we took a taxi to my apartment.

Neal and Carolyn had no money, and because Mrs. Robinson disapproved of the match, Carolyn could not ask her mother for help. Neal applied for his seaman's papers and worked at unsatisfying odd jobs such as selling encyclopedias door to door and pumping gas. His Denver friend Al Hinkle had moved to the Bay Area and soon, as he had promised, helped Neal to secure a training job with the Southern Pacific Railroad. Neal's railroad duties took him as far away as Bakersfield in Southern California, and the small, intermittent paychecks were barely enough to see the young couple through their first months together as man and wife. Their first child was on the way.

Soon after Neal followed Carolyn to San Francisco in the fall of 1947, Luanne followed Neal. At first, her presence was kept secret from Carolyn. Since they first met and made love, Luanne had known that Neal wanted her to bear a child by him and that he blamed her for not becoming pregnant. Now, with Carolyn pregnant, Neal talked Luanne into cooperating with him in securing annulment of their marriage. They traveled to Denver together and got the necessary papers. Carolyn became Mrs. Neal Cassady.

Neal continued to send Jack long letters about what he was reading and thinking, but in a letter to Allen in the spring of the following year, 1948, confessed his pessimism about fulfilling his ambition to write:

I wrote for a month straight—what came out? terrible, awful, stupid, stupid trash—it grew worse each day. Don't tell me it takes years. If I can't write one good sentence in a month of continuous effort—then, obviously, I can't realize or express.

Neal's morose verdict upon his talent was written in an-swer to a letter in which Allen had described his joy and awe at seeing the completed manuscript of *The Town and the City*. Jack already was sketching out openings for *On the Road*, showing them to John Clellon Holmes. He had written his first novel. Now it was only a matter of selling it. Then he could hit the road again. By mail Jack and Neal traded fantasies about buying a ranch together somewhere in the West.

There was no question in Jack's mind about which publisher should bring out *The Town and the City*. He sent it to Scribner's, where the patient and brilliant Maxwell Perkins had shaped Thomas Wolfe's huge manuscripts into publishable novels. Scribner's turned down Jack's book immediately. Kerouac was not discouraged, but it would be another year before the manuscript reached the hands of the network of friends who would pass it on to Harcourt, Brace and its acceptance there by Robert Giroux.

In August, 1948, Neal began pondering names for the baby Carolyn would deliver soon—"Allen Jack Cassady . . . but, to me, he's always Jacques, Jocko . . . and at times of anger 'John.'" Or if a girl, "Cathleen JoAnne Cassady . . . Cathy Jo." Cathy was born on September 7.

When the air turned cool that October Jack set aside his first attempts at *On the Road* and, working on the basis of his earnest exchanges of childhood memories with Allen and Neal, began to sketch a "novel of children and evil," using the new, impressionistic style he had developed from Neal's writing experiments. This was the germ of *Doctor Sax*. Jack's attempts to capture the spirit of the road had been less free in style, written in the formal, third-person, omniscient manner of *The Town and the City*. The successful version of *On the Road* would begin with the letter "I," with Sal Paradise, Kerouac's persona, on stage as a recorder and interpreter of events and Neal and the others at the center of his—and the reader's—attention. The book wanted to be written, but Jack could not accomplish the task until there were more travels to write about, and late in 1948 Neal arrived to help provide the impetus for them.

When Cathy was born Carolyn was waiting to begin work in Hollywood as a costume designer, and Neal awaited the vote on the full-crew railroad law that should have guaranteed him a regular job on the Southern Pacific. Neal even went so far as to assure Allen (who was pondering a career writing television scripts for children's shows) that the three of them might be able to live together comfortably on Carolyn's income alone, and that the proposed arrangement of a year earlier, a comfortable *ménage-à-trois*, was now within reach. But neither job came through, and Neal longed to get behind the wheel of a car again.

122

The car was a brand-new 1949 Hudson he had bought with the savings from his railroad work when he thought jobs and comfort lay just around the corner. Neal explained to Carolyn that he wanted a brief vacation, only a week or so in the east. Carolyn was furious, but Neal wanted to see Jack and Allen again, and he never needed a good reason to travel.

He engineered the companionship of Al Hinkle and his new bride, Helen, a quiet girl with a sternly religious upbringing. The first stop would be Denver, where Luanne was waiting for a man she planned to marry to return from overseas.

A grand round trip was sketched out. They would pick up Jack in the East and return to California by way of New Orleans, where Bill and Joan Burroughs had established housekeeping in the suburb of Algiers. By November, 1948, when Neal and Al and Helen left the Bay Area in the maroon-and-silver Hudson, Jack was in Rocky Mount, North Carolina, visiting his sister Nin and her husband, Paul. Gabrielle was there, too.

Soon after the trip began Helen Hinkle found herself unprepared for Neal's non-stop approach to crossing the country. Her pleas for meals, motels—even a chance to use the bathroom at a filling station—fell on deaf ears, and in Arizona she parted company from the rest. She would go on to New Orleans alone and rejoin her husband and the others when they reached the Burroughs' house.

Luanne Henderson:

Neal was married now and had a baby, and I had to find a life for myself. A fellow I had planned on getting married to had gone overseas. He wasn't going to be back for about two months, or three months, so I decided to go back to Denver to wait until he came back. I really didn't have anybody in San Francisco.

I'd been back there about three weeks, and about four o'clock one morning, there was a knock at the door, and I said, "Who is it?" This voice said, "Your husband. Open up." And in walked Neal, on the way to New York. That's when he stopped to pick me up, he and Al Hinkle. That was the last part of 1948, because we spent

123

Christmas with Jack in North Carolina.

We got there Christmas Day, as a matter of fact. Neal and I both in white gas-station coveralls. It was his sister's house, and when the three of us walked in, you can't even begin to imagine the shock. Here I am, with long, blonde stringy hair to my waistline. It looked like a hippie troupe of today. In those days you just didn't go around like that. It wasn't that I wanted to. I loved pretty clothes, but I didn't have any. Neal wasn't about to start dragging the suitcases and clothes, which, of course, was why Helen wound up waiting for Al Hinkle. She had started wanting to stay at motels at night and stopping for food and such nonsensical things as that, and Neal said, "That's ridiculous." Someplace in Arizona Neal told Al, "This has got to cease."

When Neal showed up he just said, "We're on our way to New York, get packed." And I said, "Okay." I wanted to go back to New York again, just wanted to go, because we were going to wind up back in San Francisco, which should have been about the time that the man that I had met should have been coming back from overseas. And I was aware that Neal was coming back to Carolyn. He was aware that I was supposed to be coming back to get married, but he wasn't accepting it. He wouldn't believe it.

When we first got to Jack's sister's house in North Carolina Jack handled it beautifully, really. He was so happy to see Neal that there wasn't the slightest hesitation or embarrassment or trying to make excuses, 'cause I'm sure his mother must have put him through a scene. I'm sure she did. But he couldn't have cared less, at least at that point, because the welcome wagon was out. We were all three just starving to death and freezing to death, and so happy to be somewhere where there was warmth and food and people happy to see us. It hadn't been an easy trip.

We had picked up this old wino and had gone two hundred miles out of our way with the promise of getting Neal some money for gas. While he took Neal out someplace to get the money, Al and I were rummaging around looking through the room for food, anything, and I found this sack of potatoes, half-rotten. He had a hot plate in the room and this greasy, dirty old frying pan. So I got the pan out, and the potatoes, and I fried up this big mess of potatoes. There was no water in the room to wash. There was nothing. I burned the pan to try to clean it as much as possible. But Neal and I and Al, we ate when Neal came back. That tasted better than any meal I could remember. Those damned potatoes tasted like the nectar of the gods to us.

So, we were hocking all the way across, and Neal of course would leap out of the car at each gas station, and pump some in and run it back to zero. It's a good thing he knew how to do it. We never would have made it.

Once we went into a tailspin on an icy road and got off in a ditch and Neal had to walk I don't know how far. Al and I sat in the car hugging each other, trying to keep warm. Neal got to a farmhouse and the farmer brought the horses over and pulled us out, and then we went on our way.

So by the time we got to Jack's house, we were really ready for a little bit of love and attention, and he gave it to us. Then Neal got renewed vigor, and we went up to Long Island, and then Jack and Neal drove back to North Carolina to get the furniture. Neal moved Jack's mother's furniture while Al and I stayed up in New York. I don't remember how long we stayed at Jack's mother's apartment, but she was lovely. From all the things that I had heard about her from Neal up to that point I was scared to death to really go there.

To me Jack and Neal were like two much younger men than they actually were, like two kids, maybe eleven, twelve years old, getting their first buddy, their arms around each other over the shoulder type of thing. They could talk, they could have fun, and it wasn't a sexual thing. Very close and very warm and discovering things together, or discovering that they had liked the same things, that they had thought the same things.

Jack was absolutely enthralled with Neal and Neal's ability with women, his ability to talk with them so easily, because it wasn't easy for Jack.

Jack was beautiful, he was a beautiful male, and you'd have thought that women weren't any problem at all, which it wasn't—as far as attracting women. But Jack didn't have the easiness that Neal did, accepting whatever the situation happened to be for what it was, for the moment. This was something that I think Jack admired in Neal, as well as his unending vitality.

And Jack was everything, I think, that Neal would like to have been: a football hero—physically, he thought Jack was magnificent—and also the stability, the ability to sit down and write. The discipline which Neal didn't have.

I think they were very jealous of each other in many respects, but not jealous in a way that it interfered with their relationship. It was just something that each would have liked to have of the other one. What one didn't have, the other gave. All during the time that we were in New York, it was really almost closer than brothers.

Until December, 1948, Jack's friend John Clellon Holmes had only heard of Neal, but never had met him. Holmes' first wife had become accustomed to, if not pleased about, Jack's frequent visits to the Holmes apartment on the West Side. For Jack the calls were a chance to break away from his mother's side and to make rounds of parties. Holmes' wife worked at a secretarial job in order to give her husband time to write his first novel, just as Jack relied on his mother's income from the shoe factory (along with disability payments from his phlebitis) in order to finish *The Town and the City*. Now Holmes, who already had met and observed Allen, Burroughs, Huncke and the rest with a novelist's eye, met the most unforgettable character of them all, Neal.

John Clellon Holmes:

Neal blew into town one day with Al Hinkle and Luanne. She was one sweet cookie. Anyway, they came in, it was just before Christmas '48. I had heard about Neal. Neal was not at that point to Jack the sort of mythic figure he became later. Jack was all excited by Neal—by his energy, by his ability to function, and so forth. So Neal and that whole crowd were there for about two weeks over that New Year's.

Neal and Luanne slept a couple of nights with me. I

don't know where they slept otherwise. With Allen, I guess. And sure, my God, I reacted to Neal the way I suppose Jack must have in the beginning. Neal was frenetic. Neal wanted to abolish time—that's why the music was always on. Neal could handle himself in situations which most of us knew nothing much about. Neal was attractive.

Neal, although to anyone with any perceptions he was immediately recognized as a con man, was not a cruel con man. He wasn't just making a score with you, he needed something to go on to the next moment, and you could come with him if you wanted to.

I never felt hustled by Neal. I must have given him twenty-five bucks over the years, which was just chicken feed, but he always returned more than that—in good feelings and in energy and discovery.

When Neal came to town, that was total, man. The wives of people and the girlfriends of people looked upon Neal as an enemy, perhaps because their men were so attracted to him. I don't mean homosexually, but attracted to the pole of this vigor and this energy and the simplicity that he seemed to offer. I mean, "Let's roll up to Harlem and see what's going on!"

Neal had a capacity to make—he didn't intend this, I don't think—some kinds of people feel inauthentic. I was always afraid I wouldn't respond in the right way. Neal never put you down. Neal never said, "Oh, come on, man, you're a square." Never anything like that, because he was always looking to the next moment. To how to move it. How to get it going. So even if you did something dumb, Neal never sneered at you. He had no sneer in him at all, not in those days, at least.

But of course, it was all brand-new to me. I mean, here was a guy who had stolen five hundred cars, or however many there were, whom I had seen seduce endless numbers of women in literally two minutes. Walk in—boom!—into the sack. He was a marvel in this way.

He concentrated, and he just poured it in. I believe Neal was a psychopath in the traditional and most rigorous sense of the term. That is, he acted out everything that occurred to him. He wasn't an ugly person, and he wasn't really a very violent person, but when he saw a chick, he poured it on and everybody melted. I suppose there must have been girls that didn't. I'm not trying to say that every female person can be had, but Neal's score was incredibly high. Many of us have tried to use that technique, but a technique is different from really feeling it, and he really did. He was indefatigable that way. By that I don't mean that he would make love all the time, but that there must have been a degree of guilt in it, so that he was constantly trying to make up for something.

When he was fastening his attention upon you he was fastening everything, and he was anticipating what you hadn't even thought of.

Jack took something in himself, fastened it on one character, and then spread it out over a lot of things. The Lost Generation's the same way. How many Julien Sorels were there, from *The Red and the Black?* People seize upon something that appears to be the embodiment of the things they themselves can't act out. And the reason why "Dean Moriarty" became the sort of image or metaphor that he did become was because people were feeling that way. Why Jack fastened on this is peculiar to him, but it's also peculiar to genius to pick out instinctively—he didn't do it cognitively—something that was going to be the next move.

Neal was always, I bet, somewhat embarrassed by this.

He had these incredibly complicated day-to-day schedules: "I've got to fuck so-and-so at two o'clock, and then I've got to rush off and do this." He had all this energy, but he never finked on anything. I can remember lending him five bucks and saying, "Look, I've got to have this back at five o'clock Thursday afternoon because, literally, we can't have dinner without it." Man, he turned up with it.

I didn't resent Jack's attraction to Neal. I didn't feel that my friendship with Jack was being drained in the other direction. I often sometimes felt that Jack was romanticizing Neal. We even talked about this occasionally. Jack couldn't articulate—at least in conversation— why he was so fixated on Neal.

I don't think that Jack and Neal were hung up sexually. I don't think that Jack's attraction to Neal was sexual at all. I think Neal made Jack feel inauthentic, too. That was his attraction. Most people never made Jack feel inauthentic, most people never made Jack feel square. Neal didn't mean to make him feel square, but Neal was real. That is, Jack got scared when Neal stole a car. Jack got scared when Neal did a scam. Jack was a very, very proper middle-class boy from a mill-town in New England. He believed that life could break open somehow. He wanted it to break open, but he didn't have the guts to do it himself. He didn't have the way to do it himself.

Neal was enormously attractive to people who sat on their ass most of the day in a dim room, biting their nails, and typing out shit.

Jack lived a much more conventional life than I did. I was married and living in the city and I knew all kinds of different worlds. Jack, basically, was living with his mother in a lower-middle-class setup, itching, as one does. He constantly wanted a wife. He constantly wanted a girl. He constantly wanted some other order than this.

Neal in effect said to everybody—his lifestyle said: "It's simple. Forget it. Toss it over." Neal was like a Zen master who hit you on the head with a bamboo stick and said, "That's *satori*." Boom!

Jack had no center to begin with. His center had begun to disintegrate with the death of his father and the move from Lowell, and he was looking for some kind of new center.

Neal seemed to offer, not a center, but a trajectory, out.

I didn't spend much time alone with Neal, two or three nights, the nights when he and Luanne stayed in my apartment. She went to bed and Neal and I would stay up, and we talked a lot. I was—Christ, I was young. He and I were almost the same age. I guess he was even younger than I am.

It was all new to me. He was so open, and he wasn't laying a trip on anybody. He didn't make me feel that I was what I really was, a sort of migraine-headache intellectual. He just gave it right on out, and I accepted it because I was ravenous for it, and interested.

Luanne Henderson:

Neal was having a bad time as time went on, and it came

closer to getting back to San Francisco. His relationship with Allen and me was deteriorating again. In the beginning of course it had been up to the mountain-top, and it was sliding back down now because I realized that the time was getting closer when we would be separating again. And Allen also realized it was getting toward the time when Neal was going to go home again.

Allen was working on a newspaper, we were living with him, and we were taking turns sleeping. Allen only had one little cot and a couch, Al Hinkle was sleeping on the couch. Neal and I were sleeping in the bed at night and then Allen would come home like six or seven in the morning, and he'd usually climb in bed with the two of us. It was just a small cot, a three-quarter bed.

I had planned on going back to New York after I got back to San Francisco then, to move in with Allen, because we were both—especially the last week— devastated because that was the end of something again. So when we left, that was shortly before Allen had a breakdown.

Neal and Jack and Al and I headed for Bill Burroughs' place in New Orleans.

In Virginia we got stopped by a cop and there was a fine attached to it if we were to get out. I had all the pot down my pants, scared to death. Immediately they asked who we were. I said, Luanne Cassady, Neal Cassady— and Neal is extremely nervous, talking a mile a minute. "I'm on my way back to my wife, and this is my ex- wife..." Automatically, this policeman's ears popped. "What are you doing with her if you're going back to your wife?" And Neal's trying to say, "It's not important. It's just enough for you to know that I'm on my way back..." But to the cop it was important. "I want to know what you're all doing together." He didn't think I was eighteen.

Al had been driving and he committed some infraction for which Neal was ready to kill poor Al. Neal was just infuriated over the fact that we'd gotten stopped. And of course, I was shaking in my boots because I'd heard so much about the small towns in the South. Here I am with all this dope down my pants and not having the least idea of how I'd even try to get rid of it, if I had to. But fortunately, it didn't come to that.

130

For Al Hinkle's young bride, Helen, the trip east from San Francisco was a honeymoon interrupted by her own discomfort in Neal's company. She had gone on to Louisiana alone to await a reunion with Al on his swing back west with Jack, Neal and Luanne.

Helen had been brought up by a family so strict that movies and lipstick were forbidden. She was an innocent, but sharp-witted enough to retain her poise as her naivete evaporated in the company of Bill and Joan Burroughs. The Burroughses made her welcome at their rambling rented house in Algiers. Only a few minutes from New Orleans, Algiers, with its unpaved streets and lush vegetation, looked like a small southern town, an odd frame for the Burroughs *ménage*. By the time Jack, Neal, Luanne, and Al reached Louisiana, Helen had accustomed herself to the more bizarre aspects of life in the house, but she was furious at her husband for his tardiness. It was not the last time Al would go off alone in this manner, nor was she the last of the circle's women to be abandoned— though Al's absences were temporary—in this way.

Helen Hinkle:

I was staying—much to Al's discomfort—at Burroughs' place, Algiers, in New Orleans. That was my very first look at Jack.

He was coming in the back door in Burroughs' place, sort of with trepidation, walking in like, "What's going to happen?" I had called repeatedly trying to reach Al at Jack's mother's home. And of course Neal arrives with a woman, whom he introduces to me as his wife. Well, I had just met his wife in San Francisco. All of this happens, and in comes Jack, dressed in a pair of black cotton pants and a white shirt.

Al and I immediately repaired to the bedroom to do some arguing. Al didn't argue. I argued. And Jack busied himself, started immediately to fill the vacuum. It was a weird scene. Burroughs was enraged, and I had known Burroughs for all of a month. So everybody's kind of embarrassed when these people walk in.

Then Jack started doing the most insane thing. He

asked to make *crêpes suzettes*. He had a recipe. Nothing was happening, so he had to start saying something. He said, "Do you have flour and eggs?" That's when Al and I left to argue.

Luanne came in and sat on one of those twig-benches that was in the room and said, "Aren't you going to screw? I'd like to watch." Aaaah.

I hadn't even been to a movie until I was twenty-one. Being so naive, I had no idea what was going on. I had no reason to be suspicious, although it was odd behavior. Joan's raking lizards off a tree all night long is odd. Bathing thirteen cats and tying them up in strings is rather odd. But then, I had met Neal Cassady, and that was pretty odd, too.

Burroughs was enraged that Neal was coming, because he knew Neal was a con man and was going to con him out of something. And I expected when Neal walked in that he was going to kick him out, or there would be a fist fight. When Neal got there, Burroughs was very nice to him, polite. But I think Jack expected fireworks. And nothing happened.

I thought that Neal was the devil incarnate. I'd never seen anybody smoke marijuana before. But he had been one of the three or four people at our wedding, and on the way over to meet Carolyn I could tell that there was something the matter with him, because he was dancing up and down and jumping and the radio was blaring, and I was saying to Al, "Is he smoking mari—"

So I had been telling Burroughs all this time what a dreadful person Neal was. He smoked marijuana. And Burroughs said, "Well-l-l, marijuana..." And he gave me the La Guardia Report on marijuana to read, and he said, "Now the thing you never want to get involved in is heroin. Now that's the real evil." Actually, at the time, according to Neal or Jack, he apparently had twenty acres of marijuana under cultivation in Texas.

At the time we met Burroughs he was thirty-five going on ninety-five. And he talked like an old man. I had met him in a Chinese restaurant, a dungeon of a place in New Orleans, told him my plight, and he nicely asked me to come and stay because I couldn't get reservations anyplace. It was Sugar Bowl week. A few days before the game I had to leave the hotel I was in.

Fortunately, somebody got me a room in a brothel a few doors up.

All I had, really, except my home address in San Francisco, was Burroughs' address and phone number. I told him my plight and he replied with a long, long speech on prefabricated housing. It was the time of *The Man in the White Suit*,* and he got into nylon hose, and Bill was shaking with rage at the nylon hose. But he nicely asked me to come, and he said, "We do have a room. Please do come over." And the crazy thing is, those people wanted to reconvert their chicken shed into an apartment for Al and I. I mean, for some crazy reason, they liked having us around. How I spent my days in order not to be a bother was, I'd get up in the morning, leave, and come back in the evening.

Now Burroughs liked Jack, and he was really pleased that he was coming and he was pleased to see him. There was no jealousy. Burroughs didn't feel like he had to protect himself against Jack. But he was enraged about Neal, and then he didn't say a damned thing. "And if that Neal Cassady comes, I can tell you right now..." Generally, he didn't speak about things personally at all. Generally he talked about anything but people—things. But I think he figured that Neal was going to con him out of something.

Al Hinkle:

I remember having a conversation with Burroughs over Westbrook Pegler. The discussion was over not what Pegler was saying, which Burroughs thought was all hogwash, but the way he was saying it. He just admired his prose, his ability to write the English language, and he'd think, like, he's the best writer writing for newspapers in the United States.

Helen Hinkle:

I left during the day. Sight-saw a lot, and then I used to get Joan one benzedrine inhaler a day. Once somebody

---

*An Alec Guinness film comedy about synthetic fiber research.

offered me a dozen and I said, "Well, no. One is enough." I asked Joan. "Oh," the druggist said, "I'd sell you a dozen because I know you wouldn't, couldn't misuse them." I said, "Misuse them?" I went back to Joan, I said, "I could have gotten you twelve today," and she said, "GOD! I hope you got them!" I said, "Well, no." And I said, "By the way, it says on those tubes that they last six months. I don't understand what you're doing." Then she showed me what she was doing.

She'd break the cap off and take the little cotton out and swallow the cotton.

The kids used her Revere Ware pots to crap in, and they were the same ones we used to cook in at night. She mopped every day, scrubbed those kids' rooms just like a hospital room, because she had to. But the kids didn't bathe. You bathed that little girl, and you could tell she hadn't been washed in ages. That little girl—she bit her arm all the time. She had great, terrible scars on her arm. Bill called the boy "Little Beast."

Joan had a limp. Very quiet. Sort of looked like an overworked, dreary housewife. Straight hair tied back with wisps hanging. She never wore a bra. There was something kind of naked about her. I don't think she ever wore shoes or hose. She looked rather childlike.

It was like going to another world then, Algiers was, and I think that Burroughs was very much horrified by his neighbors and they by him.

Joan, of course, never slept. And because the kids would be sleeping and Bill would be sleeping for part of the night, she had to do something. There was a barren tree right outside the porch. The house was L-shaped and porched all around, and there was this dead, ghastly tree. It was just covered with lizards, and she used to rake lizards off the tree at night. I don't think she killed them. Of course, they went back. That was their home. It just gave her something to do at four o'clock in the morning in the moonlight.

As we left there Burroughs was building a table that would last a thousand years. And it was absolutely eaten full of wormholes.

They ate very well. By that, I mean they ate a good deal, and well-balanced meals, and cared about what kind of meat and vegetables. I think Burroughs used marijuana for an appetite, just so it would give him some reason to eat.

He carried a gun holster, and he used to shoot those benzedrine capsules with an air gun.

Al Hinkle, 1976. Photo by Lawrence Lee.

Al Hinkle:

He'd take these benzedrine plastic things and set 'em up and then shoot them with a gun.

Helen Hinkle:

You always had to knock at his door before you'd walk through, and the easiest way to the john was directly through his room. Otherwise you had to go out on the veranda and through the kitchen. You could usually hear when he was shooting. He'd line up her benzedrine capsules and sit on the couch and: *pyoo! pyoo! pyoo!*

Then he had a shoulder holster and a side arm. The first day Jack was there he and Bill got out there in the front yard, and they each strap on guns, playing fast draw.

Al Hinkle:

Jack had one of the kids' cap guns.

Luanne Henderson:

I didn't really have any opportunity to get well acquainted with Burroughs at that time. I don't think even Neal and Jack got too much of a chance. Jack, more than Neal, was talking with Burroughs, and kind of in need of Burroughs at the time. The fact that we were going down by Burroughs really meant a great deal to Jack. When we would talk or anything, Burroughs was very much a part of him, like a teacher. He always found a way to take Burroughs aside and talk with him.

Neal kind of avoided Burroughs for some reason. I think Bill was a little unhappy with Neal at that point. I wasn't really too sure then why, what the whole thing was about, but I got the definite impression that Burroughs wasn't all that pleased about seeing Neal. It kind of put me in a position of holding back.

Joan was really involved in speed, that inhaler trip. We cleaned Algiers out and then had to start going over into New Orleans, making trips to every drugstore in town, because I think at that time—I'm not positive—she was taking about eight tubes a day.

I never saw her sleep. I don't care what time I got up or came home or anything, Joan was up, either with the broom or rake, scraping lizards off of the tree, in the kitchen washing walls, continuously scrubbing.

There were several evenings that we all sat around Burroughs' feet, him in his rocking chair. I don't think I ever saw Bill out of that rocking chair all the time we were there, except a few times outside with Jack. Listening to Bill was very interesting.

He was directing most of his conversation to Jack, more than Neal or I, concerning things in New York, and Jack's writing. And I think Neal felt all that deeply, and proceeded to agitate or irritate Bill further by some of his antics, which Neal had a tendency to do when he felt inadequate around someone. It would speed him up even more, and then he would get into things that normally weren't part of him.

After we left Algiers for California we were going through the bayous. It was midnight on this spooky little road with all the willow trees hanging down, and Jack proceeded to tell the story of the death of David Kammerer, just like we were listening to a version of *The Shadow*. It was really wild. He had me just with shivers up and down, and he was talking in that kind of voice deliberately. We'd been listening on the radio, 'cause at that time, all our spook stories were on, like *The Shadow* and some other old-time radio shows, and that's just how Jack related it. Speaking in a very low, mysterious voice, and picturing the whole thing of the river, the darkened streets. He really went into vivid detail, and I felt like I was there, and I got the shivers. Jack and Neal, of course, were giggling like they were telling ghost stories.

Then we all took our clothes off when we were going across Texas. Jack went through that thing in *On the Road*, saying I smeared them with cold cream, and all that, which was totally unreal. We did take our clothes off, because it was sweltering hot. I mean, we were just dying. We didn't have any cold cream. I would have loved to have had some. Any kind of cream.

But the most memorable part Jack didn't go into much description of. We stopped at some ruins and all of us went over there and for miles around you couldn't see a thing. You could see a car coming for a hundred miles down the road, and we were all cavorting naked through the ruins and we saw a car approaching, which we all proceeded to ignore until it was just a few hundred feet away. Then Jack and I sprinted across the highway to get back in the car. Neal struck this magnificent pose up on one of these concrete platforms. You could see the car slowing down, this elderly couple coming by. You could see this old woman on the passenger side pointing, and Jack and I were discussing exactly what she was saying. "Isn't that amazing?" Because Neal did have a beautiful body. "Isn't that a magnificent statue? And the way it's held up through the years when all this deterioration was around it." There wasn't a finger out of place. He must have stood there in that hot sun for a long while, because they just slowed down to a crawl. And of course Jack and I were getting lower and lower in the car. I guess now when I look back on it, we really were lucky none of us was ever arrested.

The ending of that trip was so abrupt, and so cold.

Neal left Jack and I on the street in San Francisco. Neal just drove away, and there was Jack and I without penny one, without anything except a lousy suitcase and each other. We just stood there looking at each other and thought, "Where do we go from here?"

It had been such a happy trip, but, of course, with nobody thinking about tomorrow.

We didn't have anything when we got to San Francisco. I think, at that point, whatever Jack had, he had given to Neal for gas and food and such. He might have given Burroughs something for the food.

There had been a point when we were in New York, close to the time when we were leaving, and Neal was feeling kind of panicky, and I recognized it. I don't really know if Jack did at that time. I know he wouldn't have discussed it with me if he had. But Neal was kind of trying to push Jack and I together, which would have eased things off for him as far as I was concerned. That

138

would have gotten one problem out of the way.

That's the way it was going, because at this point I felt a definite attraction to Jack, and I felt that he did to me. There really was no need for pushing on Neal's part, but Al said that if Neal was aware of that, he would have been very unhappy. He was later, when he found out I was really attracted to Jack, and it wasn't Neal's idea but Jack's and mine also. He was very unhappy about the situation, and he tried to reverse it, which wasn't that easy to do.

But then when Jack and I got to San Francisco we had no money for food, and I went over to this other hotel about a block from the one where Jack and I were staying. This was a girl that I had stayed with previously, and we had learned to use this iron upside down to cook on. You sit it on a wastepaper basket and turn the iron upside down. They didn't allow hot plates or anything, and the manager used to go crazy smelling coffee or food.

One of her recipes that we lived by was boiling noodles and opening a can of cream of chicken soup and just mixing it up. It was great.

I also had a problem because, as you remember, before I left I was going to be married. It was only about two weeks and he was due home in San Francisco. And here I am and I really didn't know what to do. Not only because Jack was there alone, but the thing was that I knew Jack would go to Neal, and I was very confused at that point about how I felt.

I was involved with Jack and cared a great deal about him. To me, at that time, three months was like three years, and so much had happened in the three months since my fiancé was gone, I really didn't have any idea how I felt about him any more. I'd even forgotten what he looked like, but I did know that the letters were still coming in and he was still expecting me to be writing. I had an obligation to at least give him an explanation of what was happening. He had no idea I'd been to New York.

I went over to a hotel about a block and a half away from the hotel that Jack and I had been staying at, where this girl stayed. She was a hooker, a very, very young girl that I had met when I first came out to San Francisco. I

ran into her in the bar that was downstairs from the girl
with the iron, and she was living with a guy that owned a
bar on Turk Street. I told her I had just gotten back, and
that I didn't have any money or anything and I wanted to
get a job at the bar—except that I was underage. She was
underage, too, but she was living with the owner, so I
thought maybe she might be able to help me through
him. So she said why don't I go out for dinner with him
and her and the bartender? I realized they were setting
me up, but I didn't care about that. And she also said she
would give me some money, which she did. Anyway, I
went out to dinner with them. I didn't get the job. I
didn't know a damn thing about hustling or anything at
all, and I thought she's being my friend, working with
me, but it was the other way around. She was with them
and trying to use me. It didn't work out at all.

Jack called Neal the day before I left for Denver.
Neal told him that he would pick him up, and that was
all settled and straight. Jack and I spent that whole night
talking about he and I, and we both agreed that I had to
do something as far as the man I was to marry was
concerned—do something one way or the other. And
then I was supposed to get in touch with Jack afterward
and go on from there.

As it turned out I got married, and I didn't see Jack
or Neal.

I had seen Jack in relationships with other women,
but naturally I had no idea whether he was the same with
them as he was with me. With me, Jack reverted to a
little-boy type of thing. He needed mothering. He was
extremely lovable and beautiful, but I think Jack had a
need for being taken care of.

But at that time, so did I. I needed someone—not
necessarily to take care of me financially, but I wasn't
emotionally strong enough. At least I didn't think I was. I
just didn't feel secure. Since we didn't go on with it, I
don't know if things would have changed. But I felt like
Jack leaned on me more than I leaned on him. And that
was a scary time, and I was the one who would have to
make all the decisions or all of the moves, and I wasn't
quite sure I was ready to make all the right ones. I
wanted help.

After I got older and I saw Jack, as I did, through
the years, I think that made me sadder than anything,

that Jack couldn't get away from that hang-up with his mother, the relationship with his mother, and not being able to find a good, stable relationship with a woman. He just never was able to pull himself out of that.

Neal was very, very jealous of Jack, but I don't think Jack was appreciative enough of that. I tried to tell him. I really thought it would help Jack to realize that Neal was very jealous of him as a man, because Jack always acted as though the women around would only turn to him as second-best, if Neal didn't want them. I tried to tell him it wasn't that way at all, but I don't think he ever really realized it. He thought I was just saying it to make him feel good, which I was, but not for the reasons that he thought.

I think that Neal tried to prove to himself that even if he gave his women away, he would win in the end. He had the doubt about women and everything else concerning himself, but because nobody else had that doubt, he had to live up to it. Jack wouldn't expect him to have any kind of worry concerning himself. You know, "Why worry about me with the woman? You know you can have her back anytime you want." But Neal wasn't that sure of it.

This was a pattern of Neal's with most of those who cared for him. They found themselves being left a great many times. I think Neal would feel pressure when he felt someone was relying on him that much. Neal would get panicky, too. I think all of us had a tendency to think that Neal was strong enough and infallible enough to accept anything. When someone would be depending on him a great deal, he would get panicky, not necessarily showing it as panic, but just suddenly splitting from the scene. That way he didn't have to face up to the responsibility of whatever people were expecting of him.

Carolyn Cassady:

They came back from this first trip to New York—six weeks was all—and I was on Liberty Street and Jack and Luanne were in the hotel. Neal and Jack came over and I said, "How's Luanne?"

Neal said, "Luanne who?"

I said, "Where is she?"

141

"I don't know where she is. How should I know where she is?"

And this time—*this time*—I knew he was lying, of course, so I said, "Beat it."

Somehow Neal convinced me he didn't have a place to go. They both stayed there while Neal had a job selling pots and pans. Of course that job didn't last but a week. And that is when Jack was disappointed in Luanne and went back to New York on the bus.

Jack was furious. He said that she was deceiving him, and that when he stood there and saw her get into that big car with a fat guy that she was just playing games with him. Of course he was paranoid anyway, so he just put the most paranoid interpretation on it. He was hurt and angry. She says she was doing it to get the money for him, for dinner, but he didn't believe that.

So then he went off on the bus with his fifteen sandwiches.

Neal was still telling me he didn't know where Luanne was, and there's a knock on the door, and there's Luanne. Of course, this happened to me all the time. It was up and down, up and down. He'd convince me that he was through with her, and the next thing, she'd show up again. This happened for ten years.

I had nothing against her anyway. When she had shown up in San Francisco the first time, the year before, all dressed up to the teeth ... when I'd last seen this weird little pigtailed girl in Denver, and here is this gorgeous gal, big fur collar and the gold, glistening hair. She was still seventeen, but some guy had bought her all this and brought her out there.

It was so obvious she'd come to torment Neal that I was cheering her on, because he had been rotten to her, I thought. I thought, "Boy, does he deserve it." It was a good ploy. He was really jealous as hell, and his suicide try came right after that but I didn't know it then. He'd convinced me he wasn't falling for all that show.

That had been the year before, but then when she showed up at Liberty Street after their trip to New York, I realized once more that it still wasn't over with her, and I can remember looking at the cheese toast I was cooking for Jack and Neal, pulling it out of the oven and crying over it in the kitchen.

I stayed in the kitchen while Neal and Luanne were
having their little chat. Then of course, when she left I
said, "You can go with her. One more set of lies, so go
your way. Go, go." So he left and then came back the
next day with a broken thumb. I drove him to the
hospital in the Hudson. He borrowed a nickel from me so
he could call Luanne and tell her to put all his clothes in
the street, 'cause he was absolutely through with her.
That's what he told me. Instead he called her and sobbed
about his broken thumb, and she was all sympathy and
came running down to pat him. I'm sitting in the Hudson
and here drives up Luanne in a taxi. Then Luanne and I
went back to my place together.

Of course, she was embarrassed about whose car this
was now, since I'd never been in it before and I'm
saying, "You want to drive?" I felt completely through
with Neal. This was the end—again.

Luanne and I let our hair down, and she loved
griping about all the things Neal had done to her and
how awful he was and everything, and so when they
called from the hospital and said he was ready, she didn't
quit, she just kept right on talking and said, "Let him
wait." So I kept saying, "Don't you think we ought to get
him?" And she'd say, "Aah..." And so finally we went
down to get him, and he's sitting on the curb throwing
up. We put him back in the car and took him to my
place, and he fell asleep, both of us covering him and
patting him.

Then she got up and said, "Well, I have to go."
I said, "Well, take him with you."
"I don't want him. You keep him."
"No, you take him."
"No, you take him."
He's lying there. He doesn't care.
So she said she just couldn't, because her fiancé was
coming back. He was a merchant seaman, and he was.
coming to that hotel, and Neal couldn't be there, of
course.

So I said, "What am I going to do?" I had to leave
him where he was, and he wasn't going to move,
anyway.

After he got better, I couldn't tell Neal to go to hell.
I had to let him stay with me to take care of the baby so

I could get a job, since he couldn't work. So he shaved his head and took care of Cathy. I came home from work one day and looked up at the window and there was this weird bald skull. Luanne came over when I was at work, but I didn't know it then. Then after I'd found a good job, we moved to Russell Street.

Neal still had his hand in a cast, and they had to cut off the end of his thumb when it got infected. He broke it when he had hit Luanne in the head. The first thing I said was, "My God, how's Luanne?" And he said, "Fine! God-damned, hard-headed bitch." Neal never got into fights with men, but he hit women, though no one else got injured. He knew better than to hit me.

Neal was always bored and frustrated when he wasn't working. Of course, when Jack came out, he got to play. That was my dilemma always, and why I didn't really welcome Jack at first—I knew it meant I'd be abandoned again. But, if it would make Neal happy, I'd say go ahead and ask him to come. That's why Jack came back the second time; Neal begged him to, and Jack wanted to get away from his second wife's demands for money.

Shortly after Jack left Luanne and San Francisco to return to his mother (she sent the bus fare) in January of 1949, Giroux accepted *The Town and the City* for publication by Harcourt, Brace. The advance payment was a thousand dollars, which struck Jack and Mémère as a sizeable fortune. Jack considered spending part of it to join Ed White and other Denver friends in Paris that summer, but decided instead to move to Denver himself. He bought Gabrielle a Motorola television set before leaving, explaining that he would find a house there and send for her. Now that he was about to become a successful novelist she could give up her job in the shoe factory and rely on Jack to support her, as he had promised Leo.

Jack and Robert Giroux became fast friends, and Kerouac led his editor beyond the final pages of the novel they were revising together and onto the road itself, to Denver, where Giroux stayed briefly before returning to New York.

Gabrielle came west to see the house Jack had prepared for her, but she disliked the suburban isolation and after a short stay in Colorado, Mémère went to North Carolina to help Nin recover from a difficult Caesarean section. Jack's idea of supporting his mother was mixed up in his head with his idea about living in the West, Neal's West, but Gabrielle was content with her small New York apartment and with the relative closeness to her daughter in North Carolina.

Jack's months in Denver that summer were lonely—at least so far as having old friends on hand was concerned. Ed White and Allan Temko, who had been in Denver the summer before, were away in France for a brief taste of the expatriation they had read about in Hemingway. Neal was in California, attending to Carolyn and their child.

The summer of 1949 gave Jack a chance to experience first-hand the sights and sounds of Neal's Denver boyhood. He took a job that Neal had once held, as a common laborer in the Denver wholesale produce market, and after work, during the hot summer evenings, he ranged Larimer Street. The descriptions of "redbrick neon" deadbeat Denver in *Visions of Neal/Visions of Cody* are products of this stay.

Allen, who had graduated from Columbia in February, 1949, had been arrested with Huncke, Jack Melody, and Vicki Russell that spring and, by the summer, had been released from the psychiatric confinement that had spared him trial and sentencing as an accessory in their crimes. He returned to everyday life with an ambition for more or less conventional success, stung, evidently, by the brief loss of his freedom. Neal kept writing Allen—long letters pledging friendship and concern—but it was Kerouac whom Neal summoned to join him in San Francisco that summer.

In August, 1949, Jack left Denver and went to San Francisco, planning to stay two weeks. When he arrived at the Cassadys' house Carolyn was fearful that Jack's appearance meant that Neal would leave soon. Neal's problems over money were compounded by the pain from the thumb injury and by a stubborn respiratory infection. He was bored and morose. The urge to go—anywhere—was as strong as ever. Earlier that summer, Al Hinkle had left Helen again, going to live in a separate apartment with Jim Holmes, the pool hustler, and then going on in his company to Maine and, eventually, New York, before returning west. In Al Hinkle's absence his wife Helen had become Carolyn's confessor and confidante, siding with her against Neal.

Neal's Hudson had been repossessed, and so, in order to play host to the visiting Kerouac, Neal turned to his old Denver friend Bill Tomson, who now was married and living in San Francisco. Bill had a car and, although he was sullen about it, agreed to serve as chauffeur and guide. The three men sampled San Francisco's night life, buying marijuana in black neighborhoods and smoking it while they toured the jazz clubs, including the "mixed" bars where a diagonal white stripe across the room separated the black and white contingents of the audience while they listened to such West Coast exponents of the bop style as Slim Gaillard.

As they smoked and drank and explored the city together, Neal, who despaired of pleasing Carolyn, found comfort in Jack's company. It had been three years since they first met, and although they often had talked and written of simply going on the road together, alone, the ambition had been postponed, as they saw it. The trip of the previous winter, 1948–49, had been too crowded and purposeful for them simply to experience America as it happened to them. Carolyn had done nothing to make Jack feel welcome, so they might as well set out. And there was no reason to confine their itinerary to America. This time they could continue to Europe, as they had fantasized.

But neither of them had much money. Jack had ninety dollars with him and Neal had nothing when, late in August, 1949, they left San Francisco and headed east on the trip which is retold in Part Three of *On the Road*. Although they owned no car they did not hitchhike, as popular imagination later would have it. Instead they called upon the agencies that arranged rides with other travelers or recruited drivers to take cars to their owners in other cities. The first leg of the journey, to Denver, was in the company of a prim homosexual, who drove in evident fear that Neal would rob him, or worse.

Once in Denver, the immediate goal was to find traces of Neal's now-vanished father, but the idea soon was forgotten. At a roadhouse near Denver Neal insisted on showing Jack his skills as a car thief. While Jack drank inside, Neal went to the parking lot to test-drive the customers' cars, trying to choose exactly the right one for a joy-ride into the mountains. The police were called soon after the first customers noticed their cars parked in the wrong place, but Neal escaped without arrest. He knew, however, how familiar his fingerprints were to the officers on Denver's car-theft detail, and so he and Jack wasted no time in leaving Denver. They left in style, in a Cadillac secured through legal means—from an agency. They were to drive it to its owner in Chicago.

Just outside Denver the Cadillac's speedometer cable disintegrated at 110 miles per hour, and Jack was forced to rely on higher mathematics to calculate their pace, an average of 72 miles an hour from Denver to Chicago, including all rest and food stops. In Chicago they visited a jazz bar to hear some bop, and then set out for Detroit by bus. They were too broke to afford a skid-row room and slept instead in the balcony of an all-night movie house for thirty-five cents a seat. The double feature was a singing-cowboy epic and a spy thriller with Sidney Greenstreet and Peter Lorre, and the plots and characters of the two joined and clashed in Jack's half-sleep. He was worn by the speed and near-collisions of the journey.

The last leg of the trip was with a middle-aged businessman, who charged Jack and Neal four dollars apiece to take them from Detroit to New York. In Ozone Park Gabrielle told Jack that Neal would be welcome only for a few days. Then he would have to leave.

All thoughts of going on to Europe together had been forgotten. Instead Jack turned to the final cuts and revisions of *The Town and the City*, which was scheduled for publication in February, 1950. While Jack was away that summer John Clellon Holmes had begun notes for his own chronicle of the New York scene, *Go*.

Three thousand miles from his wife and two children Neal watched with fascination as Jack was taken up by the New York literary world. As a soon-to-be published novelist Jack now tried to offer a helping hand to friends who were not so lucky.

Allan Temko:

When I came back from Europe in '49 I had written a

book, a novel, and he took me to Bob Giroux, his publisher.

Giroux was very nervous with Kerouac and me.
Giroux had gone to Columbia, and to break the ice I
came in with the manuscript. Kerouac was very generous
to bring me to his publisher and try and get my work
published. We were in the board room of one of those
New York publishing houses, imitation English upper-
class paneling, just like Louis B. Mayer.

I had met Alfred Kazin in Paris. I had brought him
some work. Giroux said, "Have you shown it to anyone?"
I said, "Well, I brought it up to Alfred Kazin, but he was
apparently eating his lunch in his hotel room." Then I
said, "He reminded me of one of these guys who used to
come up to Columbia on the subway with their corned
beef sandwich in their briefcase."

So that pissed off Giroux, Kerouac later told me,
because Giroux had done that. That got him angry at me,
so he said, "Well, we'll read this book with great interest."

I think he had a fixation on Kerouac and he didn't
want anyone else around. He doted on Jack and, of
course, Jack was not above exploiting this kind of thing.
In fact he was almost indifferent to it.

I at that time might have been insufferable, because
I didn't like Giroux's looks, and must have shown my
dislike. There was something wrong with the whole
scene. I normally would never have hit it off with him

Neal Cassady with Diana Hansen and family, Tarrytown, N.Y., 1950. Photo
courtesy of Carolyn Cassady.

anyway, but, typical of Kerouac, he said, "You guys will get along enormously." And it always turned out to be a disaster.

Well, he felt I would love Neal, which I didn't. He was always trying to get all his friends to love one another, which was an admirable trait.

Forgetting Carolyn, their daughter, the second child on its way, Luanne, San Francisco, Neal stayed on in New York in the fall of 1949, occasionally joining Jack on his forays into literary society. Cassady's immense skills as a driver equipped him superbly as a parking-lot attendant, and New York was a city full of women to be conquered. In a matter of weeks he found one woman in particular, a cultivated beauty from a well-to-do Long Island family, Diana Hansen. She was married, but soon she was pregnant by Neal. John Clellon Holmes saw the affair from its very beginning.

John Clellon Holmes:

I knew his wife, Diana. I saw him fuck her for the first time. I saw him score. That's one of those two-minute things. He walked right in and he looked at her—she was married to somebody else at that point, and I'm not sure if her husband was there—and literally scored with her immediately, and moved in with her, and had the child with her, and lived with her for I don't know how many months, but it was some months. I visited him very often up there.

She was the wife of a poet. She'd lived in Europe. She was completely New York literary establishment, and she'd never seen anything like Neal, who came roaring into her life. She gave over her entire life to him simply because of this magnetism, which she'd never felt before. It's become talk of the streetcorner now, but in the early 50's there wasn't anybody like that.

I remember going up there. The shades were always drawn, and they had a red light, or something. Neal wore a short kimono with his dork showing underneath it—just the tip. And here was Diana—how do I put this without sounding sexist?—all she wanted was for him to love her and she was willing for anything. He could fill their

149

apartment with twenty-five people. She'd never smoked pot in her life. I don't believe she'd ever heard bop, or anything. And suddenly, her whole life was transformed, but it was all riveted on Neal.

Now Carolyn found herself being nudged aside to make way for Diana. Carolyn was unwilling to step aside quietly, correctly sensing that Neal would return to San Francisco and guessing that she might be able to get him back.

As Jack moved deeper into his friendship with Giroux and his work on revising *The Town and the City* he and Neal had less time to spend together. Neal's romance with Allen had cooled into warm friendship, but his child by Diana was on the way, and he wanted to please Diana by giving the child his name. Accordingly, at long distance, divorce proceedings from Carolyn were begun, with Carolyn's grudging consent.

Neal returned to California, but he was now unwelcome at Carolyn's house in San Francisco. The railroad had recalled him to work, and he moved to Watsonville, in the Steinbeck country near Monterey, the southern division point on the Southern Pacific lines that served the San Francisco Bay Area. There he took up both with Diana, who followed him, and with Luanne, who took a job in Watsonville to be near him, as he had requested.

Carolyn Cassady:

He went back to New York and took up with Diana Hansen. He was never going to bother me again, he said, and he was really trying to change the whole pattern, thinking it was hopeless, so he lived with her, and she went to bat for him ... ran all the interference with me, and told me to get a divorce, and I said, "Let Neal ask me for one." So she wrote the letter, and he signed it. She was pregnant now, too. She and I battled all that year and many more. I had Jamie in the meantime, while Neal was gone. The divorce thing was all very strange. He went to Mexico to get a quickie, since the one I started would take too long, but instead he got pot. Diana never knew. He came back to San Francisco the next summer, but I never filed for our final papers, thinking he had gotten the Mexican divorce.

Luanne Henderson:

I moved down the coast to Watsonville, the other end of Neal's railroad run, Carolyn not knowing, once again, and I got a job at a drive-in. But Neal was so possessive, he spent one night standing in a telephone booth watching me the whole night. He was there three nights a week. I never really knew when he was coming in. I didn't know a soul there, not a soul, and I was totally alone in this boardinghouse that we had a room in. And he was just watching me constantly to see who I would go home with. I never went home with anyone, and he was always totally disappointed.

He could walk off and leave me like that at any time, regardless of the relationship, and yet he was so possessive that he would smother me. But that only lasted about a month at the most, and I told him that he was getting goofy watching me.

I told him that if he wasn't going to trust me, I couldn't live that way. This time I was getting a little older and Neal wasn't used to me being independent in any way or making my own feelings known, and I think it was kind of a shock to him. It really was a shock to him when I left. He didn't think I would, but I did. And it wasn't a mistake. It was best for him and I, Carolyn and everyone.

Carolyn Cassady:

Watsonville, that's the other end of the freight line, so instead of living in San Jose or San Francisco he had moved down there so he wouldn't be bothering me, and also so Diana could come out. He lived in San Francisco for a while in a room, too, and she was going to come out there.

He went to Watsonville so Diana would be farther away from me, but she still insisted on coming by to see me, and I told her to get lost, and then she missed her plane, she said, and came over anyway with all these little gifts for the girls, and she was out to here with his child.

But Neal thought that she had caught the plane in Oakland. So she spent the night, and he arrived on the doorstep at about six o'clock in the morning. Diana was in bed upstairs so I just made sign language and said, "Guess who's here?" And of course he'd sent her off from Watsonville with one of his big stories, but here he was at my house caught red-handed.

I felt sorry for her that time, I must say. He went up and talked to her, and I guess really put her down. She was pretty forlorn when she went off to the airport.

So then, again, I had to let him stay.

The Town and the City by John Kerouac appeared in February, 1950, to reviews that were only cordial. The publicity, and many of the notices, mentioned Jack's debt to Thomas Wolfe, but Wolfe's vision of the picaresque novel was no longer fresh enough to fire enthusiasm. The effect on Jack's mind probably was to ratify the search for a new way to tell the next story, *On the Road.* He felt certain that Giroux would buy the book for Harcourt, Brace, and that his career would continue, but in a new direction.

Jack planned a long trip that summer that would take him, first, to Denver and his friends there to celebrate *The Town and the City,* and then on to Mexico, where he would visit with Burroughs' old friend, Bill Garver. Neal also had plans to visit Mexico. His evident motive was a quick Mexican divorce from Carolyn that would let him marry Diana, if only briefly, to legitimize their child. He also wanted to buy marijuana.

There were two Kerouacs in Denver that summer: "John," who put on his dust-wrapper-photo suit to sign copies of his novel in the book department of Denver Dry Goods Company, and Neal's old buddy, Jack.

Ed White's sister decided to give a party for her brother's friend, the visiting novelist from New York. She invited her well-to-do acquaintances, and was appalled when Neal and a contingent of Larimer Street buddies crashed it.

Jack had a romance with Beverly Burford, who, with her brother, Bob, would continue to watch Jack's progress until his death. The Burfords came from a wealthy family, and Bob was able to view Kerouac, Neal, and the others with the detachment of the patron and editor of small literary magazines that he would later become.

Like White, the Burfords were cultivated and widely-read

young people who were impressed, as they should have been, by Jack's achievement with *The Town and the City*. Justin Brierly and his friends were among those who visited the department store where Jack autographed copies of his novel. Denver, then as now, was the major city for many hundreds of miles and was not an unsophisticated place, but a novelist whose advance publicity likened him to Thomas Wolfe was a social prize, and Jack, who looked striking in his dark suit, trotted out his party manners and fresh gossip about the important elbows he had rubbed in New York that season.

Jack's closest friends among Denver society were easygoing in each other's company, and Jack, Ed White, and the Burfords chose Denver's Elitch Gardens, a public park that was deserted at night, as a safe place to smoke marijuana. (They were Bohemian to that degree.) "Elitching" became their private code word for smoking grass. Ed White was a genuine friend of Al Hinkle's and found no discomfort in the company of Jim Holmes, but to Bob Burford, as to Allan Temko, Neal was an unacceptable friend.

Bob Burford:

I think that Jack just picked up the wrong hero in Neal.
There was a character treatment, and then he
exaggerated it, and he blew it out of all proportion to
anything that was real.

For example, the poolhall referred to is any poolhall
you could find along the street. It wasn't big-time sharks,
one guy hustling the other one. There was no big hustle.
They were hustling for time, snooker for time, hustling
for twenty-five cents. They were playing for a dollar.
But Kerouac wanted to see it in a much bigger way.
That's how he saw it, and that's how he wrote about it,
but it just wasn't that interesting.

I think there were many characters that he could
have written about, and really would have developed his
talent more than playing around with Cassady. Cassady
just wasn't that interesting.

It was hard for me to look at Cassady when Kerouac
himself was of interest. Cassady seemed to be nothing.
Ginsberg was just like a figure in the background there;
he was even in a shadow. He was more interesting than

Cassady. Allen kept Kerouac's interest in Neal alive, because of his own interest in Neal.

Kerouac did have an immense talent. It was only a question of where you put him. Kerouac was always in a lousy situation. You never saw him at a party where he was really having fun all night, or for many hours. He was never consistently having fun. He'd have highs listening to, say, Charlie Parker, or something like that. And he must have had some times when he was genuinely happy: alone, nature, big nights, and just writing. He loved to write. But he wasn't a happy fellow.

Jack saw more similarity than there was between himself and Neal, a blown-up picture of greatness in Kerouac and Cassady. It must be fantastic fun to read about them in your living room and then close the book and go about your business, but who would want to set this up as a thing to do in America? He got involved in something, and he was just involved, and I don't think he liked it.

Kerouac really wanted to redo things. If you call something the Lost Generation, he says "the Beat Generation." That's pretty great. That would stick. That was a way-out expression, The Beat Generation. Before beatniks, he said, "This is a beat generation." He really thought that he could will himself into being someone as great as Thomas Wolfe, or greater. I don't think he wanted to be greater, he'd just like to be that good.

Jack's trip to Mexico with Neal during that spring of 1950 provided the final episode of *On the Road*. The night before they left there was a big going-away party in the bar of a shabby hotel where Neal and his father had once lived. Brierly was there, Bill Tomson and his wife, Jim Holmes, Al Hinkle, Ed White, and Bev Burford. Another Denver friend, Frank Jeffries, was going to Mexico City with Jack and Neal.

By the time they reached Burroughs' Mexico City apartment Jack had been stricken with dysentery. Before Jack had recovered Neal either did or didn't get his Mexican divorce and left for New York and Diana, in the old Ford he was driving. The car's transmission failed, and Diana had to wire him the money to fly on from Louisiana. The day he arrived he married her, legitimizing her child, and with more money from his new wife boarded a bus to return to San Francisco and Carolyn, the wife he had just divorced.

Burroughs, always a diffident host, was deep in his studies of Aztec culture, surrounded as usual by his armamentarium of drugs. The Mexican police paid no attention to the pistol he wore everywhere.

Jack recovered slowly from the dysentery. His friendship with Neal appeared to have played out for the moment. The novel he had worked on for four years had been published to no great success, a third of its first printing left unbound. Jack began to experiment with morphine himself, and for the first time to indulge heavily in marijuana.

By October, the month that usually beckoned him home to Mémère, Jack was worried that he was on his way to addiction. He returned to Gabrielle and New York. Allen assured him that he was not an addict.

Despite the so-so reception of *The Town and the City* Jack never wavered in his perception of himself as a writer. The task now was to distill the road experiences into a publishable novel, but he needed a paying job as well. He found it in the New York offices of Twentieth Century-Fox, where he synopsized current and forthcoming novels as possible screen properties.

He resumed his correspondence with Neal who was in San Francisco with Carolyn, and at Jack's suggestion Cassady began to read Proust again. Neal had a new toy, a tape recorder, and proposed that Jack buy one, too, so that they might exchange long, soulful conversations by mail.

Allen remained in psychoanalysis, convinced that it would cure his homosexuality. One of the women he courted at this time was a slender, pretty girl named Joan Haverty. She was the mistress of a hard-drinking law student named Bill Cannastra, whom Jack had met during his bouts of partying in Manhattan. Cannastra had rigged a peephole into his bathroom in order to spy on guests, a device that displeased Jack.

While Jack was ill in Mexico Cannastra had been killed in a bizarre mishap. One evening, headed from one party to another, he boarded a subway train with some friends. While the train was still in the station Cannastra, acting out a story he was telling, thrust his head and shoulders through the window of the car. The train began to move.

Cannastra found himself wedged into place. The others tried to pull him back, but the cloth of his coat tore away in their hands. As the subway train entered the narrow tunnel Cannastra's skull was smashed and his body dragged out through the window.

According to some of their friends Joan Haverty's relationship with Cannastra had been casual, but after his death she stayed on in the apartment they had shared, treating it as a shrine to him. It was there that she lived when Jack met her that autumn, and two weeks later, on November 18, 1950, they were married.

Allen, Lucien, and Jack sang together drunkenly at the wedding, as bachelors are expected to do, but Ginsberg noted at the time that a sense of doom hovered over the proceedings.

Later Jack would tell an interviewer, "I didn't like her. She didn't like any of my friends. My friends didn't like her. But she was beautiful. I married her because she was beautiful."

Within six months they had separated, and Jack returned to Gabrielle in Ozone Park.

In late February of 1951, twenty-eight going on twenty-nine, fresh from the failure of his second marriage, Jack sat down at his typewriter and inserted the end of a roll of teletype paper that Lucien had brought him from the wire service office where he worked. Jack's thoughts went back to 1945 and the aftermath of his first marriage, and of his illness: "I first met Dean not long after my wife and I split up..."

John Clellon Holmes:

He wanted to break loose and he didn't want to have to pause for anything, so he wrote *On the Road* in one long paragraph about 120,000 words long. It was unparagraphed, using all the original names and everything.
He just flung it down. He could disassociate himself from his fingers, and he was simply following the movie in his head.

Jack was a lightning typist. Once, Jack said, "Let's write a letter to Alan Harrington." And I said, "What do you mean?" He said, "Well, you do the first page, dictate to me, and I'll take it down on the typewriter, and then

I'll do the same with you." And literally—and I was talking much faster than I'm talking now—he took it down, just as I talked to him. I tried to do it—I'm a very fast but inexact typist—and I couldn't come anywhere close.

He wrote *On the Road* in the spring of '51 when he was living with Joan in Chelsea. They had split by that point and he was then living with Lucien, or he'd moved his desk into Lucien's apartment, and he was typing it up. Typing to Jack—in Jack's career—meant rewriting. That's how he rewrote.

I remember going down there. Allan Temko was there, Lucien's then-girl, Liz Lerman was her name, was there. Lucien was there, and we were all waiting to go out and do something, and Jack had to finish typing up this chapter. It was noon. So it must have been a week after that that he finished and took it to Giroux and Harcourt, Brace.

How much longer it was after that that they rejected it, I can't remember. But it wasn't too long. Two weeks maybe. He never told me the details. He just told me that Giroux had rejected it and said that this isn't what we wanted. We wanted another novel like *The Town and the City.*

Here he was, after all the difficulty of writing the book, all the false starts, he thought he had something. So he delivered it to Big Daddy, and then when Big Daddy said no, he was both angry—he was angry on the surface—but I think much more important, he was confused.

I read *On the Road.* I read the roll, and I read it—I can't remember exactly, but it was no more than a week after he had finished it. He had not even read it. He brought it to me and it was a roll like a big piece of salami. And he was so confused and exhausted when he was finished.

It was much longer than the book is now, about a third longer, and it went on and on and on. It took me a whole day to read it. I read it like a Chinese scroll. And it was one paragraph! Of 120,000 words, with the names unchanged. We all used to do that then.

I knew it was good. I knew it was something. His work always changed my days, whenever I read anything. His enormous capacity for sense impressions and his gift for catching them on the fly somehow, always changed my reality whenever I read his stuff.

I took it to my agent, MCA, who read it and liked it, but also was kind of persnickety about it, but nevertheless took it on, and they finally—Phyllis Jackson—sent the book to Viking, and Viking said maybe. And that maybe lasted for an awful long time. Meanwhile Jack left town and became a bum, in effect. Worked on the railroad and the whole thing, and went on writing all those books for which we know and love him.

When he sent me *Visions of Cody*, and even *Doctor Sax*—*Doctor Sax* came first—I thought, man, no one's going to publish this. It's brilliant. It's youth. It's something absolutely new and unique and important, but *no one's* going to publish it. I'll never forget the afternoon. It was snowing. I was living on Forty-Eighth Street on the fifth floor of an old tenement, and I read that whole damned book *Visions of Cody* in one day. And I was depressed, not by the book, but by the fact that I knew he wasn't going to make it with this book. He wasn't going to get through. Nobody but me and Allen and a few people would ever read it, it seemed to me. I thought, "Oh, God, Jack! Why can't you write something that can get published so somebody can understand what you have?" In my foolishness it seemed he was being perverse. I was of two minds. I still am. In those years, in the fifties, it seemed to me most important that somebody come to understand him. They haven't to this day.

Giroux was deaf to Jack's explanations of a breakthrough and shocked by the form of *On the Road*, a singlespaced paragraph more than a hundred feet long. If a friend such as Giroux recoiled simply at the look of the thing, who would read it and publish it?

Jack sought a Guggenheim Foundation grant that spring, but he was turned down. Jobless when summer came, he joined Gabrielle on what would become a regular pilgrimage to Nin's house in Rocky Mount. Jack had no job there, either, but to his sister's husband and friends, he was a published novelist working on his next book.

What he worked on that summer was a long story published posthumously as the novel *Pic*. "Pic" could be read as shorthand for "pickaninny" or "picaresque," but is the nickname of a black boy christened Pictorial Review Jackson. He lives in the South and longs to hit the road with his wild older brother, Slim, for adventures on the West Coast. There is a great deal of talk in poorly handled black dialect, and the result is an embarrassingly uninformed white man's version of Langston Hughes' *Not Without Laughter*. At the end the two black brothers are standing by the road with their thumbs out. Two older travelers named Dean Moriarty and Sal Paradise give them a ride. At the very end of his life, when the words were gone, Kerouac retrieved *Pic* for consideration by Grove Press and changed the ending at Gabrielle's behest, removing the scene with Dean and Sal.

That October Jack joined Ed White one evening for a Chinese dinner at a restaurant near Columbia. In a letter to White well after the fact Jack thanked him for suggesting the new form that Kerouac called "sketching."

White had been a reader and useful critic of Jack's work all along. A year earlier, during Jack's 1950 visit to Denver, he had read the then-current draft of *On the Road*, the much-revised conventional narrative version begun in 1948.

"It had a completely different style, a very ornate sort of introduction," White recalled. "It was being told by a bootblack or shine boy. It was sort of Melvillean, real heavy prose."

By the night of the important Chinese dinner Jack had completed the teletype-roll draft of *On the Road*, which contained brief passages of impressionistic description, as *The Town and the City* had. Sketching was not a completely new method for Jack, but an intensification of traits that had been evident in all of his writing, including *The Sea Is My Brother*.

Ed White:

I think I was actually using a sketch pad then, 1951, and just suggested that he could do the same thing with notes. I think he thought about it. I don't think he said much about it, but then he began carrying his little notebooks around, filling them up. He printed faster than most of us

159

can write. He would show up with his notebook sometimes in the evening, after he'd been downtown all
day—at the library, in my apartment or wherever we
happened to be at the time; and he'd read parts aloud
he'd been writing. We'd usually end up drinking beer and
going out and listening to music.

The little notebooks provided raw material of two kinds:
diaristic details, like a reporter's notes, about events at hand
and an endless retracing in memory of all the events of his life,
reaching back to his earliest childhood memories in Lowell.

The following year, 1952, Jack adopted the sketching form
to record his dreams. A selection of these notes, published in
1961 as *Book of Dreams,* shows the depth of the psychological
forces that enrich his novels begun after sketching gave him a
way to mine the material. But these dreams, which actually mix
dreams with waking recollection, are presented as a patient
might recall them for an analyst, without theoretical interpretation of any kind.

In a significant entry in the dream journal police are
searching for Jack as an exhibitionist and he is running from
them without a pair of trousers. His search for something to
cover himself with leads him to a room crowded with his
manuscripts and poems, all of them embarrassingly revealing.
The dream makes him feel like "a sheepish guilty idiot turning
out rejectable, unpublishable manuscripts."

In another dream Leo rises from the dead again and again
to wander the streets of Lowell in search of work, but his ghost
never comes home in the evening to Jack and Mémère.

Late in 1951, utilizing this new technique, Jack had begun
to expand his early notes on Neal, which had gone unused in the
first draft of *On the Road,* into the eventual *Visions of Neal.*

Henri Cru wrote from California with another promise of
a berth on a merchant ship, but as before, when Jack arrived in
San Francisco there was no shipping job to be had. The trip did
give Jack a chance to continue writing about Neal with the
model before him.

"You going to write another book, huh?" Neal had written,
referring to the embryonic *On the Road.* "I'm trying to write
one, right? You love me, don't you? I love you, don't I? If we're
so all-fired good, then think of the funny times historians of the

future will have in digging up period in last half of '51 when K lived with C, much like Gauguin and Van Gogh, or Neitche [sic] and Wagner, or anybody ..."

Neal, as a patron, offered Jack the garret of the Cassadys' rented house on Nob Hill. This visit was Jack's first lengthy contact with Carolyn. With Neal's consent and implicit urging the two became lovers.

Matters became strained the night of Neal's twenty-sixth birthday, February 8, 1952, which was to be a quiet dinner at home for the three of them. Jack never appeared, and late at night, after Carolyn and Neal had gone to bed and made love, Jack telephoned "from the police station," as Neal told Carolyn. Cassady dressed and left. Hours passed, and neither returned.

Finally, after dawn, Jack and Neal reappeared, drunk, and Jack had with him a prostitute he led to his room in the attic. Carolyn was infuriated. Later Jack added a fresh inscription to the Cassadys' copy of *The Town and the City* and laid it on her dressing table. Carolyn had read Jack's first novel but she was avoiding the manuscript of *On the Road* because she knew it contained things about Neal and Luanne that would upset her.

Carolyn Cassady:

The inscription he wrote says, "To Carolyn, best wishes for you and your wonderful family, including the old man there, what's his name, old Neal. Love to you all, Jack Kerouac. December 19, 1951." Then underneath that he wrote that apology: "With the deepest apologies I can offer for the fiasco, the foolish tragic Saturday of Neal's birthday, all because I got drunk. Please forgive me, Carolyn, it'll never happen again."

Well, it didn't, actually. Not quite like that.

On the Road I dodged, or I just told him that I really didn't want to go through all that because I was still so sensitive about all these revelations that I didn't know about, and it would make me mad at Neal. I simply said I didn't want to hear about that trip. When I finally did get around to reading it, it was just one shock after another, but by then it didn't matter. The Diana thing I knew pretty much about because she and I'd been such close correspondents. Jack's passages about sitting around

161

in bus stations or any of that sort of thing, he'd read us, and that was great.

Like the *Visions of Cody* tapes attest they sat night after night and wanted to tell each other stories of their past and every other story they could think of, to get all the details of each other's lives and all their theories about everything. I don't think Jack had any idea at the time that he was going to use them verbatim. I think it was more a friendship thing of getting together, getting it all told, all understood.

The writing wasn't an outlet for Neal as it was for Jack. For Neal it was hard work. He did it mostly while he was babysitting. I always had the feeling that it was a forced discipline, and he would rather be out running around Little Harlem. He had to stay home, and so it helped him, but as most of his letters attest he was frantic, and that's why he had wanted Jack to come out all the time.

In 1951, Burroughs, Joan, and their children had moved to Mexico City. Morphine prescriptions were easy to come by in Mexico City, and Joan could buy her *dexedrina* over the counter rather than having to eat the drug-soaked wadding from respiratory inhalers.

Jack Kerouac, Cathy Cassady and Neal Cassady, 1952. Photo by Carolyn Cassady.

In the spring of 1952, Bill killed Joan in a game of William Tell at a party in Mexico City. It was she who put the champagne glass on her head and insisted that he fire, but, even at close range, he missed, and the bullet went through her brain. With the help of a Mexican lawyer Bill escaped charges; Joan's death was ruled accidental.

Now Burroughs, at thirty-five, began to write. He sent *Junky*, his chronicle of Huncke and Sailor and the early days of his addiction, to Allen chapter by chapter.

Allen in turn gave it to Carl Solomon, a poet he had met when both were patients at the Psychiatric Institute of Columbia-Presbyterian Hospital. One of Solomon's celebrated gestures during this period was the incident in which he threw potato salad on Wallace Markfield while the critic was lecturing on Mallarmé. Later he would become an ice cream vendor outside the United Nations, and then an author and book salesman, but in 1952 he worked as an editor for his uncle, A.A. Wyn, the publisher of Ace Books. Solomon convinced his uncle that with appropriate cutting and a distancing "medical" introduction *Junky* was publishable. Wyn bought it in April of that year for one thousand dollars.

By May the Cassadys were involved in plans to move to San Jose at the foot of San Francisco Bay.

Jack was uncomfortable with Neal's conflicting signals about the triangular relationship. He left for Mexico City, where Burroughs had begun *Queer*, a confessional book about his homosexuality intended as a sequel to *Junky*. In a few months Burroughs would press on to Morocco, and then to South America to search for a drug that fascinated him, *yage*.

In Mexico Jack turned back to his notes for a "novel of children and evil" and composed *The Shadow of Doctor Sax*, which eventually was published as *Doctor Sax*. Burroughs was still involved in his studies of Aztec culture at that time, especially interested in the psychological terror methods used by the priesthood to maintain control over the population. This trip was Jack's first real exposure to Mexican art, history, and legend; he had been too ill to pay much attention during his 1950 visit. Toltec folklore holds that the site of Mexico City was marked for its founders by an eagle with a snake in its mouth, and it was this image that Jack borrowed to furnish the ending for his apocalyptic vision of the world-snake's attack at the close of *Doctor Sax*. As the snake rises from the hill where it has slept for centuries, the storm-clouds above Lowell form themselves into the figure of a gigantic eagle, which seizes and subdues the serpent before both vanish with the morning light.

When Burroughs left Mexico City for Tangier in the summer of 1952, Jack returned to Rocky Mount, but he was uncomfortable there. In *Book of Dreams* he describes himself "like a thinner younger Major Hoople who really had a small taste of early success but then lost it and came home to live off his mother and sister but goes on 'writing' and acting like an 'author.'"

Neal asked him to return to California and Jack did, but the Cassadys and Kerouac were unable to restore the delicate balance of their three-way relationship, and so Jack withdrew to a skid-row hotel.

This particular October, 1952 marked the fulfillment of the old dream of Jack's that had begun on Mary Carney's front porch in Lowell, his ambition to work on the railroad, as Mary's father had done. Neal was working full-time on the Southern Pacific and with his help and Al Hinkle's, Jack was hired as a brakeman.

The prose that resulted was one of Kerouac's most affecting pieces, "October in the Railroad Earth," an impressionistic essay that captures the look and the feel of life on the line and in San Francisco's redbrick derelict streets.

Al Hinkle:

Jack was a poor brakeman. Neal was a natural, a good brakeman. And a good switchman. As a matter of fact he could tell from the exhaust of a steam-engine how fast the engine was going, and he could give the signs without even looking around, when he wanted them to stop. But Jack, I think, was afraid. He was afraid of the wheels. He was afraid of getting off and getting on. Neal would get on and off at twenty miles an hour; it didn't make any difference.

Because Jack was kind of afraid of it he would stay away from any of the jobs that would require a lot of experience and knowledge, instead of trying to get out and learn it.

Actually, what he wanted was to get on the Zipper, one of the long runs, and ride down to Watsonville and get off and go to the store and buy some crackers and wine, or some canned soup, and go down to the hobo jungle and sleep under the bridge of the Pajaro River and then go back to work.

But he liked the money. He liked not to cash the checks, save five or six checks up and then turn them into traveler's checks. Jack was a great one to carry all this money in traveler's checks and go down to Mexico and write a book.

I got Allen a job, too, on the railroad, when he came to San Francisco soon after that. They wouldn't hire Allen as a brakeman at the time because they wouldn't hire any Jews as brakemen. At that time there was, actually, in the union, a clause that you had to be white—and that included Jews, too. I got Allen a job as a clerk, what you call a mudhop, and it was in South San Francisco, nights. I think he lasted like a week or ten days, getting up fifty or sixty bucks, all he wanted to get anyway. Count the cars, get their number and what track they're on and make up the switch list for the switching crew so they'd move them to the industries or, if they were empties, to the inbound tracks.

Jack really wasn't that bad. We got a lot of poor brakemen. In comparison with Neal, who was very good, and myself, who's about the best as far as knowing how to do the work good, safe, fast. Neal and I worked together a couple of times and Jack and I worked together a couple of times. But because at the time we were mostly all on the extra board, just filling a vacancy as it occurred, we didn't work together that many times. But we'd run into each other off different crews down in Watsonville and do a little railroading down there. Most of the good railroading is done after the work's all over, when we'd sit down and talk about it.

Later Jack worked as a switchman in New York on one of those lines that take the boxcars and put them on the barges, take them over to New Jersey and you come back to the New York side, and then the engine goes out and pulls them off the barges and then they take them down to the different wharves. Jack wrote me about this, telling me he had gotten over his fear and could do the work now.

The toughest conductor we had on the SP was a fellow by the name of Ponteau, who was also French-Canadian and spoke French. This conductor was so *expertee* that I worked for him for four or five months as his rear brakeman on a switching crew, and I'd be standing out behind the caboose while he'd be sitting out on the main line flagging, sitting at his desk, and he'd look at his watch and say, "That crew is twenty seconds overdue to be back for the work they had to do." Then he'd start walking up to see if there was a switch off.

He was the conductor Jack worked for on his last trip. Jack caught him on the worst possible day, a Saturday, because on a Saturday he wanted you to do eight hours worth of work in two and a half hours, so he was a holy terror. You got paid for the whole day, you got eight hours pay, but this was Saturday, the start of your weekend.

So at eight o'clock in the morning, we'll say, the local goes to work out of San Jose, and Ponteau would be down there around 7:45, expecting everybody to be ready to go. If the clerks didn't have the bills ready, he was right in there screaming. If the yardmaster didn't have the train put together and put together right, he was on the speaker or would run up the stairs to the tower. And if the brakeman dared to be five minutes late he'd probably just leave him, because he'd leave at eight o'clock.

Well, Jack showed up on time, thank God, and the thing with Ponteau on a Saturday is, you got to have one foot in the air at all times. You got to move.

Jack not only can't move like that, he doesn't know what to *do*. You'd take off with a caboose and an engine and about seven or eight cars, and we're going to come tearing up through Campbell, up toward Los Gatos, and dump a couple of cars off, pick a couple of cars up, and then up to Permanente, this cement plant, and switch there, and then run down to California Avenue and switch there, the cannery, get rid of a few cars and then streak for home.

That Frenchman just went wild, because Kerouac made boo-boo after boo-boo. Which cost maybe a minute here, two minutes here. He didn't get off the engine until the engine stopped. He was supposed to get off

166

while it's still rolling and roll the two cars by. If you're
going to set two cars out, for example, when the engine
gets the speed down to about ten miles an hour you drop
off the engine, and when he stops, you're right at the two
cars. The minute he stops, or maybe even a little before,
still only moving a mile or two an hour, you reach in,
turn the hand-cock, pull the cutting lever—because a
good engineer will have the cars bunched so that you're
able to pull them—and give him the highball and then
grab by him, because then the engine doesn't even have
to stop. You've made the cut and away you go. This is
the way Ponteau wanted it done on a Saturday.

You didn't stop that engine and get off and walk
back two cars and turn the hand-cock and give the
engineer the sign. This is the way you would do it if you
were stalling for overtime, but this was the only way Jack
could do it, and he'd have to look at his list to see if this
was the right car. He'd look at the list and then look at
the car number. You're supposed to have this stuff in
your head.

Ponteau just chewed on him. I think Jack was going
to split in a week or five days, something real short, but
that did it for him. He never went to work again. He told
me he'd cut this job and talked to me before, and he
thought he was going to get along with Ponteau real
good. He was French-Canadian, too. At least these two
Canucks could talk to each other in French, but Ponteau
wasn't interested in anything on Saturday but getting
through.

After his autumn on the railroad Jack moved in briefly
with Carolyn and Neal again, but the three quarrelled, and so
Jack returned to New York City. It was clear that he was not a
recognized novelist, that *The Town and the City* had not
guaranteed him publication of further work, or even a cordial
welcome from the major publishers. But *The Railroad Earth*
was a very great work of prose, one whose merits must have
been plain to the author, and the railroad job provided another
way for him to buy the freedom to travel and to keep writing.
Gabrielle was well enough to take care of herself, and in a pinch
Jack could claim New York state disability payments on the

grounds—which were proper—that his phlebitis prevented him from working without endangering his health.

Heartened by his success in selling Burroughs' first manuscript to A.A. Wyn, Allen had become an active advocate and promoter of his friends' reputations. John Clellon Holmes finished his novel of the New York scene in the late 1940's and gave it to Allen, who in turn passed it along to Ace Books. Solomon rejected it, but Scribner's—Thomas Wolfe's publisher—accepted it. The Scribner edition consisted of only 2,500 copies, but *Go*—a title Jack suggested to Holmes—later would be picked up for paperback publication at a price of $20,000. Holmes' success stung Jack because *On the Road*, crowded with many of the same characters and some of the same situations, was unpublished. Both men knew that Jack's was the better book. Holmes would later call *Go* "almost literal truth, sometimes a truth too literal to be poetically true, which is the only truth that matters in literature."

Kerouac had followed Holmes' progress on *Go* since his friend began the book in earnest in 1949. He encouraged Holmes, and never expressed his jealousy to Holmes' face.

John Clellon Holmes:

Jack read it chapter to chapter as I wrote it, and, of course, when I came to writing Allen's visions, I talked to Allen about them the week before, wrote them—tried to write them—gave it to him, and he said, "Well, that's close enough."

Most of Jack's comments were tremendously helpful, but they were technical. He never said, "Oh, that's not the way it was." He said, "Why don't you skip from this to this, cut that out." Jack had a tremendous aesthetic gift. He could tell when it got dull, when you were straining, when you were padding. Most of the advice he gave was like that. It was awfully valuable.

He got resentful when I got to that part in the book where I have him fuck my wife, because he didn't. That was me intervening, trying to be a novelist, to explain my own screwing around with somebody else. Jack was kind of resentful about that, but we never had any con-

168

frontation about it. He didn't like that bloody glow thrown on his beard.

Within six weeks of finishing *Go*, it was accepted by Scribner's. Jack was on the West Coast. I'll never forget the day. I guess it's a day one doesn't forget. I was working at a place in downtown New York with Allen Ginsberg, NORC it was called, National Opinion Research Corporation. Allen had been working there longer than I had, and he was my boss, in effect, on this particular survey. A phone call came in about eleven o'clock in the morning for me. I picked it up and my agent said, "Scribner's is taking your book." Here are twenty-five people in the room and I was, of course, happy—though my marriage was breaking up, I was really more concerned with my personal problems—but I said to Allen, "Let's have lunch together. My book's been taken."

When the break came, around noon, down we went in the clanking elevator, and I said, "We gotta telegraph Jack. Wow!" "Yes," he said, "That's what we'll do." So we did. We sent Jack a telegram simply saying that the book had been taken. Then Allen and I went out and had a couple of drinks and some lunch.

Jack, on the West Coast, later became very resentful, in effect, that *On the Road* had been turned down while my book had been taken. And then, of course, when I got a big paperback deal, he was angry at me. Not angry at me perhaps, but angry that I'd broken through in a way that he really wanted to.

It all turned out to be dross, the way it does.

I was living in a cold-water flat on Forty-eighth Street and Second Avenue, and Jack came back. Allen came over to my house. We were expecting Jack, just back off the road, man, and so I put on my tape and we recorded the first ten minutes of our getting together again, the three of us.

By this point Jack was very purified. Nothing like the road to rub all the sand out of your soul. He didn't resent me any more. He never resented me personally. He just resented the fact he was eating shit and suddenly the Lord had smiled on me.

I had moved out from my wife. I was supporting her, but I had moved to another joint, this cold-water flat. When Jack came back, it was just as it always had been. It was different because my situation was different, but he used to sleep in my house then just the same. I was writing what would be my second novel, which has not been published yet, and doing articles—that first Beat Generation article and all that.

Allen Ginsberg:

... Kerouac encouraged Holmes to develop a certain intellectual style in mythology about Neal and about himself and about me. And then Kerouac got upset when Holmes actually performed that in a novel and made use of it, and later felt that Holmes had stolen ideas from him, or used ideas from him and didn't give him enough credit. So that made Holmes feel very upset and intimidated maybe. Jack did that with me occasionally. He accused me of stealing things from him which I thought were sort of common mythological property.

The provenance of the phrase "Beat Generation" is hazy. Jack and his friends picked up the word "beat" from Huncke, but in the drug scene the word has a special meaning: cheated, robbed, or emotionally and physically exhausted. In a "beat deal," a user puts his money down for heroin and takes home a packet of sugar. Both Holmes and Kerouac used "Beat Generation" in a casual way in *Go* and *On the Road*, and it was Gilbert Millstein, the literary journalist of the *New York Times*, who noticed the phrase in an advance copy of Holmes' novel and was intrigued by it. It had been a good thirty years since the emergence of a full-fledged American literary generation, the Lost one.

John Clellon Holmes:

The Beat Generation article came up as a fluke in October of '52. Gil Millstein had reviewed *Go* for the *Times*—the review had not been published yet—and he called me up and said, "What in hell is this whole 'Beat Generation' thing? What is this? Come in and let's talk about it." So I went over.

Scribner's was not going to do anything for the book. First novel, who cares? So I thought I'd do anything I could.

I went over and talked to Millstein, who was a very intelligent and interesting and perceptive kind of journalist guy, kind of man I respect. He said, "What is this?" And I said, "Well, I don't know yet." "Okay, do you feel like doing something for the Sunday section?" And I said, "Well, I'll give it a shot." So I went back, and in two days I wrote "This Is the Beat Generation" and sent it in. I didn't really know what it was, so I took two days thinking about it and writing it—not a very long piece— trying to define it. It looks silly to me now to some degree.

"This Is the Beat Generation" was their title. I delivered it to them and they liked it. I had to cut it somewhat. I had things about non-virgin clubs and all kinds of sexual things that they wouldn't swallow. I was taken in. They called me over and said, "We adore your piece. It's terrific. It's going to run, but..."

They took me in to see Louis Bergman, who was head of the Sunday Magazine section, and Gil said to me, "Look, he won't stand still for these non-virgin clubs." Through the Midwest in those years there was something called the non-virgin club. Kids formed clubs to deflower young ladies, and young ladies joined these clubs to be deflowered. I put this in as an example of changing mores. That had to go.

They published the piece, and it was a huge success.

"This Is the Beat Generation" ranges well beyond the small circle of New York intellectuals and party-goers portrayed in *Go*. Holmes' vision of the Beat Generation includes veterans of the Korean war who vanish into large corporations because their belief in the survival of small business has been destroyed, and teen-agers arrested for smoking marijuana, daring to question whether the drug is really evil. He finds their faces flooded with innocence.

One of Holmes' examples is a hipster mechanic with elements of Neal's character: "... [T] he giggling nihilist, eating up the highway at ninety miles an hour and steering with his feet is no Harry Crosby, the poet of the Lost Generation who planned to fly his plane into the sun one day because he could no longer accept the modern world. On the contrary, the hot-rod driver invites death only to outwit it."

For his closest historical comparison Holmes reached all the way back to his first literary discussions with Jack: "Dostoevski wrote in the early 1880's that 'Young Russia is talking of nothing but the eternal questions now.' With appropriate changes, something very like this is beginning to happen in America, in an American way."

The conventional popular image of the Beat Generation was still more than four years away. It would be drawn from reporting about Jack's personal situation and friends at the time that *On the Road* was finally published, bringing the phrase back into use, and from the humorously insulting coinage, "beatnik," invented by San Francisco gossip columnist Herb Caen. For those who required labeled goods Holmes made a label.

Soon after Holmes' article appeared, Allen made a personal breakthrough. A psychiatrist offered the opinion that Ginsberg was as sane as the physician himself, and Allen accepted this for the fact that it was. His poetry had begun to move in a new direction, toward the "eternal questions" considered in a revolutionary way. He was at work on "Howl," a full-throated roar on behalf of "the best minds of my generation" destroyed by the repressive society he now believed that it would be madness to join, or to surrender to.

For Allen the rushing threnody of "Howl" was a new style, a change in literary strategy equivalent to Jack's single-sitting draft of *On the Road*. Ginsberg turned his back on formal nineteenth-century scansion and the rhymed construction he had borrowed from models such as Yeats. Rhapsody was the motive force now, and his catalogue of modern horrors was dedicated to his former fellow psychiatric inmate, Carl Solomon.

From Solomon and his uncle, A.A. Wyn, Allen had wangled a three-book option for Jack, but when Kerouac submitted *On the Road* and *Visions of Neal*, the books were rejected. It is likely that Solomon could read their value clearly, but Ace Books was not a literary house. It produced instead very cheap paperbacks for sales in drugstores and bus stations. Later, of course, *On the Road* would sell in exactly such marketplaces, but in 1953 it was too early for that.

That spring Jack began another book, one that he hoped Solomon and Wyn might approve, a novel of late adolescence with Mary Carney at the center, *Springtime Mary*, also known as *Springtime Sixteen*. Like the other books set in Lowell this novel has a special brightness and clarity. Scotty, G.J., and all the other boys are here, and Jack's relationship with Mary Carney is presented with tenderness and poignancy, but Jack is in control of his sentiments and succeeds in suggesting the way in which his intellect and ambitions cut him off from the girl he loved in high school.

The book also had a distinct place in Jack's larger scheme, *The Duluoz Legend*—between *Doctor Sax* and *Vanity of Duluoz*. Five years after documentary evidence shows that the idea of the book-of-many-books was growing in Jack's mind, he was at work on it. *Springtime Mary* covered much of the same period of time that Jack had treated in the first half of *The Town and the City*, but he was writing about those years in the new style, which remained unconfirmed by publication or acceptance. In *The Town and the City* Francis' thwarted affair with "Mary Gilhooley" had been a brief episode used to draw that brother's character. Now it was a book unto itself.

Wyn rejected *Springtime Mary* as well, and Jack's option with Ace lapsed. On Holmes' recommendation, all of Jack's properties, including *On the Road*, were taken up by Phyllis Jackson at the MCA literary agency.

Jack went to California to spend the summer of 1953. The Cassadys had moved to their new house in San Jose, but Neal, who had been injured in a railroad switching accident (his foot nearly amputated by a wheel), was far from his effusive self. After a week or so, he and Jack quarrelled. It happened during a discussion about the pork chops Carolyn had served for dinner, and Jack came to feel that Neal had accused him of sponging. Jack retired to his room, where he prepared his own meals on a hot plate, and then to San Francisco, to one of the skid row hotels. Carolyn remembers visiting him there with her children. She was appalled by his fascination with the flaking paint, the buzzing neon signs and the derelicts snoring in the doorways. As soon as he could get a ship, Jack was on his way home to New York, via Panama, a journey he recounts in his essay "Slobs of the Kitchen Sea."

Home in New York he found a new woman. Mémère, still working as a skiver, had moved to Richmond Hill in Queens, but Jack took up his old alternation between her kitchen and the apartments of his friends in Manhattan, especially Allen, who lived on the Lower East Side, well before his neighborhood became "the East Village."

Jack's new romance was with a strikingly beautiful black woman who served as the model for Mardou Fox in *The Subterraneans*. [In the present volume she is, at her request, identified as "Irene May," Jack's name for her in *Book of Dreams*.]

She grew up in the most rural of the city's five boroughs, and played hookey from high school to explore the city, just as Jack had done when he went to Horace Mann. To a teen-ager from a quiet, small place, Manhattan was overwhelming and noisy, but, because of its comfortable scale, she found Greenwich Village appealing from her first discovery of it and she moved there when she began working in the city.

She worked as a telephone operator in the nearby Chelsea district and then for a social service agency headquartered off Astor Place on the Village's eastern fringes.

Several of Irene's friends had been patients in an experimental program for gifted people at the Psychiatric Institute of Columbia-Presbyterian Hospital. Kerouac appears never to have considered turning to psychiatry for insights or comfort, and Allen's rejection of psychiatry with the aid of the analyst who recognized the value of Ginsberg's dissatisfactions was a turning point in Allen's creative life. But for many Villagers and other New Yorkers of the 1950's, analysis was a secular religion which set forth the prospect of salvation through personal accommodation to a world which established a definition of sanity through normative behavior. Thus, for many, a simple refusal to adjust to the psychoanalytic view of the world as it was became a charged act of rebellion.

In the early 1950's, Irene worked for a health book company operated by an editor of New York's defunct left-wing newspaper, *P.M.*

"Irene May":

We were putting out books like *Blackstrap Molasses, Sauerkraut, Urine: Water of Life.* I felt, you know, here we are and what are we doing? And why am I in this office, typing up these bills, answering this correspondence? How can you get your bearings if you're doing things like this? The people who wrote us letters were in their 60's and 70's and looking for medical help. I was taking art and craft courses. The office manager was writing a biography of Virginia Woolf.

In the 50's world it seemed before you could do what you wanted to do, you had to be able to function in the straight business world. And a lot of people were having trouble coming to terms with it.

Eisenhower was telling us, "Everything is fine," and most Americans seemed happy with the way things were, and were making money or trying to. The impact of Madison Avenue was beginning to be felt in the early 50's. Someone would say: "Are you going to sell out to Madison Avenue?" And even the people Madison Avenue certainly didn't want, we all felt better. None of us was going to sell out!

Jack was incredibly good-looking, really handsome. He had big blue eyes and black, Indian-type hair. He had an openness, a brash quality. He could be very winning and lovable. I was always surprised at people's acceptance and caring for Jack. If you saw him with his friends, even if he were stone-drunk, he was accepted and loved. He was comfortable with them. No matter what he did, it didn't bother them.

I *liked* Jack, at times almost like a brother, someone I knew very well. We used to walk a lot, and sometimes we just goofed, sat around and talked and did nothing. When he came into Manhattan, he reminded me of kids from Brooklyn or Jersey coming to the big city, wanting to do something, wanting to go places. And it was fun up to a certain point.

At that time, I was barely able to do anything (or I had talked myself into thinking I couldn't without my therapist's approval), and Jack in his own way was helpless. We were both really play-acting at serious life.

But he was so busy wanting to get involved and

know this one group of people who didn't want to know him. They couldn't understand why he was coming at them in this incredible manner.

The New Yorker had a devastating review of *The Subterraneans* in which it was stated, "Mardou got tired of his writiness." I got tired of what was going on in conjunction with all the drinking, and barging in on people and going this place and the other.

Jack was insecure and paranoid to the point where if I went into the hall, he imagined I was sleeping with someone in the hall. If he was outside the door, I was in bed with someone.

Jack and I went to visit Lucien and his first wife, who had just had a baby. This was the first time I had met them. Lucien inquired with great politeness and seriousness: "And what part of India are you from?" I stared at him, perplexed. "India?" Jack had told him I was Indian.

Jack showed me *The Subterraneans* probably four or five days after he wrote it. He sent me a telegram: "Have soul surprise! Wait for me. See you Friday." Like a child who was going to receive a magical gift, I waited.

He walked in, we sat down before the fireplace and he handed me the manuscript. I started reading and I went into shock. A lot of it was still raw.

I could look at it one way and feel it was like a little boy bringing a decapitated rat to me and saying, "Look, here's my present for you." These were not the times as I knew them and the people, with the exception of his friends, were not as I knew them.

He said, "If you want me to, I'll throw it in the fire." I have to laugh. Jack would never have brought his only original manuscript to throw in the fire. I just don't believe it, but I did then, though.

The Subterraneans documents the frantic rounds of Leo Percepied and Mardou through the Village's various scenes. Record producer Jerry Newman, novelist William Gaddis, bop sax-man Alan Eager and poets Alan Ansen and David Burnett are all here, under other names. Kerouac chronicles Irene's fatigue and dissatisfaction with their life and records his search among their small quarrels for the one which will afford him a chance to separate from her. The chance comes following their encounter with Yuri Gligoric [Gregory Corso].

A native of Greenwich Village, reared in a series of foster homes, Corso's childhood echoed Cassady's. He became a street thief, and he discovered Stendhal and Dostoevski while serving a three-year sentence that ended in 1950, when he was twenty. Corso met Allen that year—and Jack, too, but only briefly. Kerouac and Corso did not become close until the autumn of 1953.

In the most memorable episode of *The Subterraneans* Yuri Gligoric engineers the theft of a vendor's pushcart as a prank, enraging Adam Moorad [Allen]. Ginsberg had been sensitized against such pranks, even a midnight misdemeanor like this, by his arrest with Huncke, Melody, and Vicki Russell. A few pages later Yuri and Leo Percepied [Jack] are bickering over Irene. Leo settles upon a trivial incident as his cue to break up with Mardou, and then wanders alone to a freightyard, where he has a vision of his mother.

The Subterraneans, as published, takes place in a curious terrain. The names of places are streets and neighborhoods in San Francisco, adopted to make the book appear to be entirely a fiction, any similarities between its characters and actual persons, living or dead, a coincidence. The pushcart episode happened on the flat terrain of lower Manhattan, for example, but as it appears in the novel would have involved a killing hill. San Francisco has no pushcart vendors. The freightyard in the final pages of *The Subterraneans* is the "railroad earth" of the Southern Pacific yards in South San Francisco. It is possible that Jack's calming vision of his mother happened in the switching yard near their old apartment in Ozone Park. What seems certain is that Jack's thoughts really did turn from Irene to his mother. He was thirty-one years old.

Gregory Corso:

In *The Subterraneans* Jack was very pissed at me, which he had no right to be because I was not then his close Gregory Corso friend as it is today. In those days I had just met him.

To me, friends were very hard to make, especially in prison. If you're going to make a friend, it was *hard*. But coming out of prison, you're a poet and the other guy's a poet, automatically you were friends, you see. I didn't see it that way. It took a little while before I became friends with these guys.

He writes in *The Subterraneans* where I was there hanging around 'cause I had no place to stay. I said, "There's no place for me to write." He mentions that. And he called me a mooch in the book, yet, 'cause I asked him for a couple of dollars. So there was not a friendship built up yet by it. Something was not yet formed because it was just happening—just in the beginning. And being that Jack recorded all the things that went down, it seems like when people read it, well, here's an old friend of Kerouac's doing this thing which is not so. I was a new friend.

I was the instigator of the pushcart episode. We had come out of Fugazi's Bar and we were walking through Washington Square Park and there was this pushcart. I said, "Well, wouldn't it be nice if you got in there and I pushed you to Ginsberg's place?"—And they said, "Yeah, it would be nice." And I said, "Well, great, get in." So they got in and I pushed and they were looking up at the stars and it was beautiful. And I was really pushing that thing beautifully. It was a happy scene.

I park it in front of Allen's place. Now that wasn't very cool, 'cause there was the evidence in front of Ginsy's secure home, right? The landlord wondered what was that pushcart doing in front of the place where Allen lived? So he went to investigate.

Allen and Jack had a little fuss. It was not a big deal, but nonetheless, the pride of Kerouac came out, and he threw the key down and said to Allen, "Here's your key," 'cause Allen said, "You screwed up the security of my home." With the pushcart, but not only that, but Allen's warmth for the poor bum who owned the pushcart.

So I tried to ease off Allen on that by saying, "No, the bum does not own the pushcart, the pushcart comes from these mothers who use the bum to pick this cardboard to sell." So really, it belongs to the Mafia who get all the paper and then recycle it. He should not have had that much worry about the poor bum, because it's a bum, it's many bums who go in daily and they dispose of

178

the pushcart, they can't pick up any cardboard. Anyway, we had the nicest time in that pushcart that that pushcart ever had.

The security of the house and Jack laying down the key and saying, "Well, fuck you and your security of the house. Here's your key back." And me, I'm sitting there like, "Uh oh, I fucked up again, I did something wrong." I caused friends to argue and åll that. Really, I was like a real pain in the ass sometimes, but in a nice way, I thought, because all it was was a nice pushcart scene.

Gregory Corso in New York, May 1972. Photo by Marshall Clements.

So I might have caused a little screw-up with them by me using the pushcart and leaving it in front of Allen's and getting screwed up with the two friends.

I'm in it as a kind of guy who gets in there and is fucking up the scene with his dopey actions. But most of them to me were all spontaneous. They weren't planned, and they were happy moments.

Allen Ginsberg:

If anybody had brought a pushcart to Jack's house on Long Island, he would have screamed like a stuck pig.

Gregory Corso:

Oh, yeah. It would bother him. But you see, if nobody had ever brought the pushcart, nothing would have happened. There would have been nothing to write about. I ain't that dumb out of it. See, you didn't get into the main ballgame. The main ballgame was in the push-cart, looking up in New York City streets at the sky and the stars—if you see stars in New York City. Lying back with the buildings straight up, closing in.

Allen Ginsberg

That's not the main ballgame. The main ballgame was probably me and Burroughs at home in the apartment when you guys stole the pushcart.

Gregory Corso

Bill was the one that looked at me really being the guilty one. It was so funny. Allen and Jack arguing and all that, and I'm just sitting back and not getting any weight laid on me, whereas I'm the one that said, "Hey, a pushcart. You wanna ride?"

I was under the impression that Jack dug women. That's as much as I knew. My impression of him was that he dug chicks and that his mother was very heavy on him in a way. For instance, a crucifix over the bed in the

180

house. If you came over, if you were married, you could fuck in that bed, but if you weren't married, you could not fuck. A very Catholic—French-Canadian-Catholic—number. He was anchored very much with something very noble, taking care of the mother. He didn't know who was going to take care of her. "I've got to take care of her, Gregory." I said, "You're right."

But a lot of people confuse his sexuality with that, that she's the one then who screwed him up at that. He didn't really make it well with women. There was not one that could fold any long way with him, except at the end he went back to his old girlfriend—Greek girl, Stella—and married her at the end of the ballgame.

And what'd he lay on her? "Take care of my mother when I'm gone."

Helen Hinkle:

Jack fell in love with every woman he ever saw. They were *gorgeous*. They were *marvelous*. He was a *lover*. He loved women.

Lucien Carr:

Jack and I were *so* different—intellectually, emotionally, prejudice-wise—all the things that make a man. So different. We were close because we loved each other, but we were able to understand each other because we were so apposite.

We never agreed on a woman—I mean that we both wanted. "*Man*, that's a *great* woman for you," and he'd say, "That's a *great* woman for *you*." We never really lusted after the same woman.

Allan Temko:

Kerouac's sex life is very ambiguous, so one doesn't know. Those guys hated women, all of them. Either they maltreated women or took women who were at a hopeless social disadvantage. They were at a loss with educated women.

181

"Irene May":

Women liked him. I think he was very fond of women, but I don't think he was up to the responsibility of taking on a wife who was going to be dependent on him. He needed someone to take care of him.

The San Remo. The San Remo used to be very crowded. Two girls used to come in, they wore very heavy eye makeup and they had bangs—very attractive— and they used to sit on a low refrigerator unit in the corner of the bar, a large room filled with over a hundred people, peeking out and looking at everything. We called them the birdwatchers.

We were all like that. We were standing there on these black-and-white tile squares, like a checkerboard where you take up a position.

I remember Gore Vidal standing at the bar and leaning, with one foot on the rail. Jack—I had gotten used to this pattern—was well on his way to being drunk and didn't want to stop. "I've got to see Gore Vidal! It's a historic literary occasion!" To me, that just meant a drunken occasion.

We went outside where we had this little scene. I tried to drag him away so he wouldn't go on drinking all night. He stood on his head to convince me he was sober and knew what he was doing. He used to do that quite often.

Gore Vidal:

We'd spent the early part of the evening with William Burroughs, who had just come up from Mexico, and Burroughs had written Jack a letter saying that he wanted to meet me because I looked so "pretty" on the dust-jacket of *The Judgment of Paris*. (I was sent a copy of the letter a couple of years ago.) So the three of us went to dinner and got rather drunk.

Then Jack decided that it was time that he and I went to bed together. As the evening waxed, it seemed to me like a less good idea, as the drink increased and the morning was near. Finally, Burroughs disappeared into the night, and Jack and I ended up at the Chelsea Hotel.

182

I have a perfectly vivid memory, as indeed did Jack, of what then transpired. For those curious, they can read the early chapters of *The City and the Pillar* if you want to get exactly an impression of what happened.

Jack was in a very cheery mood about it all, in spite of a hangover the next day. He'd run out of money, and he asked me to lend him a dollar. He gets that right in the book. I gave him the money and I said, "And now you owe me a dollar." Those were my last words to him as we parted.

I didn't see him again until *The Dharma Bums* was published, which was '58. Meanwhile I had read *The Subterraneans*, and I said, "Why didn't you really describe what happened that night at the Chelsea?"

He said, "Oh, I forgot."

I said, "You didn't forget."

"Well, maybe I wanted to forget."

And I said, "And this is the method that you are trying to peddle to the world? Your honest, straightforward, absolutely truthful tell-it-like-it-is literature. Is this it?"

He had no answer to that. I think that's what he *thought* he was doing. But he was basically timid—

Then I was doing a Studio One play for television, and a guy called Jack Barefield, who worked for the McCann-Erikson advertising agency, said that he was in the San Remo and this crazy guy suddenly got up and shouted, "I blew Gore Vidal!" Jack Barefield came to me and said, "I don't think this is very good publicity for you, Gore." And I said, "Well, describe him." And it was Kerouac.

Fag-baiting was the national sport in the forties and fifties, and it was particularly intense in the New York literary scene, and the few editors who were faggots were certainly hung high in the deepest and darkest of closets. *The Partisan Review* was, from the high-brow point of view, the most venomous on the subject while the *New York Times* conducted the holy war on behalf of the middle-brows. The idea that there was a comintern of faggot writers and editors perverting and seducing innocent talent is just nonsense.

Jack was bisexual, and Jack was not above using it, and his physical charms, to get his way. In one instance he may—and I'm putting this very tactfully—have done exactly that in order to advance his career as a writer.

Did Allen tell you about what Kerouac's mother said? He said that Jack took him home to Lowell to meet his mother, and he said, "Now, for Christ's sake, Allen, don't camp around and just play it cool. My mother's an old-fashioned, Roman Catholic, French-Canadian lady and..." He was very nervous about bringing Allen in. This is pre-beard. Allen looked like a young advertising executive, which he was—still is, I should think, at heart.

So Allen behaved very well, he thought, and then as soon as Jack was out of the room, Mrs. Kerouac turned to him and said, "Are you a faggot?" Or whatever word she used. "Pansy" was probably the word. And he said, "Yeah, I guess I am." She said, "That's so interesting, because, you know, I always thought Jack's father was." And she started a long speech about her suspicions about the father, not about Jack.

Allen Ginsberg:

It didn't happen, but I can believe that Jack told Gore Vidal that it had...

Except by reference occasionally in his writings ...Jack avoided his own homosexual encounters, rare as they were. He completely blanked out on that aspect of me, in life he actually was upset about it. He was upset when he was confronted with it. I'm puritanical myself.

I remember once in New York, in '48 or so, we were sitting around Neal's house. Neal, I think, just had a little Chinese dressing gown on, and I had my hand on Neal's thigh for about an hour, in a long conversation, and Jack finally, irritably said, "Why don't you take your damn hand off his thigh...feeling him up all the time." Really funny, like his mother, an echo of his mother, which might have been God knows what. Perception? Or jealousy? Or perceptive to my aggressiveness?...

Neal finally had to rebuke Jack and say, "Now mind your business, Jack," or whatever he said, something like, "What's the matter, Jack? I like it." I don't know what it was, but anyway, he defended me.

He would bait me quite a bit...drunken humor...particularly on the telephone, until I realized what he was doing and started baiting him back...He

184

was just sort of like testing out how egocentrically hung up I was in whatever position I thought I was defending... I probably was hurt that he was accusing me of "corrupting little boys," but I probably should have said, "You're absolutely right. You're next, get in there and take off your pants!" Then he would have come down and stopped making a big scene. Or if I'd said, "Yes, but not so shady a corrupt as your mother with her fishy cunt, your father with his corpse-like implications..." he would then come down, and just get on to an ordinary conversation.

The Subterraneans, which Jack had written in the space of three nights. assisted by benzedrine, joined the rest of Kerouac's shadow-legend in the files of his agent, Phyllis Jackson.

Burroughs left New York for Colombia, in pursuit of *yage*. In next-door Panama he gathered the impressions of banana-republic soldiers and civil servants whom he would satirize in *Naked Lunch*. Allen began planning his own expedition to Latin America and, beyond that, considered staying with kinsmen in Southern California or doing post-graduate work at the University of California at Berkeley.

Jack traveled to the little town of Los Gatos, west of San Jose at the foot of San Francisco Bay. Neal and Carolyn were settled there in a ranch-style house with a large yard, but, for the first time, there was no spare room set aside for Jack. He said nothing about it, but Carolyn felt his discomfort. Rather than sleep on the living-room couch, he pitched camp on the patio, where the Cassadys' cocker spaniel would lick his face to awaken him in the morning. His phlebitis was bothering him again, and Carolyn watched him stand on his head for long minutes to get relief as the blood drained from his legs.

Since their last time together, the Cassadys had become serious students of the American prophet and healer Edgar Cayce. When Neal and Carolyn attempted to share their enthusiasm about Cayce, Jack countered with Buddhist aphorisms. Allen, for his own part, would later begin to study Hinduism in India, and whether Jack's interest in the Buddhists had begun with Professor Weaver's reading-list in the mid-1940's or was a later discovery, he now became absorbed in the subject, vanishing often into the San Jose Public Library to read their collection of books in the field. His main source of raw material was a volume that collected the essential texts of Buddhism, Dwight Goddard's *The Buddhist Bible*. In its 700-odd pages he found concepts of historical cycles so gigantic that they dwarfed Spengler's. He found, as well, the notion of *dharma*, the same self-regulating principle of the universe that he had proposed himself in the closing pages of *Doctor Sax*. *Maya*, the illusory play of reality, matched the vision of his personal insignificance, which had been inspired by the starry August sky that long-ago night on his mother's back porch in Lowell.

Using his sketching technique Jack converted the texts in *The Buddhist Bible* into his own words, the still-unpublished journals, *Some of the Dharma*. Jack never abandoned his Catholicism, but a philosophy that began with the premise that all life is suffering helped him to make sense of his own situation.

After a few months with Neal and Carolyn the three argued over the division of some marijuana they had bought together, and in March, 1954, Jack moved back to his Mission Street hotel in San Francisco. There he composed *San Francisco Blues*, a downbeat sequence of poems about streetlife and winos, some of the verses tinged with the first Buddhist phrases and ideas to enter Jack's published writing.

Little, Brown turned down *On the Road* in June, but later that summer the critic and editor Malcolm Cowley, who was associated with Viking, wrote Jack for permission to propose an excerpt from the book to Arabelle Porter, an editor of *New World Writing*, a quality review published in paperback form by Signet Books. Jack had bitterly abandoned his relationship with MCA after Phyllis Jackson's failure to place the book, but Cowley was struck by its freshness and became Kerouac's champion, praising the manuscript in his 1954 survey *The Literary Situation:*

> There was one fairly large group that refused to conform and waged a dogged sort of rebellion—against what it is hard to say, because the group had no program, but possibly against the whole body of laws, customs, fears, habits of thought, and literary standards that had been accepted by other members of the generation.... Often they talked about being "underground" and called themselves "the beat generation." It was John Kerouac who invented the second phrase, and his

186

unpublished long narrative, *On the Road,* is the best record of their lives. In two respects they were like the conventional majority of young people: they had no interest in politics, even as a spectator sport, and they were looking for something to believe, an essentially religious faith that would permit them to live at peace with their world.

Malcolm Cowley:

My first notice of Kerouac was the submission of the manuscript of *On the Road* to the Viking Press, and specifically to me at the Viking Press. I don't remember how it came in. Allen Ginsberg may have brought it. It had, by that time, passed through several stages. At some stage it was revised and retyped so that when it came into the Viking Press it was a conventional paged manuscript.

I read it with great interest and enthusiasm, and I told a Viking meeting about it and got a couple more readings for it, but no, they wouldn't publish. It was very much a matter on my mind. I thought, "Here is something new. Here is something that ought to get to people. A way has to be prepared for it."

Viking was then a rather conservative house, and they thought this was too much out of the beaten path for our salesmen to place in the bookstores, so the manuscript stayed on my desk. Kerouac came in to see me several times, and I said, "What you will have to do first is to get some of this published in magazines." So I excerpted the section called "The Mexican Girl" and gave it to *Paris Review,* which accepted it with some enthusiasm. Then I looked for what other section could stand by itself. It was the one on jazz in San Francisco, and Arabelle Porter took that for *New World Writing.*

Time goes on. I continued to see Jack and then, sometimes, Allen Ginsberg coming in with him. I remember one night Jack and I went out on the town. I wanted him to show me the new dives in Greenwich Village with which I was totally unfamiliar, not having been a Villager for twenty years. And he took me down. I remember his saying portentously that in fifty years there will be only two religions left in the world. I said with curiosity, "Which two?" And he said,

"Mohammedanism and Buddhism." That rather surprised me because Jack's Catholic upbringing was one of the steady strands in his nature.

So I was seeing Jack and seeing Allen Ginsberg and giving advice from time to time. I think Allen had the idea that perhaps I could act as a sort of elderly grandfather for the Beats, which idea did not appeal to me.

Arabelle Porter paid Jack $120 for "Jazz of the Beat Generation," and went along with his insistence that it be published under the name "Jean-Louis." Jack was fearful of publishing anything under his real name, lest his ex-wife, Joan Haverty, sue him for support of her daughter, whose paternity Kerouac denied. The piece was scheduled for publication the following spring, 1955.

In October of 1954, Jack went all the way home, a visit to Lowell. Back in Mémère's flat in Richmond Hill he tried to explain to her the comfort he had found in his Buddhist studies, but Gabrielle stubbornly insisted on regarding that philosophy as a pagan religion. The quarrel would worsen in the years ahead.

Mémère went to Rocky Mount alone that Christmas. Jack stayed on in Richmond Hill to continue revising *On the Road*, hopeful that Cowley's plan would work, that Porter's publication of the excerpt would spark interest at some house that had not yet rejected the manuscript.

Despite the fact that Jack was broke, drawing aid to the disabled on the basis of his persistent phlebitis attacks, Joan Haverty brought her suit for child-support. With Allen's lawyer brother, Eugene Brooks, defending him, Jack convinced the judge that he was destitute. The question of paternity remained moot, although in later years it was plain to Jack's closest friends that Joan's daughter was his, too.

In truth Jack's phlebitis was worse. It had begun with his benzedrine binges while writing *The Town and the City*, and worsened with his increasing reliance on drink in the early fifties. He could secure relief only by taping his legs to contain the swelling, and he often was forced to type in bed with a portable machine on a board across his lap.

Jack translated the agony into a strengthened faith in the message of the Buddha. In Rocky Mount in the spring of 1955 he began *Wake Up*, a biography of the Buddha. Nin and her husband were discouraged by Jack's drinking, and baffled by his attempts to rationalize Buddhism to them. The appearance of the issue of *New World Writing* with the story "Jazz of the Beat Generation," did nothing to restore his reputation in their eyes.

Before leaving for North Carolina Jack had secured a new agent with Giroux's help, Stanley Colbert of the firm of Sterling Lord. Colbert submitted Jack's new version of *On the Road*, now retitled *Beat Generation* with an eye to the market, to Alfred A. Knopf, who quickly turned it down. But now Cowley had a new ally at Viking.

Malcolm Cowley:

Viking had acquired a new editor, Keith Jennison, and Keith read the manuscript with great enthusiasm, and he had force and conviction in presenting his case. And Keith, this time, with my aid, put *On the Road* past the Viking meeting. It was finally accepted.

In addition to the sale of the section based on Bea Franco to *The Paris Review*, Cowley engineered a $200 grant from the Academy of Arts and Letters to help tide Jack over until his royalties from Viking began. With that grant and his small advance check from Viking, Jack went to Mexico in the summer of 1955 to join Bill Garver in Burroughs' old apartment. Burroughs was in Tangier, writing the sketches that would be assembled as *Naked Lunch*.

A story that Jack wrote that spring shows the way that Ginsberg, Burroughs, and Kerouac shared themes and approaches. "cityCityCITY" is Jack's only published work of science fiction. It evidently grew from his dream of a "city of refuge." The style of "cityCityCITY," with its dangerous and alluring "No-Zone," its computer-dispensed drugs, and its mysterious forces of Activation, guerrilla fighters on behalf of real life and free love, are highly reminiscent of the control systems Burroughs explored in much of his less-than-literal work.

189

Jack "chippied" at morphine use that summer, and under the influence of marijuana continued his experiments with poetry. The result was *Mexico City Blues*, regarded as his best set of poems. "I want to be considered a jazz poet blowing a long blues in an afternoon jam session on Sunday. I take 242 choruses; my ideas vary and sometimes roll from chorus to chorus or from halfway through a chorus to halfway into the next." Each chorus represented a single sitting. Every important aspect of Jack's life to this point is contained in these sketch-works, if only as an echo, and Kerouac's analogy with jazz is exact. Some of the choruses read like scat singing played back at slow speed, words "blown" for their musical values or their punning link to the subject matter that Kerouac had in mind.

William Burroughs:

Jack'd sit and write for hours on end. Longhand, longhand. He'd just sit down in a corner and say, "I don't want to be disturbed," and I wouldn't pay any attention to him. He worked away.

Kerouac's method of writing worked for him. That doesn't mean it would work for anyone else. It doesn't work for me at all. I don't write that way. I edit. He always said the first version is best. I said, "It may be best for you, but it's not for me." I take three versions at least before I get it into any kind of shape. It is very much, of course, in the tradition of Wolfe. The method of composition was very similar. It's the flow and writing at great speed.

At that time, in Mexico, his whole theory was pretty well developed. That is, of sketching with words, and of the flow and using the first version—the first words that came.

Gregory Corso:

When we saw him writing *Mexico City Blues* was the first time I saw him smoking pot. I was living downstairs with Peter [Orlovsky] and Allen and Bill Garver, who lived next door and was a morphine addict.

Jack was going across the street to a bar, and I remember him looking at his palms. I was saying, "Now look at his hands." I said they were like Clark Gable hands—real strong, manly-type thing. And I looked and said, "Those hands are gonna make it."

He was very much into trying to help out this junkie Mexican chick, Tristessa in the book [Jack's novel, *Tristessa*], and he took me up to see her, and it was this strange Mexican building. It was like glass, only you walked on a glass floor. A very small room, and she was out of it. He had this great feeling towards her. I don't think he knew what a junkie was like, 'cause there's nothing you can do but just give them some junk and they'll feel better. There's no way of trying to ease them out unless you give them their medicine.

"Tristessa's" real name was Esperanza Villanueva.

By now Jack had adopted the Buddhist code of celibacy, doubtlessly assisted by the morphine and the pain of his phlebitis. When he returned to Mexico a year later, in 1956, he professed his love to her, but she regarded his declaration with the cold eye of the addict accustomed to selling her body for a fix. Jack added her portrait to those of Mardou Fox and Maggie Cassidy in his chronicles of unhappy love affairs. The novel *Tristessa* paints Duluoz as an innocent adrift in a world of everyday evil.

Kerouac's October pilgrimage in 1955 was to San Francisco, where Ginsberg had gone to visit the Cassadys. After a stay at Neal's, Allen worked for a year in San Francisco, wrote "Howl", and then moved to Berkeley where he lived in a cottage on Milvia Street. His initial intention was to enroll at the University and get an M.A. degree, but this was not to be.

San Francisco had always had a rich and varied tradition of poets, many of whom had come to the city from other places, as would Ginsberg, Corso, and the other Easterners. Michael McClure, for example, was a midwesterner drawn by the presence of the abstract expressionist Clyfford Still. In the fall of 1955 the Bay Area's poetry scene was like a super-saturated solution, waiting for the single crystal that would solidify it. "Howl" turned out to be that crystal.

191

Much of Allen's newfound calmness and faith in himself as a poet probably came from his intense affair with a handsome, blond young man named Peter Orlovsky. The painter Robert LaVigne provided the unusual connection between the two men.

Peter Orlovsky:

I came out of a very poor family. My father's Russian, and he didn't have any friends and was always occupied in his business, making ties, silk-screening ties in New York. One business went to another, one failure to another failure, and so he was spending all his time at work, hardly any time at home. My mother was deaf, and she had half her face paralyzed from a bad operation. She stayed up all night and drank—they drank a lot in the daytime through the forties, when I was growing up. The house was very disorganized and messy, and it was just a bad situation. I had three brothers and a sister. I was the third oldest. Then I went off to the Army, and I got stationed in San Francisco at Letterman Hospital. There I met Robert LaVigne, an artist. I was living with him for a year, and then Allen saw a painting that LaVigne did of me, naked.

Allen saw that and fell in love with me, and then we got together. I fell in love with Allen because he was so smart. He knew so much, and he recited so much poetry from memory, and he loved me, so I was thrilled.

I went back East in early '56 to get my brother, Lafcadio, who wasn't doing too well at home, and we came back to San Francisco and were living there, and Jack would come over and visit and Neal would come over a lot. In '55 Jack came around and got into an argument with Allen, accusing Allen of being lecherous toward me, and banged a crack in the bathroom door, calling Allen a lecher. After young boys, you know. His Catholic upbringing, I guess.

I took a liking to Jack right away. He was very rugged-looking, healthy and strong, an athlete. Jack was talking about Buddhism, about the ten directions of space, *tathagata*, and *gandharvas* and eternity, and they had Dwight Goddard's *Buddhist Bible*, so Allen started

Chris MacLaine, Peter Orlovsky and Gregory Corso, San Francisco, 1957.
Photo by Gui de Angulo.

reading the Diamond Sutra and the Heart Sutra and the
Lankavatara Sutra.

We went up one day to Alan Watts, where he was
giving lectures at the Asian Society, and we were outside
those big luxurious houses up there in that Nob Hill area.
I was trying to impress Jack, and we had a nice long
conversation in the street about how all of a sudden you
got to love everybody and be kind to everyone. I got that
from Allen and from reading a little of the poetry that
Allen gave me to read and reading those passages in *The*

Idiot where Mishkin says you got to love everyone or Father Zossima says it's all based on love and being kind and being good.

Jack would stand on the street and write things down. The amount of literary talk, talking about what they were reading, it was endless and it was always amazing, 'cause they always were able to keep at it for hours and hours, and then they would look over poems that Gregory wrote or Allen wrote or Jack wrote or Neal wrote or Bill wrote. It was an endless interest in words, an endless flow of words.

Jack practiced so much, just like a sitter, a Buddhist sitter. Sitting-writing-sitting. Sat at the typewriter. Jack really went home and wrote for hours and hours and hours, continuously over the years. That's a writing-sitting, or a composing-sitting or creative-art-sitting. It's not the same as letting go. That's another kind, just being aware of mind in space, or mingling of mind and space, or just paying attention to your breath leaving your nose.

In courtly fashion (the letter of introduction was from William Carlos Williams, a resident of Rutherford, near Paterson, N. J.), Ginsberg sought the company of Kenneth Rexroth. Rexroth was scholarly without seeking the shelter of the academy. As a poet, critic, translator, and literary Barnum in a city that demanded conformity to local color, his house very nearly had become the Bohemian Embassy. Presentation of portfolio was an important ritual for a new poet in town.

In a spirit of goodwill Rexroth brought together the writers who would stage the Six Gallery reading in November of 1955. In the two decades since that evening happened it has come to be regarded as a watershed, such as the Armory Show was for American painting or the première of *Le Sacre du Printemps* was to modern composition.

Lawrence Ferlinghetti:

I had an old Austin, and I drove Allen and Kerouac and Corso to the Six Gallery reading. The car was weighted down to the axle, this little tiny car, and we went to this little tiny garage, which was the Six Gallery.

Kerouac, at that reading, was drinking wine. He had

a jug of wine and he was lying on the floor up near the stage in the front. The whole building was just a remodeled garage, about twenty-five feet deep and twenty feet wide. Sometimes Kerouac would flake out, and people would think he was passed out or something, but he was taking everything down in his head.

Michael McClure:

Just a few months before our reading there, earlier that year, 1955, Robert Duncan had read his *Faust Foutou* play. And I guess that's what gave Wally Hedrick the idea of having a poetry reading at his Six Gallery, so he asked me if I would set up the reading. In the meantime my wife Joanna was pregnant and I was working at the museum, and I ran into Allen on the street. He said, "What are you doing? What's happening?" I said, "I've been asked to set up a poetry reading, but I'm really in a kind of crunch of time and life at this moment." And he said he'd do it. So then Allen took it over and set up the reading for us.

Michael McClure, Philip Lamantia, John Wieners and David Meltzer, San Francisco, 1958. Photo by Gui de Angulo.

It's very possible that Allen was already looking for a place for a poetry reading, because he took the possibility of the Six Gallery with such alacrity. He must already have had it in mind, and he might have even mentioned it to me at the time.

I hadn't seen Phil Whalen or Gary Snyder before. They were new to me that night. Of course, Lamantia and Rexroth I knew. That was my first poetry reading, and it looked like a lot of people to me.

I would guess that there were a hundred and twenty-five. I was very nervous, but I thought it was a totally delightful and beautiful evening. I did enjoy everyone's work, and was very distracted by the circumstances.

Everybody was drinking a lot. Contributions were taken. People were going out to get wine. There was a lot of yelling. I read a letter from Jack Spicer, who was trying to get a job back in San Francisco so he could come back from Boston, and people were talking about that.

Lamantia already had quite a reputation, but I don't think Lamantia's reputation was public. It was a literary reputation. So that in essence Lamantia was new. I think that's really the mystery of it. There was certainly some distance between Allen and Robert Duncan that I was in a position, in an odd way, of trying to bridge. I don't think Robert ever realized that, or probably would have been grateful for the fact that I was doing it if he'd known.

What really was holding things together was camaraderie, and there was a different spirit between, say, the six of us who read at that gallery and the older, very beautiful, and potent literary scene that had been here. Duncan and Rexroth and Everson and Jimmy Broughton and Maddie Gleason and various other individuals had been part of a literary scene that had been developing since the forties. We were all standing on our feet enough so that I think we all influenced each other enormously.

Jack rooted Ginsberg and the others on, as one would encourage a jazzman to sustain a brilliant solo. For Jack the most important figure on the stage of the little waterfront gallery was Gary Snyder, then a Berkeley graduate student who pursued Oriental language studies in order to satisfy his hunger for Buddhist texts in their original form, especially the works of the Zen masters, who were then little-known or understood in America.

Allen Ginsberg:

In San Francisco Kenneth Rexroth was "at home" one day a week. I must have gone with Gary Snyder at one time or another, I went by myself once or twice, I went there once with Phil Whalen and Jack and Gary and Peter. Kenneth had a house with a large library and lots of copies of the *I Ching* and *Secret of the Golden Flower* and Chinese poetry, Japanese poetry, and old English, German dictionaries...a great library.

He knew Gary already. He connected me with Gary originally, actually, and thus connected Gary with Kerouac. I forgot whom I went to his house with—maybe McClure—for the first time. Or maybe Robert Duncan, or Lawrence Ferlinghetti. I had a letter of introduction to him from William Carlos Williams, and I guess what I did was bring him a copy of my book *Empty Mirror*, with Williams' introduction. I think I gave it to him, and he said to give it to Duncan. And I may have brought him Kerouac's *Visions of Cody*. I was carrying *Visions of Cody*, maybe *Yage Letters*, *Empty Mirror*, a whole bunch of stuff around with me and to the West Coast, finally. I brought it all and showed it to him.

...Anyway, I once went to Rexroth's *salon* with Jack. Rexroth had read his work, knew of his reputation, admired him a great deal, had said that he was the greatest unpublished writer in America. Or maybe he told that to Cowley, maybe that's where Cowley got it. Jack was a little drunk and, unless I'm mistaken, was sitting on the floor laughing, and Rexroth got upset that Jack was going to wake his baby—his daughter—and got mad at him, called him a son of a bitch and ordered him out. Or got mad at him later, after we left, but was upset. Well, Kerouac was a little drunk, but just sort of a Friday-afternoon tipsy, not a big scene, and certainly not violent or anything like that. So Rexroth was a little extra apprehensive...I think he misunderstood the situation...he asked us to leave. His excuse was that it was scaring the children, but the children weren't there, they were in the bedroom sleeping or something. I don't think Jack actually literally scared the children.

...Then I misbehaved once very badly. I was a little drunk there, and I'd just read "Howl" and I realized it was within Rexroth's *genre*. He had just written "You Killed Dylan Thomas, You Son of a Bitch in the Grey Flannel Suit." That's a famous, early, sort of beatnik poem by Rexroth, self-righteously accusing the man in the Brooks Brothers suit of killing Dylan Thomas. It was a good-hearted poem, but it was not very classy, not very strong as poetics. So I got drunk and was comparing that poem with "Howl"—in my mind doing it—and I said, "Rexroth, I'm a better poet than you are, and I'm only twenty-one years old" or twenty-eight, or thirty, or whatever it was [he was twenty-nine], which was terrible behavior to him, because it was mocking him. Just like kids do to me all the time now.

But he took it very badly and thought it was some like awful, awful juvenile delinquent's arrogance. Which it was, but it wasn't that serious. I was just drunk, and it was the first time I realized I was really a poet, and was coming on...and in some odd way I thought I was being sincere, or friendly, or open, or frank, or something like that—actually communicating. I don't know what it was, but I didn't think I was being cruel. But he thought I was being evil...

The Six Gallery reading had come about when Wally Hedrick, who was a painter and one of the major people there, asked Rexroth if he knew any poets that would put on a reading. Maybe Rexroth asked McClure to organize it and McClure didn't know how or didn't have time. Rexroth asked me, so I met McClure and Rexroth suggested I go visit another poet who was living in Berkeley, which was Gary. So I went right over to Gary's house and immediately had a meeting of minds with him over William Carlos Williams, 'cause I had written *Empty Mirror* at that time and he had begun *Myths and Texts*, or *The Berry Feast*, or something, and he told me about his friend Philip Whalen who was due in town the next day. And I told him about my friend Kerouac who was in town that day, and within three or four days we all met....

Jack and I were coming from Berkeley, and had just

arrived in San Francisco at the Key System Terminal, the bus terminal there, and we met right out on First and Mission, by accident. Gary was with Phil and I was with Jack, and we all went off immediately and started talking. And then Philip Lamantia was in town, whom I'd known from '48 in New York, and then there was Michael McClure. So there was a whole complement of poets. Then Gary and I decided we ought to invite Rexroth to be the sixth—sixth poet—to introduce at the Six Gallery, be the elder, since he had linked us up.

Robert Duncan, who was in Europe in the fall of 1955, was second only to Rexroth among San Francisco poets in terms of near and distant recognition. He was closely associated with the poets Robert Creeley and Charles Olson, all of whom taught at Black Mountain College in the fifties. He watched the disintegration of the friendship between Rexroth and the others with detachment.

Robert Duncan:

Rexroth, in the beginning, was really sponsoring and very friendly to Ginsberg and to the fact of a new movement. He continued for a period to write about the Beats with a good deal of understanding and goodwill. It was the first appearance of street poetry, and Rexroth had wanted to be a popular poet, and here was a popular poetry, a popular writing, that was taking the town—his town—as a matter of fact, his territory.

I was in Europe at the time that the big break-through came, but I saw blocks of Kerouac's writing as well as Burroughs' earlier, because Ginsberg, before he came to San Francisco, which was '54, had sent blocks of stuff to Rexroth, and Rexroth handed it around. He said, "Wow, did you ever see anything like this?" Ginsberg had only the poems of *Empty Mirror* and that preface of William Carlos Williams'. *Empty Mirror* turned me off. It was, "I don't have a fuck, I don't have anything, I'm a poor-looking specimen." Ginsberg always lived in the romance that he was going to know overwhelming writers. Allen came to San Francisco because of Rexroth, because of Rexroth and Patchen. Even meeting me, and I

was nothing, was to him overwhelming, as Kerouac had
been and Burroughs was. He invented the sky with new
stars in it, and his invention of it was a poet's. That
interested me.

I came back from Europe in 1956. En route, I taught
at Black Mountain for two terms, and I arrived in San
Francisco in August or September of '56. Within the first
couple of weeks there was an invasion of the whole little
gang. I don't know if Kerouac was along in that gang, but
I know that Ginsberg, Corso and Orlovsky were
streaming into our house. They said, "We came to see
Duncan," and came roaring into the apartment like an
invasion. Which they were.

Robert Duncan, Berkeley, 1952. Photo by Gui de Angulo.

Almost immediately after meeting Snyder, Jack regarded him as a new hero. As he had done with Neal, Jack apprenticed himself to his new friend, and in October of 1955 earned the title "the Buddha known as the great quitter" during a trip with Snyder to climb Matterhorn Peak in the Northern Sierras. Their companion on the climb was the bookish and distracted John Montgomery.

Gary Snyder:

When I was a graduate student at Berkeley studying Chinese and Japanese and planning to go to the Orient, in a perhaps excessively orderly fashion I decided I should get my teeth fixed. I didn't realize they had dentists all over the place. Anyway, I signed up with the University of California dental school, and for two years I bicycled from Berkeley to San Francisco once a week and put myself in the hands of a Japanese-American dental student. On one of those occasions I took along *New World Writing No. 7*, and I read the little thing by a fellow named Jean-Louis, which was one of the most entertaining things I'd read in a long time, and it always stuck in my mind. I didn't know anything of Jack or Allen at that time, but I never forgot that little piece of prose, "Jazz of the Beat Generation." It was the first time I saw the term Beat Generation. What I liked was the writing, of course, and the energy that was in it, and the evocation of people. Of course it didn't say "Jack Kerouac," it said "Jean-Louis."

Later I met Allen. Shortly after that, I met Jack. When I met Jack, and hearing Allen speak of his projects and hearing Jack speak, I flashed that he was Jean-Louis.

Allen asked Rexroth who was doing interesting poetry in the area. Allen had the idea of trying to put together some kind of poetry reading, and Kenneth mentioned my name as one person he might want to look up. So Allen just turned up at my place when I was fixing my bicycle in the backyard, and said that he had been talking to Kenneth. So we sat down and started comparing who we knew and what we were thinking about.

Jack was, in a sense, a twentieth-century American mythographer. And that's why maybe those novels will stand up, because they will be one of the best statements of the myth of the twentieth century. Just as Ginsberg represents one clear archetypal aspect of twentieth-century America, I think Jack saw me, in a funny way, as being another archetypal twentieth-century American of the West, of the anarchist, libertarian, IWW tradition, of a tradition of working outdoors and fitting in already with his fascination with the hobo, railroad bum, working man. I was another dimension on that.

Like on one occasion I remember we spent a number of hours in which I simply explained to him how logging camps worked and what all the steps in a logging operation are. Now I don't believe he ever used that in a book, but he was collecting that kind of information and enthusiastically digesting it all the time.

If my life and work is in some sense a kind of an odd extension, in its own way, of what Thoreau, Whitman, John Muir, etcetera, are doing, then Jack hooked into that and he saw that as valuable to him for his purposes in this century.

And Allen was the New York radical, Jewish intelligentsia. Jack really was skillful in identifying these types, recognizing them as being a particular image that would become part of the mythology of America that he was working at. When he talked about his great novel that he was writing, it was like Ovid's *Metamorphoses*, a collection of stories which sketch out the view of the times. And he saw himself on the scale of a mythographer. The legend of Duluoz.

The dialectic that I observed in Jack, which was kind of charming, really, and you see it at work in his novels, was that he could play the fool and he could play the student very well. "But see, I really don't know anything about this. Teach me!" "Wow! You really know how to do that?" and lead you on. That was balanced by sometimes great authoritativeness and great arrogance, and he would suddenly say, "I am the authority." But then he would get out of that again. It was partly maybe like a really skillful novelist's con, to get people to speak. And he uses that as a literary device in his novels, where he presents himself often as the straight guy and he lets the other guys be smart.

I much appreciated what he had to say about spontaneous prose, although I never wrote prose. I think it influenced my journal writing a lot, some of which would, say, be registered in the book *Earth House Hold*. I think that I owe a lot to Jack in my prose style, actually. And my sense of poetics has been touched by Jack for sure.

Our interchanges on Buddhism were on the playful and delightful level of exchanging the lore, exchanging what we knew about it, what he thought of Mahayana. He made up names. He would follow on the Mahayana Sutra invention of lists, and he would invent more lists, like the names of all the past Buddhas, the names of all the future Buddhas, the names of all the other universes. He was great at that. But it was not like a pair of young French intellectuals sitting down comparing their structural comprehension of something. We exchanged lore. And I would tell him, "Now look. Here are these Chinese Buddhists," and that's how we ended up talking about the Han-shan texts together, and I introduced him to the texts that give the anecdotes of the dialogues and confrontations between T'ang Dynasty masters and disciples, and of course he was delighted by that. Anybody is. That's what we did.

I didn't then, and I don't now, think in terms of whether or not people are genuinely committed Buddhists or not. We're working with all of these things, and it doesn't matter what words you give to them, and if I thought that there was some point where I would say, "Jack, you're thinking too much about how the world's a bad place," that would be my sense of a corrective and his understanding of the Buddha-dharma, but that wasn't in my interest, or anybody else's interest, to think: "Is this guy a real Buddhist or not a real Buddhist?" He was worried about it later, but I never was, and I don't think Philip Whalen ever was, or anybody else.

When Jack came I was living over on Hillegass, and Philip had come back from the mountains. I had spent the summer up in the Sierra Nevada working on a trail crew and, naturally, we were talking a lot about the mountains. We were just back fresh from it, from the season's work, and I had rucksacks and climbing rope and ice-axes hanging on the walls around my place. Naturally we talked some about all of that.

I perceived that there was a kind of freedom and mobility that one gained in the world, somewhat analogous to the wandering Buddhist monk of ancient times, that was permitted you by having a proper pack and sleeping bag, so that you could go out on the road and through the mountains into the countryside. The word for Zen monk in Chinese, *yun shui*, means literally "clouds and water," and it's taken from a line in Chinese poetry, "To float like clouds, to flow like water," which indicates the freedom and mobility of Zen monks walking around all over China and Tibet and Mongolia on foot.

With that in mind I said to Jack, "You know, real Buddhists are able to walk around the countryside." So he said, "Sure. Let's go backpacking." I think John Montgomery said, "There's time for one more trip into the mountains before it gets too much colder." It was around the end of October.

So we headed up over Sonora Pass, leaving at night in Berkeley, and went over to Bridgeport, up to Twin Lakes and went in from there, over Sonora Pass.

It was very funny. It's very beautifully described in *The Dharma Bums*, actually. It was very cold. It was late autumn. The aspens were yellow, and it went well below freezing in the night and left frost on the little creek in the canyon we were camped at. There was a sprinkle of fresh white snow up on the ridges and peaks. We made it up to the top of the Matterhorn and came back down again. Actually, Jack didn't. I guess I was the only one that went up there. I was the persistent one.

Despite the others on hand at the Six reading in November 1955 it was Ginsberg's performance—"reading" is the wrong word—of "Howl" that signaled a shift in the wind, but Jack left California for New York before the reaction had crested. Neal's companion at the gallery that night was a troubled woman named Natalie Jackson. In typical fashion Cassady left her in Kerouac's care for a time, but Jack couldn't deal with her. She told him she had written her confessions and they were all doomed. The day after the afternoon Jack spent with her, trying to calm her with Buddhist aphorisms, she jumped to her death from the window of her rented room. The episode disturbed Jack greatly, and he returned to Rocky Mount, before Christmas, to meet Mémère at Nin's.

In January, 1956, still in North Carolina, he wrote the affecting memoir of his brother's death when Jack was four, *Visions of Gerard*. Working from the portrait that Mémère and the nuns had given him of Gerard as a near-holy figure, Jack saints his brother, in Buddhist terms, and lays him to rest in Nashua, N.H., after a poetic storm of recollection that reaches from his father's printshop to narcotized conversations with Bill Burroughs.

In letters to Cowley, Jack had made plain the scheme of *The Duluoz Legend*, and he had arranged to work with Cowley on revisions of *On the Road* when the editor came West to teach at Stanford University in Palo Alto, not far from the Cassadys' home. Cowley had expressed fear that the novel might be unpublishable, because its characters were not fictional inventions but real people who might sue Viking for real dollars. Jack reassured him that he was close enough to all involved to secure releases. Perhaps cuts or revisions would be exacted from him by his friends who were portrayed, but that was permissible because the characters would simply be expressing themselves by modifying their portraits.

Later he suggested the tactic of deepening the disguises. Justin Brierly, "Denver D. Doll" in the published book, was "Beattie G. Davies" at that stage of the game. Jack proposed that he be made into a Greek-American proprietor of a chain of bowling alleys in Colorado, but that his interest in the education of young men be retained.

By the time Jack returned to California in April, 1956, Cowley had left Stanford. By mail they pursued the process of securing releases against libel and defamation actions. Some portrayals, like that of Brierly, were considerably shortened or softened. Jack had mentioned to Cowley that, with the advent of rock and roll and the startling publicity that Ginsberg and the other poets had garnered after the Six reading, the time was ripe for *On the Road*, but the legal and literary demands that Viking made, and with which Jack was slow to deal, stretched out for another full year.

Malcolm Cowley:

Jack and his memory are very, very unfair to me.
Blaming me for putting in or taking out commas and
caps and what-not in *On the Road*. I didn't really give
much of a damn about that. I knew that Jack wrote well.
Jack wrote well naturally. His style reminded me a great
deal of Thomas Wolfe, who was an early enthusiasm of
Jack's. Jack never lost his enthusiasm for Thomas Wolfe.
That same way of writing: headlong, but at the same
time in periods.

I should place Wolfe, outside of Ginsberg, as the
greatest influence on Jack. He speaks of Proust instead,
but Proust and Wolfe were alike in one thing: not in
genius, but in the fact that their whole work was
essentially based on memory. They were the great
rememberers. So, just as Wolfe was going to do his whole
life as one more or less connected novel, Jack was going
to do his whole life as one more or less connected novel.
I know that I mentioned Wolfe to him a couple of times
and he said, perhaps hauntedly, "I don't like Wolfe now,
but I think he's good."

On the Road was good prose. I wasn't worried about
the prose. I was worried about the structure of the book.
It seemed to me that in the original draft the story kept
swinging back and forth across the continental United
States like a pendulum. And one thing that I kept putting
forward to Jack was, "Why don't you consolidate some
of these episodes so that your hero doesn't swing across
the country quite so often and so that the book has more
movement?"

Well, Jack did something that he would never admit
to later. He did a good deal of revision, and it was very
good revision. Oh, he would never, never admit to that,
because it was his feeling that the stuff ought to come out
like toothpaste from a tube and not be changed, and that
every word that passed from his typewriter was holy. On
the contrary he revised, and revised well.

He also turned out a great deal of original material during
1955 and 1956. In addition to *Visions of Gerard* there would be
Tristessa, his long story about Esperanza Villanueva; the prose-

poem *Old Angel Midnight*; *The Angels in the World*, the first section of the first of two novels eventually published together as *Desolation Angels*; and a home-made *sutra* called *The Scripture of the Golden Eternity*, the last written to, and for, Gary Snyder that spring while they shared a cabin in Marin County behind the home of Locke McCorkle, a young carpenter interested in Buddhism.

Locke McCorkle:

Jack was really easy to be with. The only time he got kind of violent was when he was drunk, but then it was just like noisy.

One time he said, "I want you to get an experience of what it's like to be a wino." I says, "Great, how do we do that?" He says, "Well, we each get a poorboy of Muscatel, we go down on Howard Street, and we duck in and out of doorways and drink it and just sit down there and do the same things they do." So we did, but you get a kind of different experience, because you can walk out at the end of the act.

I definitely thought that he didn't think of himself as being better or worse than anyone else. He really had a Buddhist view of that—of equality of everybody. In a sense, though, I think he made up his Buddhism. I think his intuitions were right. He didn't know a lot about it, didn't have a lot of training in it. This is what Gary Snyder liked. Gary was always involved in the form and sometimes—in his own view—felt he missed the essence, and Jack caught it in a way that Gary never did—or wasn't, or didn't think he was.

Bev Burford, Jack's old girlfriend from his Denver summer in 1950, was living in the Bay Area that year, and remembers his high spirits as he faced the prospect of being a published novelist once more.

Bev Burford:

I worked in San Francisco and lived in Sausalito. I came

to my little apartment and found a note: "Am borrowing hi-fi. Big party Mill Valley this weekend. Pick you up Friday. Love, Jack." So my hi-fi was gone. I never locked the place, but he found me, where I lived, and so that party was a big weekend in Mill Valley. But we ended up many times in San Francisco.

In those days women wore a hat and gloves to work. After work they'd meet me, or have me meet them, at The Place—North Beach—and then we'd get back across the bridge. One time, one Sunday, we flipped a coin: do we get a bottle of wine or do we take the ferry back? Well, we got our bus tickets and went to the wrong place for the bus, and ended up walking all over San Francisco. How depleted of people it is on Sunday. We had a great time all day. And then we finally got back to Sausalito, and he went on to Mill Valley. A little fat taxi driver in Sausalito took him up for nothing because he liked Jack.

I ended up in the hospital with tuberculosis, a light case, and Jack came to see me a few times. We wrote a little, but I wasn't involved in hitchhiking across the country. Even in Mill Valley, at the parties everyone would sit around smoking pot. I didn't. Actually, he was more like a brother to me. My own brother, the one living in San Francisco, I think came to see me once in the hospital. That was it. But Jack was more like a brother all the way.

I know of many girls that were in and out of his life occasionally. One-night-stand girls. And Neal was out there. Carolyn happened to end up as ballet teacher to my other brother's daughter. And at one time she was very involved with a progressive priest that she was going to marry and dump Neal. And Neal was living so many lives—by the clock, by his stopwatch. Everything was by his stopwatch. He had one life in San Jose, the other life in San Francisco, and Kerouac was in and out of it a little bit.

Locke McCorkle:

We really enjoyed each other. I enjoyed him much more as a person than I did as a writer. I mean, he was the only person of that whole group who my wife would trust to babysit the children, which probably breaks a lot of reality with a lot of people.

I was being a carpenter for a living, and a Buddhist as an avocation. That was how I met Gary. We all had been social revolutionaries at one time. I'd have been a communist, except that the party wasn't active enough in my area to get me into it when I was eighteen years old, and by the time I was in my twenties, I had found a better means of revolution, which was Buddhism. I got converted by Alan Watts in one radio program. When I heard what he had to say, it was what I'd been wanting to hear all my life and nobody'd ever said to me. It was almost like I'd said it to myself. That was the beginning of the era that led to my knowing Gary and Jack and everybody. I studied with Alan Watts at the American Academy of Asian Studies. Zen and Bengali and Sanskrit and Hinduism and all that stuff. I had a ball! Loved it!

When they talked about enlightenment I thought, "Well, that's what I'll have." You know, it's like you look at a menu and they say "filet mignon with mushroom sauce." I was that enlightened when I first heard about it that I didn't make any big deal out of it. Later on, I made a big deal out of it and made it hard to get, impossible, and all that bullshit that people do that makes it take twenty years sitting in rows and being hit with sticks to catch on again.

When the poetry scene first started it was really very fresh and casual. The whole audience drank wine and hooted and hollered like it was a baseball game and cheered the people on, and just took that whole academic stuffiness out of the literary world. We had a great ball with it.

Jack was very easy to have around. He was shy and he didn't run around much, and mostly he'd write things. I remember he came down one morning and he'd written *The Scripture of the Golden Eternity*, and he said, "Last night, Locke, I knew exactly what it meant." This morning he had no idea—gone.

We would have parties in Mill Valley where everybody took all their clothes off and danced. It was really innocent, in a way, compared with the hardcore pornography stuff that goes around now, and he would just sit there and leave his clothes on and watch.

Jack told me, "They won't publish my stuff because I won't change the names." That was the big thing that was going on with Viking. I said, "Well, if they publish them, what will happen?" He says, "Oh, I'll be a famous writer." And I said, "Do you like being a famous writer?" And he says, "No, I hated it the first time." And I says, "Well, why are you doing it again? Why not just forget the whole thing and do something else?"

But he didn't choose to do that. He had six or seven novels at that time that were unpublished, and then he finally backed off his position and said what he was going to do—said that he was going to change all the names, which he did slightly. I thought he was writing a novel. I didn't see the people that he based those things on anything like he did. If I wrote a book covering the same period you wouldn't recognize them, including me. He definitely saw things the way he saw them, so I figured that it was fiction. He didn't have any problem with it. He made it all up. Which we all do. He isn't any different than anybody else.

With Snyder's help Jack arranged to spend two months of the summer of 1956 on Desolation Peak in the Cascade Mountains at the upper left-hand corner of Washington State. Following his stay with Snyder that spring Kerouac hitchhiked north to Desolation.

Once ensconced on the mountain he was totally alone. When Cowley reacted against the Buddhism that suffused *Visions of Gerard* Jack had sought to assure him that it was a passing phase which would have little effect on his future work. But sitting in his lookout tower facing the dark, sheer face of Mount Hozomeen to the north Jack was still involved in his flirtation with The Void.

Gary Snyder:

Jack was taken, after going up in the Sierra Nevada that fall and talking with Philip and me and Kenneth and others, by the power of the Sierra Nevada and the power of wilderness and the archetypal paradisical nature of the high country, and he wanted to get back into it.

210

The high country is heaven, actually. It's heaven on earth, and the imagery of heaven is an imagery of mountains and mountain meadows and mountain flowers and gardens, actually, in many cases in the world. Maud Bodkin, in her book *Archetypal Patterns in Poetry*, discusses the archetype of the mountain and the mountain meadow as an image of paradise. It really does resonate in the mind and in the body to spend time in the high country.

The Maidu people who lived where I live now, when they wanted to get healing power—shaman power—they would go up to the high country and spend a month or two up there, generally eating very little, and sitting near a waterfall or a lake at the foot of the peak, until they got a song and a dream, which would be a healing song, and then they would return to the lower villages again. It's really there. So Jack tuned into that. That really gave him the desire and the energy to follow through and go up on Desolation and try to do what me and Philip had been talking about.

To my knowledge Jack never evinced at any point in his life the desire to be anybody but who he was, on the path that he was on. Now there may well have been a deep level of suffering and fear and self-awareness of contradictions, but to my knowledge he didn't express it, nor did he make any of the moves that might have helped draw him out of it. And the friends that did try to draw him out of it in various ways weren't encouraged.

That spring Jack was doing a little *haiku* even prior to when he started showing us his *Mexico City Blues* manuscript. During that spring I saw the manuscript of *Mexico City Blues*, and I gave a reading of it to the Berkeley Buddhist Church study group one Friday evening. It was a Japanese-American Jodo Shin sect, a very old, established, traditional Buddhist group. It's still in Berkeley. I gave a reading from *Mexico City Blues*, from the Buddhist poems, and said, "Now these are interesting contemporary Buddhist poems." They published some of them in the *Berkeley Bussei*, which was the annual of the Young Buddhist Association.

Allen made the comment that Jack's about the only one we knew who was able to spontaneously compose *haiku* that wasn't boring, without sitting on it for a long time. You know, in one of Basho's essays he says that for some reason the most practiced old-time *haiku* people can't do as well as someone who's just heard of the form for the first time and tries their hand at it. That that freshness and quickness is what makes it.

Jack had a lot of that kind of mind, and he knew how to use it. How to take that first thought-best thought and bring it right out. And he did beautiful little *haiku*.

Talking with Jack was like being in a handball court where you were playing with two or three balls at the same time, and the pleasure of it was actually playing the game and knowing that there were several balls always going around the room and coming back to each one of them, more or less, in the appropriate way as they bounce about. I guess that's where that image "off the wall" comes from. So it's delightful. Conversation with Jack was always, strictly speaking, poetical. It was full of imaginative, intuitive and unpredictable jumps, which made excellent sense if your minds are together and you're talking in the same way. Jack's mind and my mind were often together, and we could talk that way for hours. It wasn't just games, it was very strong, creative, exciting kind of communication, which I have with a few other people in the world, but not too many. If for no other reason, I would say because of that particular quality of Jack's, he was a real poet. His mind worked in an amazing, fast, unpredictable, but appropriate way.

Jack didn't live in a way that a reliable relationship could be established. Now, two people sharing a cabin for a few months, as we were, with no real commitments or obligations to each other, could come and go and be gone four or five days and come back, unpredictably, and not know when you're going to come back, and so forth. That's easy to do, but Jack was not about to order his life in such a way that he could be responsible to another person. And he never did demonstrate any interest in doing that.

Jack's touching back with his mother was a function of the way he was, and it was understood by most of his friends because they felt that that was, in some way, part of the quality of his genius. "The creative genius sort of thing will be irresponsible and can't be held to the same rules that other people are held to, and they're hell on their wives." That's a kind of image of the artist that's been current, definitely, since Rimbaud. The mystique of the Beat Generation or, to put it more accurately, the liberating thing that we felt in our lives about that time, mid-fifties up, was the sense that you can actually do what you want to do. That, as a liberating thing, required that some of us actually demonstrate it quite literally and be not terribly responsible to each other, and that was a very fresh, liberating feeling for many people then. Jack kind of led the way, it was his style, but no woman, or other man, say, that wanted to really be together with him in anything could hope to do it. He had an inability to be together on that plane.

Now you could say that was his genius, if you wanted to romanticize genius, or you could say it was adolescent and immature, if you wanted to be critical. But the objective fact is, he wasn't able to do it. Also the objective fact is that a lot of the energy of his art and his writing seemed somehow tied to the way he lived. He was a little bit like an old skid-row wino that rambles in and out from place to place, he liked that image for himself.

Jack would stay in hotels down near the railroad tracks, which was where the working men stayed when they came into town, and Jack had put his time in on the road. In harking back to the American hobo, Jack was harking back one of the few models—myths—of freedom and freshness and mobility and detachment, detachment from the world of scrambling for power and prestige—that was available to us at that time.

In a way the Beat Generation is a gathering together of all the available models and myths of freedom in America that had existed heretofore, namely: Whitman, John Muir, Thoreau, and the American bum. We put them together and opened them out again, and it becomes like a literary motif, and then we added some Buddhism to it.

The Dharma Bums is a real statement of that synthesis, through Jack. I don't know if Jack believed it, but I did. Not only intuitively, but rationally, and intellectually. I'm an old anthropolgist. I'm a student of two-thousand-year human cycles. And the vision of the fifties and sixties taps a deep archetypal vein in the

American consciousness, which in turn is tied to a sub-theme running throughout the history of Occidental culture, which manifests itself periodically as heretical branches of Christianity. That stream is there consistently in Occidental history.

America, in its origins, is a reflection in part of that. Then we're not done with that karma, and to nourish that karma and to try to send it off into the future and develop it more is a good political move, which is something I consciously realized in the fifties.

Allen Ginsberg:

Jack read very extensively in a lot of basic texts and he understood them very early, in a very perceptive way, for someone who had no teacher. So I think Gary, in the mid-fifties when he first met Jack, was moved by his grasp of the basic terms of existence: suffering, transitoriness, and egolessness.

Neal had picked up on Edgar Cayce, which involved theories of reincarnation and theosophical Oriental ideas. There's a letter from Jack to me saying, "It's like Billy Sunday in a suit," babbling away about Cayce, trying to convince me that Cayce is some kind of a supernatural prophet. Jack thought this was like crude American, so he went to go find the background behind Neal's ideas of reincarnation—or Cayce's...

But because he didn't sit, the non-theistic portion didn't settle in. There was still some element of theism... Finally, Buddha-Christ were the same tender person, but they were still a "Person" behind the universe.

I don't know how it was at the very end, but there was still some final reliance on Bhakti, or devotion to Christ. I don't know if it's a Catholic Christ, or a Blakean Christ, or just Jack's old human Christ of the suffering—man suffering, his father suffering on the deathbed, himself, all of us. We are going through life and dying. In Buddhism, the four noble truths: the first noble truth is the truth of suffering. Existence contains suffering. Suffering is what was born.

Suffering is a primary characteristic or theme of his

writing. Second is transitoriness, that sense of mellow-cello—"memorial cello-time." That Rembrandtian brown sense of time, receding in ghost phantoms flitting through new life with their vanity, taking it all seriously, but they're nothing but ghosts. And the third aspect was, through their vanity, the show of emptiness, "the emptiness behind the show of personality." Those, in basic Buddhist theory, are known as the three marks of existence: suffering, transitoriness, and *an-atma*—no soul, no self.

The first Buddhism I learned was from Jack, and maybe some of the deepest. I just simply had a juvenile objection to the idea of existence as suffering. I didn't want it to be suffering, that's all. And I thought it was mean. And he would constantly be cutting through and cutting me down—cutting the ground out from under me—by pointing out that it was all transitory and suffering in vain, and it was just a show of personality getting up and screaming in public, with beards.

I didn't begin taking it more seriously until the mid-fifties, when Gary and Philip presented it in a slightly cooler way and as part of the cultural context. At first I thought it was some mean old discovery on Jack's part that was intended to be anti-Semitic. Kind of a Jehovah or something, a Jack-Jehovah. So I don't think I took it seriously at all until I went to Japan, in the sense of fully understood, that it was just a description of nature rather than an imposition of a philosophy on nature. That suffering was not the imposition of an attitude or a way of life, it was just a description of the facts of being born in the meat body.

I once asked Gary how he thought Jack would do in a Zen monastery in terms of responding to *koans*, and he said that probably Kerouac could just cut through and get them.

After rooming with Gary Snyder when both were students at Reed College in Portland, Oregon (the third apartment-mate being Lew Welch), Philip Whalen also moved to San Francisco. Along with Snyder he came under the tutelage of Kenneth Rexroth, and soon emerged as a highly individualized poet in his own right.

215

Philip Whalen:

Jack carried a copy of Dwight Goddard's book called *A Buddhist Bible* around with him. As far as I could see, he was interested in the very large, big, wonderful ideas about Buddhism and about the language. He liked the extravagant language that appeared in those translations. They talked in terms of vast distances and vast lengths of time and huge quantities of everything and lots of

Philip Whalen, 1976. Photo by Sarah Satterlee.

flowers and doves and one thing and another, so it's quite a fantastical language trip, for one thing. He had had a great many profound religious experiences himself, which he later would tell about, and he picked up on the fact, I think, that the Buddhist scriptures were about experience, that they were based on meditational experience. So this interested him.

He was quite incapable of sitting for more than a few minutes at a time. His knees were ruined by playing football, so he couldn't sit much with his knees up. He never learned how to sit in that sort of proper meditation position. Even had he been able to, his head wouldn't have stopped long enough for him to endure it. He was too nervous, but he thought it was a good idea.

When push came to shove, what he was hung up on was the Little Flower of Jesus, St. Thérèse of Lisieux, various other Catholic saints, and that's what he really believed in and got the most out of and kept returning to. This made it possible, for example, for him to have long, earnest, illuminating, marvelous discussions with Philip Lamantia, who was raised as a Catholic and at that time was a practicing Catholic, and had just gone back into the church again.

It was also heavily connected with his mother, Gabrielle, who was a practicing Catholic who went frequently to church and confession, and who wore religious medals pinned to the strap of her slip.

As far as I can see, honestly, his interest in Buddhism was pretty much literary, and the idea that people were actually trying to do it was interesting to him as exhibitions of their character, possibly, as facets of their character. The idea that Gary was this very active man— very learned and very active person who liked to live outdoors and who had a very exciting social life—would be interested in Buddhism and practicing it, or trying to practice it, and presently went off to Japan to start in formal Zen training, this was interesting for Jack as a manifestation of character more than Buddhism as such was interesting to him.

He would go just so far with it, and then he'd say, "Ah, well. It's wonderful, but I really believe in sweet baby Jesus," or "little lamby Jesus" or "my brother Gerard." Much of what's in the book *Visions of Gerard* he'd refer to in conversation, stories about what happened when Gerard died, and so on.

Everybody loved Jack. Everybody was interested in him and everybody found him a very ambiguous figure, because he was quite conscious of the interest people had in him. He had so much lack of self-confidence that he would turn on that and say, "Awww—you're crazy, because I'm a failure. I'm a big flop, and so your interest is misplaced. I'm not interesting, I'm just sort of a dirty, grimy old guy." That's what the "Sunflower Sutra" that Allen wrote is about. Allen and Jack and I were down at the railroad yard and Allen, who'd apparently never seen a sunflower before, saw this dead one and was very taken with it. Some of the time Jack would be up and would be very open and very lively and very funny and very sunny and very simple and childlike. Other times, he would be very down and very sad and be coming on with this, "Aw, we're all gonna die" nonsense, about how everything is worn out and everybody is dying and nobody is doing anything and he can't get his books published and nobody likes him and he's no good and all he can do is sort of goof along and not worry, but, at the same time, it's a nice thing that we can go to church, that St. Thérèse of Lisieux is there.

But down, really down, and not only down but how you're fucking up yourself. "Why did you do this or that?" A very direct, very harsh attack on me or whoever got to him at some point. Really very mean.

This was very interesting, very disturbing. Why did he do that? You'd figure, well, he's just drunk and quarrelsome. It's a very strange business. You'd get angry with him, and at the same time, when he was on, when he was going along on some more even keel, he was very interesting because he always *saw* so much, he always was so aware of his own experience, and that's what he was seeing, what he was hearing, what he remembered. He had a lot of funny ideas and a lot of strange notions that he'd come up with, so that he was fun to be with, even though he'd go through these terrific changes where he'd suddenly be attacking you and saying everything was bad, everything was dirty, everything was ugly.

Remember, he'd been brought up in this very tough parochial school. He'd tell dreadful stories about the nuns who worked there. It must have been quite a harrowing experience. American Jansenist Catholicism is a rough go. It's Puritanism raised to about nineteen degrees higher than ordinary Protestant Puritanism. It's heretical, also. Jansenius was denounced as a heretic years and years ago—not exactly, but at least Jansen's ideas were officially condemned by Clement XI in the bull *Unigentus*. But still American Catholicism is Jansenist, and it takes this tough line about how the body is evil, the things that people do with their bodies—like take baths—somehow, they expose themselves and rub their organs with soap and think, "My God, we're going to burn, sizzle, and fry in hell on account of this." And the idea of a man getting an erection! Saints preserve us. Literally.

You better get all the saints and God and everybody else to forgive you, because the flesh has just doomed you to total destruction. All you can do is just pray and hope for the best. He had this trip about "dirty me." He had that going and this helped complicate his life and make him sad.

John Clellon Holmes:

Jack's ground was always Catholicism—Christianity, that is. He looked at things in terms of good and evil.

In terms of the books and in terms of Jack's personality, Jack's youth, Jack's sense of continuity, Jack's sense of family, Lowell, all the rest of that, is totally Catholic.

The *On the Road* experience, all the eruptive books in between, so disturbed him that he—I believe—kept saying to himself, "Why are you doing this?" His faith—his religious faith—put it down or made it easy for him to say, "Stop doing it," but he did it anyway, and that's where Buddhism came in. All faiths are the same, really. They're just stages. They're just stages.

A Zen master would have said about Kerouac, "He is a seeker." He was a seeker. Jack wasn't a Zen, he was a Mahayana Buddhist. He always thought Zen was intellectual. The point is that Jack was struggling with the meaning of life. "Why am I alive? Why should I stay alive?" This was his biggest question: "Why should I stay alive? It's just pain." For him it was just pain he felt.

Jack was, and remained to the end, a Catholic—in terms of the highest idea of the Catholic vision of the world. He didn't look upon life as chaos, even in the Zen sense of happenings that come to something or don't. He tried like mad with Buddhism. Nobody understood Buddhism as deeply as Jack that I have ever known.

At the end of the summer of 1956 Jack came down from Desolation Peak with a journal of his lonely months there. He fantasized in those pages the arrival of "400 naked Nagas" pursuing the rumor that the Buddha was living in his fire-tower, that he, in fact, was the Buddha, a fact as valid as any other fact, since "there is no Buddha, no awakener, and there is no Meaning, no Dharma, and it is all only the wile of Maya." After pausing in Seattle, where he attended a burlesque show, he returned to San Francisco and walked into a war among the poets.

Lawrence Ferlinghetti, co-proprietor of City Lights Bookstore, had brought out Allen's "Howl" in a small paperback format, which created a large-scale civil liberties battle when the U.S. Customs Service attempted, and failed, to ban the import of the printed sheets from a press in England. Soon Ginsberg would be the familiar bearded figure continuing his role as agent for his literary friends, making the introductions and recommendations that led to the *Evergreen Review*'s issue on the San Francisco group, which was a natural, since Jack had already made arrangements to publish with Grove Press. Hiking together on San Francisco's Mount Tamalpais twenty years after that disputatious season, Michael McClure and Philip Whalen looked back on the period of Allen's captaincy.

Michael McClure:

I said, "Phil, you know, I used to have so much trouble. We were so fucking hard on each other." I also knew that we supported each other. You know, it was our camaraderie that brought us all through it, actually forced new

220

literary territories and new kinds of poems and things into existence by the pressure that we were exerting on each other.

And Phil said, "Well, Michael, I thought you were the only one who knew what they were doing, knew what direction they were going in. Allen was real hard on me a lot."

And I said, "By God, you know, you're right. I realize now, twenty years later, that you were taking a lot of shit from everybody—at least from Allen." I was giving Allen a lot of shit, too, let's face it, and I had a couple of showdowns with Allen and with Kerouac.

It was that one time down in the Who Cares bar when Allen decided that we were all going to knuckle under and be part of the Beat Generation and do it his way. And he had Gregory to back him up. I was supposed to bring Robert Duncan, but Robert didn't go, and I ended up defending Robert to Gregory and Allen.

And Allen was saying, "Now listen. We're all going to Mexico. Everybody's got to go to Mexico blah-blah-blah-blah." And I'm saying, "Robert Duncan is the most important poet on the West Coast blah-blah-blah-blah." Gregory's jumping up and down and saying, "Michael, you're blah-blah-blah-blah."

And finally, I got up and swirled on my scarf and pushed out the door, and Kerouac said—what did he say? He said something lovely like, "You gotta be the toughest guy around," or "You really can fight," or "That's the best show I've ever seen." Some lovely thing as I went out the door that really capped it.

It was a wonderful argument. It was one of those once-in-a-lifetime arguments, where everybody basically settles out their individuality so that you know who you are and always in the future you're going to know why you are. If there's a few bruises, you're still going to be friends.

Rexroth, who had brought the poets together, was now estranged from the invaders from the East. To those unfamiliar with the private details of the schism it seemed to be an advanced case of regional chauvinism, but its real roots lay in a personal affair, a serious misunderstanding wherein Rexroth

resented what he mistakenly considered Jack and Allen's—
especially Jack's—adversary participation. From this time on
Rexroth reviled Kerouac both privately and publicly,
removing himself from his position as defender of the Beats.

Allen Ginsberg:

When, later, '58 or so, or whenever it was *Mexico City
Blues* came out [it was 1959], Rexroth wrote a really
damning, terrible [*New York Times*] review saying that
this form of poetry separated the men from the boys, and
Kerouac was obviously a boy and couldn't write, and it
was a disgrace that he would present this book in public.

Around the same time Rexroth was in London, and I
think he said that I had "probably written myself out"
with "Howl." This is just as I was finishing "Kaddish." So
he was telling the *London Times* that the Beat phenomenon in America was a transitory hallucination of the Luce
organization, which he regretted having anything to do
with, and we were a bunch of juvenile delinquents, and
no-talents, and we probably had so few talents that we'd
written ourselves out.... I think he was getting a lot of
flack from literary people who all along had felt that as a
radical decentralist anarchist he had now "shown his true
colors" by backing a group of unholy, barbarian, no-
account, no-good people—Beatnik, unwashed, dirty,
badmen of letters who didn't have anything on the ball.
So he may have felt vulnerable that he originally had
been so friendly, literarily, and had backed us up. Then
also, probably, he had a good prophetic or historical
insight that we didn't know what we were doing
historically at all...

In terms of history and Marxism and anarchism and
theory we were just operating on the seat of the pants,
whereas he and Paul Goodman had very complex
historical notions of what went wrong with the
Petrochevsky circle in 1870 in Moscow, or what went
wrong with the 1905 revolution, and what went wrong
with the Stalinist Trotskyites, and...

The thing is, I thought we were arriving as
reinforcements rather than competition at the time. Then
it turned out that we wound up in the position of "media

Allen Ginsberg, San Francisco, 1952. Photo by Gui de Angulo.

stars," me especially at first, so I did everything I could
at that point to spread the recognition of the San
Francisco thing, to make sure that *Evergreen Review*
carried Duncan's work. And I intervened between
Duncan, who didn't want to be published, and Don Allen
to make sure that that long poem, "A Poem Beginning
With a Line by Pindar," was published in *Evergreen* and
in the *New American Poetry* anthology.

When I came back from San Francisco I brought
with me not only Kerouac's and my and Corso's manuscripts and booklets, but also Gary's, Duncan's, Philip
Whalen, some of Ed Dorn, Robert Creeley, Denise
Levertov, Lamantia, McClure. A pile of that submitted as

223

soon as I got back to New York to Louis Simpson for the Simpson-Donald Hall *New Poets of England and America* package.

So what I actually was trying to do was a cooperative thing, it seemed to me that they had prepared a cultural theater in San Francisco and it was a legitimate community, but I thought we were part of it. I was a little upset that they felt resentful about that, what I tried to do was actually try and be worthy of the role that I had to carry, which was of "spokesman" for the "San Francisco Renaissance." I circulated all that material to *The Partisan Review*, communicated with *The Hudson Review*, brought a lot of it to John Hall Wheelock at Scribner's and talked to John Hollander, as an agent...

Maybe I'm too busybody, I don't know. See, Neal and I and Peter and Jack and Gregory did somewhat plan things together. Like to be in Tangier, we were all in Tangier together and we were all in Mexico City together, we all followed Neal and went to San Francisco together. And Gary and I went off together to the Northwest, and so there was comradeship, running around together. We were running around together. My own view was the old communist thing of "in unity there is strength," thinking that we had to fight the whole western capitalist culture, and the poets all ought to get together...a certain poets' republic. I couldn't understand why there was this dissension, when it certainly should have been a unified field.

...It used to be a big drag that there was this sense of rivalry. I wonder, by hindsight now, how much of it was my own over-presumption or forcing.

Early in 1957, when the "San Francisco" issue of *Evergreen Review* appeared, the Beat phenomenon was in full flower and had begun its penetration of the popular media. In this manner the way was prepared for the spectacular reaction that *On the Road* would achieve when it was published that September.

Throughout their editor-author relationship Jack sent Malcolm Cowley his stories and novels as they were completed. None struck Cowley as publishable by Viking, although he later came to regret, deeply, having passed up the chance to bring out *Doctor Sax*. But if Viking's editors were uninterested in Kerouac's rucksack *oeuvre*, Barney Rosset of Grove Press was not. He bought *The Subterraneans*, giving Jack enough money to join Allen, Gregory, and Peter for a trip to Tangier, where Burroughs was writing *Naked Lunch*.

Peter Orlovsky:

Allen and Jack went to work on Bill's *Naked Lunch*, editing it and typing it up, selecting parts, and Jack was typing it out—very busy typing it out. I was smoking hash, reading, listening to conversations, getting to know Bill. We didn't get along too good together somewhat, but after a while I could see he was very funny. His routines, his stories, his sense of humor. So I took a liking to him. We used to cook up dinners together and eat down in his room.

Jack in Tangier, 1957. Photo by William Burroughs.

John Clellon Holmes:

Jack [told me he] rather liked the time in Tangier with Bill and Allen. Then he went to Marseilles—homeland! French! And then he encountered the fact that he spoke French-Canadian, and the Parisian French put down people from ten miles out.

Jack thought he could hitchhike up from Marseilles to Paris somehow, the way he'd do it in the States, but in those days, in the late fifties, you couldn't do that in France. Nobody picked him up, so he finally took a bus and like many of Jack's idealistic notions about remaking tomorrow, it all came to details. What do you do? When he got to Paris he was already pretty dragged by the whole thing.

Back from Europe, Jack prepared *The Subterraneans* for publication and devised a new scheme to move Mémêre to the West Coast. At the same time he laid plans with his new girlfriend, Joyce Glassman, for her to quit her job and join him and Gabrielle in Berkeley. Perhaps he believed that *On the Road*, due out in a matter of weeks, would permit him to establish a conventional household: the successful novelist, his wife, and his elderly mother, at last retired from her long labors, Jack's promise to Leo kept.

So Jack and Mémêre packed up their belongings and gave the moving company Philip Whalen's address on Milvia Street in Berkeley. Jack planned to be there well in advance, in time to find a cottage of their own and have Philip direct the movers to the new address. By Greyhound bus, Jack and Mémêre crossed the "groaning" continent, stopping on the way to offer their prayers in a Ciudad Juarez church, just across the border from El Paso.

Upon arriving at their final destination Jack saw to it that Mémêre was comfortably installed in a hotel on Shattuck Avenue, and then went to see Phil Whalen. Before knocking on the door Kerouac peeked through the front window and spied Whalen entranced over his books. Jack was delighted, and waited a few moments before interrupting him. When he finally did Whalen greeted him warmly, expalining that he had just been observing a beautiful moth that had landed between the pages of the Lankavatara Sutra.

Jack found an apartment the next day, on Berkeley Way,

just off busy University Avenue. It was hardly Jack's dream of a peaceful "cottage in the Western night," and Gabrielle despised the Bay Area weather. She was completely unprepared for the summer climate, day after day of chilly fog, and she missed being close to Nin and her family. Jack wrote Joyce, who already had moved out of her apartment in New York, not to join him in California. He was coming back.

While he and Gabrielle were still in their shabby little apartment in Berkeley—Mémère was shopping at the time—a carton arrived from Viking Press: the bound advance copies of *On the Road*. At just that moment, he heard visitors outside. It was Neal and Luanne with Al and Helen Hinkle.

Al Hinkle:

Jack was just kind of standing there dumbfounded. He dug the books out. He had thrown them under the bed. I guess maybe he thought he was going to lose all six copies.

He'd finally broken open the books and Neal had gotten hold of one of them and started reading from it. This was out in a garage in this funny building out back, and there was a couple of metal bars off the rafters, and in between reading passages of it, Neal was chinning himself and swinging from these things and playing monkey.

Helen Hinkle:

Jack said, "You're all going to be mad at me."

Al Hinkle:

But he didn't elaborate on it. And everybody told him, "That's impossible." We couldn't care one way or the other. In fact, I don't know whether that day was kind of a let-down for him, because we got interested in doing other things.

Luanne Henderson:

He was going through all these scenes of, "Now you have to understand why I wrote this." And he was giving all these explanations and apologies.

Of course, none of us cared. We were reading a line here and a line there and reliving it and laughing and remembering. So none of us, Neal or Al Hinkle or I, were into looking to see what he had written. We were just back to remembering what had happened. But Jack's whole reaction was apology and why he had written this.

Of course, after I had read the book, I saw that so much of it was either left out or added on to. Of course, it was Jack's reaction. All of us were reacting in different ways, so I had to remember that this was the way Jack was feeling it and seeing it.

Al Hinkle:

Neal's running around with Jack's book still in his hand, but we went over back to the city to have a beer.

Jack, dressed in a lumberjack's shirt and his watch-cap, squeezed into the car with the others, headed to San Francisco for the small celebration that seemed appropriate.

When the party reached their chosen bar on Sixth Street, they were ejected by the owner because Luanne, now in her mid-twenties, had no identification with her to prove that she was of age. Al Hinkle was late for his job on the railroad, and so the celebration was aborted.

Luanne Henderson:

I imagine that Jack probably did feel the same way he and I felt the night that Neal drove away [and stranded us in San Francisco]—that he was kind of deserted.

It had been more than seven years since Jack's first novel, a novel with echoes of his real life in Lowell and New York, but still and clearly a novel. *On the Road* and the still-unpublished body of his work that had followed were something new, something more than that. Malcolm Cowley had known so for years, and Gilbert Millstein, who had commissioned Holmes' article certifying the new generation, would shortly herald Jack's new book with uncommon praise. Success, however, would taste like ashes, because Kerouac's work was so close to the truth that the art of its telling would be forgotten in the American marketplace of images.

4 THE CITY REVISITED

I asked Jack, "Well, how do you like fame?" He said, "It's like old newspapers blowing down Bleecker Street."

—IRENE MAY

< Jack Kerouac, New York, 1953. Photo courtesy of Allen Ginsberg

The America Kerouac portrayed in *On the Road* was an entirely different country from Eisenhower's America, which received the book. The novel was a traveler's tale from an alternate nation with the same language, cities, highways, and movie stars that its readers were familiar with, but separated in some important way from the motives and energies that drove most Americans of the 1950's. The events of *On the Road* had taken place ten years before the book finally appeared, but despite clear references to dates in Jack's novel, so little of it was topical that it read as news, and the news was about a strange group of men and women as exempt from the cold war as they had been from the killing war that preceded it.

Midcentury America was a country of families: Father, Mother, and the children, watching television programs about fathers, mothers, and children. The men and women of *On the Road* coupled and begat with little care for the expectations of church or society, and they seemed intent on banding together into something both larger and less than a family. Father went to a job every morning, a place with desks or a time-clock, where the business of business was conducted for forty hours a week. Dean Moriarty took a job only as a last resort, and Sal Paradise wanted nothing more from his work than food for the night or a bus ticket to take him someplace else. Eisenhower, the general who had prosecuted the hot war, spoke to his constituents in a slow and patient manner, explaining the necessity for the arms race and the bomb shelters in the way a grandfather might explain a frightening noise in the night to a child. Some of what went on in the night he did not mention at

231

all, and his fears about the "military-industrial complex" were never acted upon, but were reserved for the valedictory in which he coined the phrase.

For the great majority of white Americans it was a way of life that worked very well. The Hudson of *On the Road* was a familiar symbol to them, the streamlined car that every G. I. under Ike's command had promised himself when the war was done and the factories had finished manufacturing guns. Every Sunday after church, the family got in the car and drove to the country. The son of the family could look forward to the day when he got the keys to the car from Father, because, for most young men of that day, the expansive back seat became the first couch of love. But every Sunday it was necessary at some point to turn around and go home. Every drive-in date was a deadline mission. Dean Moriarty was different. The road, not a suburban driveway, was the place for a car. Nobody sat waiting up for Dean's girls to be home by midnight. Dean didn't turn around at four o'clock on a Sunday afternoon, he kept going.

Ginsberg and Burroughs had gone to the trouble of leaving the country in obligatory literary fashion, looking back on America with the perspective offered by Mexico, Panama, or North Africa. When Jack traveled, his mind's eye was busy recording the at-hand. He did not look over his shoulder. The same was true during his travels through the country he called *fellaheen* America. He had reached into Oswald Spengler's massive rhapsody of pessimism, *The Decline of the West*, to borrow the word the German historian had used to name the world's underclass. Jack's *fellaheen* were not the *grundrisse* of theoretical Marxism or the Third World of present-day politics, but simply the bulk of the planet's people, conducting their lives oblivious to the machinations of culture and power that functioned so well without their help. Jack's portrayal of Americans who preferred murky personal goals to clear-cut official ones was subversive without being political. Jack had shocked his friends with an occasional defense of Senator Joseph McCarthy and his paranoiac Communist-hunting of the early 1950's, and when asked for whom he voted in 1956, Eisenhower or Adlai Stevenson, Jack replied that he had not voted, but would have voted for Eisenhower. Kerouac shared neither Burroughs' patrician disdain for the annoying bureaucracy of American power, nor the principled, left-labor analysis of the political situation that Ginsberg inherited from his parents. In *On the Road*, the first book written in his swift and direct new style, Jack had simply set down "the unspeakable visions of the individual," and now they were published to a nation where the fact of individualism had been very nearly sacrificed in the name of the pure idea.

It would be fatuous to categorize Jack as a Spenglerian or to search for other borrowed themes in the Duluoz Legend, for the story relies only upon itself, creating a separate world in the way that the very greatest novels do. It is how Dickens worked, and Stendhal and Proust. But Spengler himself, drafting one of his charts of the future on the eve of World War I, had done an excellent job of forecasting the top-culture that would appraise Jack's work and appropriate it for its own uses: "Existence without inner form. Megapolitan art as a commonplace: luxury, sport, nerve-excitement. Rapidly-changing fashions in art."

In the seven years since *The Town and the City* had appeared, and the six since Giroux had refused to take *On the Road* seriously, Jack had constructed the bulk of his legend. When Malcolm Cowley had offered sympathy and a degree of understanding Jack eagerly explained *On the Road*'s place in a sequence of autobiographical novels of great ambition, but Cowley and his colleagues found *Springtime Mary* slight, *Visions of Gerard* marred by its reliance on the technical vocabulary of a completely alien religion, *Doctor Sax* obsessive and skirting dangerously near, perhaps beyond, the boundaries of coherence. *Visions of Neal*, in which Jack's profound full attention to his friend's nature and character provided the unifying element, owed little to anyone's idea of what a novel was. Lawrence Ferlinghetti turned down a chance to publish it because Jack wanted him to accept it blindly, without having read it, and New Directions, which finally did, would bring out only "excerpts" from it.

Although Jack's desire for conventional literary success was strong enough for him to achieve it, John Clellon Holmes observed him on the very eve of that success as a man who had learned to live quite well without it.

John Clellon Holmes:

Jack came to see me with Allen just before they all went to Europe in '57. Allen hadn't even gotten into Buddhism and Jack was a complete Bodhisattva then. He carried everything on his back.

He showed me *Tristessa* then. He showed me the first part of *Desolation Angels*. And he was pure as the driven snow. That is, he had been worn down. This is before *On the Road* came out. I knew nothing about Buddhism then. I had read Zen in '53 because of Allen, but Jack was living it, and he had changed from the guy that I had known earlier.

It's one of the most mysterious periods in his life, I suspect, because it's before the real drinking took hold and it's after the fury of the creative work.

It was a period of calm. He was winsome and withdrawn.

Jack's companion in that year of his tardy triumph was a twenty-one-year-old secretary at the MCA literary agency. The government's anti-trust lawyers had not yet forced that company to choose between being a literary and talent agency or a motion picture studio. Today it is known chiefly as Universal Studios, but then its power in every aspect of the public arts was immense.

Joyce Glassman:

I met him around January or February of 1957, coming in from California. That famous reading of "Howl" had happened in the fall of the previous year, and I remembered seeing an article in the *New York Times* describing it. And I had known Allen a little bit up at Columbia, when I was a student at Barnard. I ran around with an older crowd at college, people who had been to school with Allen. Carl Solomon lived around the corner in the horrible Yorkshire Hotel. I remember meeting Burroughs when I was sixteen. I began college when I was very young.

I read *The Town and the City* after I met Jack, and he was anticipating the publication of *On the Road*. He was very broke, and he was about to go off to Tangiers to be with Burroughs and then to go to France. He was very excited about the whole trip to France. He thought it would be like getting in touch with his ancestors, the Kerouacs of Normandy. He was always talking about his ancestors.

He had very little money. He was one of those people who knew how to live on nothing. He really just owned the clothes on his back.

My best friend in college was a woman named Elise Cowen, who is no longer alive, who was a very close friend of Allen Ginsberg's and was involved with him for quite a while, on and off. She had met Allen while she was going to Barnard, and then he reappeared on his way back from the coast and Allen suggested to her that I meet Jack, that Jack was lonely. He had just split up with someone, he was broke, he was depressed and so on. And so this strange blind date was arranged.

I was over visiting my friend Elise one day, and I got this phone call from this person who said he was Jack Kerouac. He had heard about me, he'd very much like to meet me, and if I would come to the Howard Johnson's on Eighth Street, I could identify him because he'd be wearing a red and black lumberjack shirt and would be sitting at the counter having a cup of coffee. Allen had set this up. Jack said he was feeling terrible, and he'd just been kicked out of this hotel that he was at, and he'd gotten short-changed, had no money. He told me all this on the phone. I was to come down and meet him. So I went down and I met him and we talked, and we ended up going uptown to my place, which was up around Columbia, which pleased him because he said he had great affection for the whole Columbia area—the West End Bar and so on.

And so we became involved and were together until he actually went off to Tangier, which was not more than two months.

I remember when I was in college a discussion I had with Elise, who had been taken by Allen to a bar in the Village called Fugazi's, which was a hangout at the time. She came back and said there were all these women there, and they all looked terrific, and they sat around on barstools and didn't say a word, they just looked cool.

The whole Beat scene had very little to do with the

participation of women as artists themselves. The real communication was going on between the men, and the women were there as onlookers. Their old ladies. You kept your mouth shut, and if you were intelligent and interested in things you might pick up what you could. It was a very masculine aesthetic.

I kind of accepted it. I expected it somehow. It didn't bother me too much at the time, and it was very exciting and I felt that I was learning things.

Jack and I talked a lot about writing because I was writing my novel. It took me some years to write, and he was very interested in what I was doing and very encouraging, and would tell me I was the best woman writer in America, and so on. He really took it seriously, which was very important to me.

I wrote in a very, very different way than he did. He would write down his dreams. He had little notebooks. In the fall of '57, I believe, he began what became *Dharma Bums*. He was always writing poems. It was a constant thing. He'd even write little poems in his letters. I admired his spontaneity. I envied it. I was one of those people who worked things over very painfully, writing and rewriting. I knew that he disapproved, but that was the way I did it. He would give me suggestions for titles. He wanted me to call the book I was writing *Pay Me the Penny After*. He just liked it. It was called *Come and Join the Dance*. From *Alice in Wonderland*. But he liked *Pay Me the Penny After*.

He had this sense of anticipation, that something was about to happen to him. He was frenetic at times about seeing people, but he really was a very withdrawn person, a very shy person, who basically liked to sit around the house not doing much. I remember a lot of real silences. They didn't bother me particularly. I kind of accepted them. He had an extraordinary memory, of course. He could meet a stranger and say, "Oh yeah. I remember you. I met you five years ago in the West End Bar. It was in October. We discussed the baseball game." It was that kind of a minute memory—really extraordinary.

He was into Buddhism at the time, not Catholicism. I knew that it was a very serious thing for him. I thought it had to do with his preoccupation with death, which was

236

something he always talked about to me. He had really been ill. He had been in the Veterans Administration Hospital, and he had a problem with blood clots. He was very, very aware of it. He had this sense that his life was going to be cut short, that it could happen at any time. He was really much more preoccupied with it than anyone realized, in the sense of time passing, and so on. It was all very much related to this very real fear he had of being killed off.

Jack's relationship with women was very troubled. I didn't have the sense that our relationship was going to last, although it went on for about two years and was very important to me. Once or twice we talked about getting married, but I never took it seriously. I thought of it as, "Well, I'm having this experience now, and it will probably end, but I will have had these two years." It was a kind of realistic notion. He talked about his marriage with Joan—what a disaster it was. He denied that the child she had could have been his and showed me a picture of this kid with his face and said, "This isn't my kid. How could this kid be mine?" I said, "Well, you know she looks like you. What can I say? Looks just like you."

I think the idea of having children was very frightening to him. I don't know why exactly. I think it had to do with his feeling of mortality, that we're all brought here to die. Having that sense of doom. The general doom. Also, he knew that he couldn't be the father that his own father was. That was impossible, and so he would fail if he were ever a father.

He would stay with me and go away again. This happened about three or four times. He wanted me to come to San Francisco and stay with him out there.

I decided I was ready to do this, and it coincided with selling my first novel and getting half the advance, which was five hundred dollars. I felt I could live on that five hundred dollars for months, which was possible back then. I was working at a new job at Farrar, Straus at that time, and I had gotten a promotion and this offer on my novel on the same day, and the next day I went in and said, "I'm quitting. I'm going to San Francisco." And I quit.

Then more correspondence ensued with Jack, whose

mother was with him by this time. He still wanted me to come out there. We'd get together with Neal. (I never met Neal. I never really wanted to. He seemed to me a kind of scary and unappealing person. His attitude toward women was really awful.) I was ready to go, and then I got this letter saying San Francisco was really a down place, terrible vibes, "I can't stay here any longer, I'm very depressed, I'm going to Mexico City. Meet me in Mexico City." And then he schlepped his mother to Florida and he went to Mexico City. So *I* was going to go to Mexico City, and then I got this letter from Mexico City saying, "It's really awful here. I have dysentery," and so on. "I'm going to recuperate at my mother's house and then I'm coming to New York. Get an apartment in New York."

Well, I had had this apartment that I had moved out of. I was staying with a friend, and then it all seemed to go on, so I had moved into the Yorkshire Hotel—the dreaded Yorkshire Hotel, which was full of troubled people who had something to do with Columbia. So I found an apartment on Sixty-seventh Street between Columbus and Central Park West.

Jack came into town about the day before *On the Road* was published. Keith Jennison from Viking sent up this case of champagne, and Jack was very excited and happy. And then—a whole lot of drinking.

Then that Millstein review came out in the *New York Times*, which was very crucial for that book. It was a daily review, obviously something very big and much more than he ever expected, and he was overwhelmed by it and frightened, I think, because he wasn't the kind of person who did very well being in the public eye.

John Clellon Holmes:

Gil Millstein gave a party for Jack. Gil Millstein wrote that review that tried to establish *On the Road* some- where in the literature, and he was all excited about it. He called me up because he had reviewed *Go* years and years before, and he used his review of *Go* and stuff that I'd written in the article that he'd commissioned in his review of Jack's book. He quoted from my article two or

Books of The Times

"ON THE ROAD"* is the second novel by Jack Kerouac, and its publication is a historic occasion in so far as the exposure of an authentic work of art is of any great moment in an age in which the attention is fragmented and the sensibilities are blunted by the superlatives of fashion (multiplied a millionfold by the speed and pound of communications).

This book requires exegesis and a detailing of background. It is possible that it will be condescended to by, or make uneasy, the neo-academicians and the "official" avant-garde critics, and that it will be dealt with superficially elsewhere as merely "absorbing" or "intriguing" or "picaresque" or any of a dozen convenient banalities, not excluding "off-beat." But the fact is that "On the Road" is the most beautifully executed, the clearest and the most important utterance yet made by the generation Kerouac himself named years ago as "beat," and whose principal avatar he is.

Just as, more than any other novel of the Twenties, "The Sun Also Rises" came to be regarded as the testament of the "Lost Generation," so it seems certain that "On the Road" will come to be known as that of the "Beat Generation." There is, otherwise, no similarity between the two; technically and philosophically, Hemingway and Kerouac are, at the very least, a depression and a world war apart.

The 'Beat' Bear Stigmata

Much has been made of the phenomenon that a good deal of the writing, the poetry and the painting of this generation (to say nothing of its deep interest in modern jazz) has emerged in the so-called "San Francisco Renaissance," which, while true, is irrelevant. It cannot be localized. (Many of the San Francisco group, a highly mobile lot in any case, are no longer resident in that benign city, or only intermittently.) The "Beat Generation" and its artists display readily recognizable stigmata.

Outwardly, these may be summed up as the frenzied pursuit of every possible sensory impression, an extreme exacerbation of the nerves, a constant outraging of the body. (One gets "kicks"; one "digs" everything, whether it be drink, drugs, sexual promiscuity, driving at high speeds or absorbing Zen Buddhism.)

Inwardly, these excesses are made to serve a spiritual purpose, the purpose of an affirmation still unfocused, still to be defined, unsystematic. It is markedly distinct from the protest of the "Lost Generation" or the political protest of the "Depression Generation."

The "Beat Generation" was born disillusioned; it takes for granted the imminence of war, the barrenness of politics and the hostility of the rest of society. It is not even impressed by (although it never pretends to scorn) material well-being (as distinguished from materialism). It does not know what refuge it is seeking, but it is seeking.

As John Aldridge has put it in his critical work, "After the Lost Generation," there were four choices open to the post war writer: novelistic journalism or journalistic novel-writing; what little subject-matter that had not been fully exploited already (homosexuality, racial conflict), pure technique (for lack of something to say), or the course I feel Kerouac has taken—assertion "of the need for belief even though it is upon a background in which belief is impossible and in which the symbols are lacking for a genuine affirmation in genuine terms."

Five years ago, in the Sunday magazine of this newspaper, a young novelist, Clellon Holmes, the author of a book called "Go," and a friend of Kerouac's, attempted to define the generation Kerouac had labeled. In doing so, he carried Aldridge's premise further. He said, among many other pertinent things, that to his kind "the absence of personal and social values * * * is not a revelation shaking the ground beneath them, but a problem demanding a day-to-day solution. *How* to live seems to them much more crucial than *why*." He added that the difference between the "Lost" and the "Beat" may lie in the latter's "will to believe even in the face of an inability to do so in conventional terms"; that they exhibited "on every side and in a bewildering number of facets a perfect craving to believe."

Those Who Burn, Burn, Burn

That is the meaning of "On the Road." What does its narrator, Sal Paradise, say? "* * * The only people for me are the mad ones, the ones who are mad to live, mad to talk, mad to be saved, desirous of everything at the same time, the ones who never yawn or say a commonplace thing, but burn, burn, burn like fabulous yellow roman candles. * * *"

And what does Dean Moriarity, Sal's American hero-saint say? "And of course no one can tell us that there is no God. We've passed through all forms. * * * Everything is fine, God exists, we know time. * * * God exists without qualms. As we roll along this way I am positive beyond doubt that everything will be taken care of for us— that even you, as you drive, fearful of the wheel * * * the thing will go along of itself and you won't go off the road and I can sleep."

This search for affirmation takes Sal on the road to Denver and San Francisco; Los Angeles and Texas and Mexico; sometimes with Dean, sometimes without; sometimes in the company of other beat individuals whose tics vary, but whose search is very much the same (not infrequently ending in death or derangement; the search for belief is very likely the most violent known to man).

There are sections of "On the Road" in which the writing is of a beauty almost breathtaking. There is a description of a cross-country automobile ride fully the equal, for example, of the train ride told by Thomas Wolfe in "Of Time and the River." There are the details of a trip to Mexico (and an interlude in a Mexican bordello) that are, by turns, awesome, tender and funny. And, finally, there is some writing on jazz that has never been equaled in American fiction, either for insight, style or technical virtuosity. "On the Road" is a major novel.

© 1957 by The New York Times Company.

three paragraphs, just giving people a way to think about it.

So he called me up and said, "I'm giving 'a party for Jack." He had never met Jack at that point. "Come in." Well, I did come in. We were up in Connecticut. I went in alone. Hours went by and people kept piling in, and no Jack.

Then the phone rang in the bedroom, and it was Jack. He wouldn't talk to Gil and he wouldn't talk to Gil's wife. He wanted to talk to me. So I talked to him, and he was at Joyce's place. He said, "I can't come down. I'm hung over. I'm shivering. I've got the D.T.'s, but I know you've come into town. Can you get out and come up and see me?" And I said, "Sure."

So I took Gil aside and explained. Jack was not very good about facing up to certain situations. When he had to cop out, he usually tried to slip out. He wouldn't talk to Gil and say, "Look, I can't make your party for me." He talked to me, and I took Gil aside and said, "Look, Jack's in trouble. He's feeling bad. He's sick, and he can't make it, and I'm going to slip out because I'm in town really to see him, and I'm going to run up and see him." Gil understood this completely. So it was one of those ludicrous situations in which, here were thirty or forty people collected in this apartment to see this new, young Marlon Brando of literature, who had just called up to say he couldn't make it, he was in bed.

So I slipped out and ran uptown and spent a couple of hours with him and Joyce. He'd just had too much. He wasn't boozed, really. Hardly enough. Later on it became absolute booze, but it wasn't booze then. It was just that he'd been interviewed by television people five or six times, newspaper people. He didn't know who he was, and he was just terrified. He was lying there in bed, holding his head.

Most books that come out are contained. That is, "I want to read that book." But what happened when *On the Road* came out was, "I want to know that man." It wasn't the book so much as it was the man. He became more and more confused as it went on.

He was on John Wingate's television show, and two minutes after that show had aired, I had phone calls from people that I knew saying, "I've got to meet this man.

240

Got to. You know him. I've got to meet him." And I said, "What are you talking about? Read his book." "No; no. It's not that. He knows everything..." Women saying, "I've got to fuck him." People came to Joyce and said, "Look, you're with him. You're twenty years old, but I've only got so many years left. I've got to fuck him now." They just wanted the experience, and all this was profoundly confusing to a guy like Kerouac, who was a terribly simple and conventional genius.

This so discombobulated him that for the rest of his life he never, never got his needle back on true north.

Never.

Joyce Glassman:

Suddenly he would go to all these literary parties. He was to be on radio. He was to be on television. Appearances at campuses. It was heavy, and it went on for months. And he would make these appearances or be interviewed, and the tone of the interviewing would often be extremely hostile. You know, "You say this about the Beat Generation. These are terribly immoral people. They take drugs. What are you talking about? These people are awful."

Jack was pretty innocent in a lot of ways. He'd meet an interviewer, and he'd really try to communicate with this interviewer and think that he had somehow reached him as a person, and then the interview would come out in some distorted form. He'd see his own words all twisted around, and it was very, very upsetting for him. The only way he could get through this was to drink a lot.

I was going with him to the parties. The parties were a nightmare. I had a dream about him once. We had been to a poetry reading out in Brooklyn College and he was practically mobbed by all these kids. I had this dream that I had gone with him somewhere and people were literally tearing him limb from limb. I felt this kind of anger in people. They were fascinated by him. They also thought he was very threatening. They hated him. All the men wanted to fight him. All the women wanted to fuck him, not in a nice way, but in an aggressive way.

It was dreadful. I decided I never wanted to be a famous person.

Sometimes he would go out alone and somebody would try to beat him up, knowing who he was. I think people identified him more with the Dean Moriarty character in *On the Road* than with the Sal Paradise character. That was another reason why he had to drink, to live up to that extroverted image. Give them what they wanted. He was really backed into a corner, and it just got very bad.

Then we went away with Lucien Carr up to Cherry Plain. The idea was, we'd all go up there and then we were going to leave Jack there. Jack had said he wanted to be alone, like he was on Desolation, retreat there. He was going to stay a week or so just by himself. A day later I came home from the office and I was amazed to find Jack back in the apartment. He had the horrors. He had to come back. He couldn't stay there by himself.

It was October, the month to go home. When Jack joined Mémère at Nin's new home in Orlando that fall, *On the Road* was on the *New York Times* best-seller list. He need no longer feel ashamed to accept the hospitality of his brother-in-law, Paul. Whatever Jack wrote next was going to sell.

Viking had the right of first refusal on Jack's next novel after *On the Road*. Keith Jennison and Malcolm Cowley had seen most of the books Jack had carried through the 1950's in his trunk or rucksack, but Viking was not interested in bringing out a quirky legend, merely books. Just as Giroux had wanted another *The Town and the City*, Viking wanted another *On the Road*.

Malcolm Cowley:

These other manuscripts did not arouse my enthusiasm, such as the one about the girl in Lowell, *Maggie Cassidy*. *Doctor Sax* I think I was completely wrong about. I think I should have forced *Doctor Sax* down Viking's throat. I couldn't do it, but that was the best of them. *Visions of Cody*, in the shape I saw it then, I didn't much like.

242

But then somebody at Viking said, "Why don't you just carry on what you were doing in *On the Road*? And Jack sat down and did his *Dharma Bums*. And I had nothing at all to do with that.

It's very acceptable prose, but this time he had a terrible fight with Viking about the changes that his editor and the copy-editing department had made in the style. Later on he got mixed up and thought I was responsible for them. I never saw the manuscript of *The Dharma Bums*. I read it as a book. I never liked *The Dharma Bums* very much, because it had no people in it except Jack—and oh, yes, Gary Snyder's in there, too; he's the only other one.

The novels which *The Dharma Bums* most closely resembles are *Tristessa* and *The Subterraneans*. That is, the book chronicles Jack Duluoz's close relationship with a single other person, an intellectual and religious relationship in the case of Gary Snyder. It was written with the swiftness of *On the Road*, *Tristessa*, and *The Subterraneans*, and Jack may have composed it in the way that *On the Road* itself was composed,

Malcolm Cowley, 1977. Photo by Lawrence Lee.

with a specific reader in mind. Jack said that *On the Road* was addressed to his second wife, Joan, although it was written at the end of their brief winter's marriage. He would use the device again, writing his last novel, *Vanity of Duluoz*, as direct address to his third wife. *The Dharma Bums* is written with an air of patient explanation, as though addressed to a book editor.

John Clellon Holmes:

He wrote *The Dharma Bums* in three weeks, or maybe a month. They wouldn't publish *The Subterraneans*. They wouldn't publish any of the other books that he'd written, so he wrote *The Dharma Bums*.

He was a guy who had been in the underground for years, and suddenly, second time around, it seemed again he had a chance to live by his pen. He'd been writing relentlessly. He'd written eight books in between the rejection of *On the Road* and its final publication.

Jack wasn't a saint. Jack believed he could somehow escape everything. There's a terrible moment when you feel good about yourself and you feel you're in charge of your talent—that is, it's invested in you, you embody it. There's an awful moment when someone comes to you and says write a book that will fit in and you say, "I can do that on Friday." You feel strong, you feel powerful, and you feel you can't hurt yourself, you can't sell yourself, you can't besmirch your own perceptions about things. That's, I'm sure, what Jack must have felt when it came to *The Dharma Bums*. "Sure, I'll write you a book about the rucksack saints." And he did.

But it wasn't impelled by the stuff that made the good books good. It was impelled by an understanding that he had, a perception that he had and experiences that he'd had, and it's valuable and it's fine. But the prose is lax.

It was, in fact, the third work that Jack started while he was in Florida. The first was a play called *The Beat Generation*, which never has been published or performed. The second was another novel of boyhood in Lowell, entitled *Memory Babe*. Its place in the Duluoz Legend would have been between *Visions of Gerard* and *Doctor Sax*.

Even before *On the Road* had appeared, Jack had found a sympathetic publisher in Barney Rosset, scion of a Chicago banking family who had founded his Grove Press in New York. Rosset set out to market the *avant-garde* in aggressive fashion. He had begun with Genet, Borges, and Ionesco, but the emergence of the Beat Generation provided stars for his *Evergreen Review* and, in the cases of Burroughs and Kerouac, his trade list. After *On the Road* succeeded he quickly purchased *Doctor Sax*. His contract for *The Subterraneans* had given Jack the money for the trip to Tangier in the summer of 1957, and that novel was being rushed to press to capitalize on the success of *On the Road*. In time Rosset would bring out the travel sketches collected as *Lonesome Traveler*, including "The Railroad Earth", *Mexico City Blues*, Jack's ad-libbed narration for the Robert Frank film *Pull My Daisy*, and later *Satori in Paris* and *Pic*.

As the editors at Harcourt, Brace and at Viking had not, the publisher of Samuel Beckett and Alain Robbe-Grillet comprehended the prose that Jack had explained in his brief forenote for a foreign edition of *The Subterraneans*: "what I believe to be the prose of the future, from both the conscious top and the unconscious bottom of the mind, limited only by the limitations of time flying by as your mind flies with it."

While Rosset readied what he considered to be the best of the existing body of Kerouac's work, Jack's new agent, Sterling Lord, sold the twice-rejected *Tristessa* and *Maggie Cassidy* to Avon Books for publication as cheap paperbacks. He did not, however, conclude an agreement which would result in a movie of *On the Road*, although reports were published that M-G-M would film it with Brando as Dean Moriarty.

Because of the demands of publicity, which Jack still was willing to answer, and of editorial work on half a dozen separate manuscripts, Jack returned to New York and to Joyce.

In December of that year he used his fame to fulfill an old dream, that of becoming a jazz performer. Ever since his apprenticeship to Seymour Wyse and George Avakian during his first year in New York City, Jack had understood what it is that happens in jazz. Although he played no instrument his scat-singing of a Miles Davis solo, for example, was entirely accurate, and something more than a simple imitation. He always felt an affinity between his poetic method and the technique of jazz soloists, a link stated plainly in his notes for *Mexico City Blues*.

When Jack stepped onto the stage of the Village Vanguard, it was as a poet leading a jazz ensemble. His sidemen included such distinguished pure-jazz stars as tenormen Al Cohn and Zoot Sims, and Steve Allen, who was then at the height of his fame as a television performer. Two months before, Jack had given the first jazz poetry readings in N.Y. with poets Philip Lamantia, Howard Hart and a young musician named David Amram, who then stood at the beginning of his career as a classical composer and conductor, jazz French horn player, multi-instrumentalist and social chronicler.

David Amram:

Jack, if you'd ride around on the subway with him, or just go out on the street, would talk to everybody and be natural and real with anybody. We used to walk around New York's streets for hours. One time we were hanging out with Allen Ginsberg, and there was a guy we met in the Bowery. He was a full-time wino named Buddy the wino. "Come on, we'll go up to Allen's place and we'll all read poems." I just listened. I didn't have any instruments with me and I was glad just to be a listener for a change. So I went up and listened to Jack, Allen and Buddy the wino all night long. Jack had *Mexico City Blues* which was neatly typed on a big roll of shelving paper. It took the whole night. Allen would read a poem and Buddy, who was drinking wine, would say, "Yeah, that's pretty nice. I can dig that. That's nice. That's all right." Then, when Jack would read his poems, Buddy would flip out and scream with laughter and slap his knee and do a lot of really wigged-out cracking up, falling on the floor. He liked Allen's poems, too, but he really identified with Jack's. And Jack said, real quietly while Allen was reading a poem, "These guys are where I get so much inspiration from and learn so much from. They are the true poets of the streets." And the way he said it, wasn't like a sociologist saying, "Now I'm descending into the lower depths to chronicle the primitive speech patterns of the proletariat drop-outs." He meant it in the sense that he actually saw past all that misery and degradation and suffering, with his own drinking habit himself, and he could see the soulfulness, the tragedy, and the true poetic vision some of these people really had—as if they were in touch with this great beatific light.

Jack didn't mean to imply that everybody should just lie around in the Bowery and drink Sterno, in order to become a better writer. That wasn't the point of what he was saying, and he never tried to encourage people to do that. He wished that he could have a more stable life, stay more sober and not drink as much, although he loved to drink. When he was drunk he had a ball. Still, he knew it was killing him and it was bad, and that he was doing it because he was so shy, and because drinking

David Amram, 1976. Photo by Lawrence Lee.

killed his shyness, and eased his pain. The pain and pressures ironically came from frustrated English-major types, who were outraged by his non-literary life style.

People would come up and say all these hostile things to him. After *On the Road* came out I remember seeing a guy on Sheridan Square in Greenwich Village with a big Colonel Blimp-type moustache. He was in his late forties, I guess, with a super Ivy League ad-agency, great-looking tweed coat, those Oxford gray pants with the loafers all shined up with tassles on them, probably had twenty-five-dollar socks on. Very distinguished, looked like the old-time *Esquire* magazine executive. And he was saying, "Where's that fucking Jack Kerouac? I want to meet that bastard. He can't write. That shit isn't writing. Any junior-high-school student... Shit, he doesn't even use any punctuation. That fucking bastard. I want to meet that moron." The guy was raving like a lunatic, hoping that someone in Sheridan Square could introduce him to Jack Kerouac so he could have a fantastic, Ernest Hemingway, three-day literary punchout. And the irony of it was that Jack was in fact, a deeply intellectual person. He knew so much about Céline, Rimbaud, all kinds of poets, French history, music. He was into everything. He was incredibly intellectual, literate and spiritual. And he didn't see being a literate person as acting like he possessed the secret to the literary atomic bomb, or we're going to blow everybody off the face of the earth if they got too close to you to try to find out what you knew, that enabled you to get your work out to the public.

Jack would tell anybody what he knew about writing, who would listen. Jack used to say to me that a writer should be like a shadow, just be part of the side-walk like a shadow. He said that one afternoon as we were strolling around shadow-style on MacDougal Street in December, 1957, the day after our first jazz-poetry reading at the Circle-in-the-Square Theater. He would usually avoid trouble, but sometimes he'd be with people who were in a more negative groove. He got punched out, I remember, 'cause he was with a guy who acted real obnoxious 'cause he was with Jack, and Jack didn't want to just stand there and let the guy, who was stoned out, get beaten up. He had so much loyalty to this guy, who was ripping him off, that he wound up taking his punches when he tried to be a peacemaker. But that was mostly when he drank, and he drank mostly when he came to New York.

At the Vanguard he got real shy. It was hard for him to read there. The Vanguard's a tough place to work if you've never performed in New York. I've played there, and love it, but it took me twenty-five, thirty years to learn how to be in places like that and feel comfortable and have a ball. That's a special art. It's just like a boxer being able to enjoy working out in a gym. You have to just get used to that groove and go with it. But if you come in there and you don't know what's happening, you just get claustrophobia and feel like you're down in a hole of some kind. The Vanguard has a certain kind of crazy subterranean nineteenth-century Parisian vibe that no place else does.

Jack was just freaked out by it, started drinking a lot and getting embarrassed. When we did our jazz-poetry readings a month before he played at the Vanguard, Philip Lamantia, Howard Hart and an army of friends all used to go outside and drink that Thunderbird wine during intermission and get stoned. I'd sit during intermission and play the piano in the hallway of the Circle in the Square while people were going out to try to talk to Jack. Then they'd all come back again and yell for Jack to read something. Half the time, he wouldn't come back for a half-hour. That's when I first learned to ad lib songs with rhymes from suggestions in the audience just to fill time.

One night, the lighting designer came down and said, "What can I do for you? What kind of lighting do you want when Jack comes on? Does he want something different?" Howard Hart said, "Just do whatever you feel." So the lighting designer flipped out. That was the first time in his life he ever had what he considered to be a spontaneous lighting jam session. No more lighting cues. It was his big chance to wail. They'd be reading all these insane poems and there'd be this crazy light. This was way before psychedelic lighting or strobe lights. Not only flashing lights and airport and highway high beams in the audience's faces, but all kinds of wild faces and traveling fog lights and search lights. It was the first

Jack Kerouac in New York City, 1953. Photo courtesy of Coach House Press, Toronto.

chance he ever had to express himself, and the things he'd do would be so crazy that we would make sounds to go along with what the lighting was like. Half the stuff was just improvised and Jack would start scat-singing. It was really amazing. It was audience-attack, but always with a cosmic sense of humor.

250

People would scream out things to him and he'd answer in a real, super down-home party style. It was a definite contrast to the grim world of cocktail-party quality lit. And everything was so conservative in 1957 that what we did to close out the year was really out there.

Lucien Carr:

Jack really was a fuckin' peasant... like when he was in the Village Vanguard. Steve Allen took an interest in Jack, right? Oh man, but Steve Allen suddenly became a great, wonderful thing. So Jack was in the Vanguard, reading his poetry, with Steve Allen playing the piano. Which was a very bad combination. They didn't really seem to go together, but it did just lift Jack up that here's this millionaire number one.... There he was, sort of playing piano, and Jack was reading. They might start out with twenty people, and by the end of the thing it'd be ten.

I'd go every night. I'd say, "Let's see what's happening tonight, Jack." He was so embarrassed, he was saying, "I haven't got my shoes on, I can't do my fingers, read this sunumbitch..." In total sort of shyness. Steve Allen would say, "Come on, Jack!"

I really think that between the two there was some real feeling, but Jack was just so far behind in bull-shitting—Jack was not *good* at bullshitting. Every time he bullshitted he thought about it for three days.

I tell you, you will never find as pure a man as that.

Jack had not told Irene that *The Subterraneans* was to be published in 1958. She had signed a release a year earlier consenting to its publication in a literary magazine, but had heard nothing more of the story, and was satisfied that it had been forgotten. Now she was to be the central character in a best-selling author's next work.

Oddly, in September of 1957, she had dreamed of Jack the night before an adulatory review of *On the Road* appeared in the *New York Times,* and she contacted him. Despite everything, Irene was happy for him. Later that fall they arranged to meet and celebrate his success.

"Irene May"

Jack came by, and we went out and had a drink. He said, "I'm going with this ballet dancer." And I said, "Fine, why don't you call her up and invite her down? I'd like to meet her."

We went to the Vanguard together. Jack was speaking on the stage, and he was drunk—you know, jazz poetry. Jimmy Baldwin said in an article, "If any jazz musicians heard Jack reading jazz poetry, they'd stone him to death." It was all out of kilter and awful.

We went back to my place and Jack and his girl had some little altercation. He was very drunk and she stood there arguing with him like, "You can't do this to me, this, that, and the other." I thought that was very charming, anyone taking all that time to talk to Jack and explain to him again what he could and couldn't do.

That was the night he told me *The Subterraneans* was coming out. I asked: "Which magazine?" He said, "It's not in a magazine, it's a book." He said, originally, a magazine was publishing it, and now he tells me it's a book.

I said, "You said it was coming out in a magazine on the West Coast."

He said, "That's what you wanted to hear."

And that was that.

Later, I don't know whether it was in the late fifties or the early sixties, I asked Jack, "Well, how do you like fame?" He said, "It's like old newspapers blowing down Bleecker Street."

In the early fifties everyone had the feeling something was going to happen—waiting for someone to make a move. But what happened, I don't think anybody expected.

Now in '57, I thought, "This is going to happen. Some new generation is being made up that somehow shouldn't exist in this way, and part of it is just going to be pure media hype."

No one was quite prepared for the way all of this broke upon the scene, *On the Road*, pot smoking, LSD, the coffee shops started opening up and the poetry readings began. Suddenly there were millions more people on earth, and they all seemed to be coming to Greenwich Village. I had the feeling things were getting a little out of hand here. This big media maw, also these millions of kids. Three, four, a hundred, fine, but not millions. It's mind-staggering. And I think a lot of people felt that way. It was just a sheer mass—or mess—of numbers, and the whole game, everything just sort of changed.

I just remember being terribly frightened and wanting to hold on to some inner reality and not get caught up.

When *The Dharma Bums* was published by Viking the following October Ginsberg used it as the platform for a *Voice* review that spent more time trying to rescue Jack from his own publicity than appraising the book itself, which Allen found to be the work of a man now "weary of the world and prose." Written like a telegram, Allen's piece began, "A few facts to clear up a lot of bull," and then accurately explained Jack's plight. But this was the *Village Voice*. *Time* and its siblings found the Beats an attractive sideshow. Soon, espresso houses with flat black walls, and bars called The Cellar were opening for business in places like Milwaukee and Fort Worth. Berets came back. Allen had no way to stop the mechanism he had set in motion three years earlier with his careful choreography of the San Francisco scene. In the very first paragraph of his review Millstein had said the publication of *On the Road* was a historic occasion "insofar as the exposure of an authentic work of art is of any great moment in an age in which the attention is fragmented and the sensibilities are blunted by the superlatives of fashion (multiplied a millionfold by the speed and pound of communications)." Fashion triumphed.

Jack's own defenses became peevish. "I am an artful story-teller, a *writer* in the great French narrative tradition, not a 'spokesman' for a million hoods," he wrote in the liner notes for his album with Steve Allen. At times he played with fame like a toy. On a trip upstate with Lucien and his wife, Jack and Allen Ginsberg surprised two college-age women at a service station. "I'm Jack Kerouac." "I'm Allen Ginsberg." They had stopped near Vassar, and the young women's expressions made it obvious that they had never heard of the pair, who retreated in embarrassment.

Bars were a happy and natural social setting for Jack, but in the bars of New York City he could not go unrecognized for long. He was now "King of the Beats," a phrase he thoroughly detested, and certain of the pretenders continued to press their claim in trial by combat. Now he was always a besotted king. The heavy drinking had begun as light anesthesia, or as bottled courage before facing the crowd at the Village Vanguard. Soon, however, he was drinking with the motivation and precision of the intelligent alcoholic, and every moment of his descent became a permanent entry in his awesome memory.

John Clellon Holmes:

He was really fleeing from what to him was a monster image of the King of the Beats. He was fleeing from that, and he wanted oblivion, which is where the drink comes in. He always drank badly. He always drank too much. All of us did, some of us still do, but Jack drank seriously. That is, he wasn't just casual about it. He was drinking for reasons.

Lucien Carr:

When Jack was on the football team at dear old Columbia, they all went down to the Village, the football team, to do the usual thing that football teams do when they aren't punishing each other. And they ran some little guy with a violin around a corner into an alley, three or four of them, and busted the violin over the guy's head. That never left Jack. It was his one guilty thing, the one thing he'd done. He went with the fullback, the left end or whatever, and cornered this poor little fag in an alley with his violin and busted it over his head. No, that never left Jack—the violence of it, against someone else. He used to get drunk and say, "We should never have hit that man with his violin."

We'd go into a bar, I'd be talking with somebody, and the next thing I knew, it was a big brawl. I'd stand there and there'd be Kerouac smacking this guy that way and I would be on the back of somebody else, and Kerouac would have to knock the guy over before I had both his eyeballs out.

I'd say, "Well, well—they all left, didn't they?" And Jack'd say, "Why did you climb on that guy's back and grab his eyes?" And I'd say, "Well, it was either that or his throat, John."

If you hurt his ego he would flinch. If you stuck your finger in his eye, he would flinch—but he had no feeling that he should hit you back.

And in later days, when he used to get drunk and really just passed out, I'd say, "Jack, you gotta get up." And I'd try to pick him up, I'd try it again. I'd kick him, pick him up and what-not, drunk, pick him up, pick him up, get him up so he's standing up, then you belt him a few times, and then—you know, he'd—but he had no hatred in him. He was a man without hate—without hate.

Broken-hearted? No. . . . a heart as strong as a boy's.

Gregory Corso:

I know him never having touched another human being. Even when one touched him, he would not touch back. There was that awful scene I witnessed when somebody was hitting his head on the curb. I was screaming like mad to the guy, "Stop! Stop!"

It was in a bar, and we were drinking, and when Jack drank he got very loud, but never boisterous. But some creep there took him as being abusive, or something. The images are very horrid of him hitting Jack's head on the pavement, and I was screaming and it was over. The guy stopped and it was over. I don't know what happened afterwards. I have no idea, but it was one of the most awful things I've ever seen—somebody's head being hit like that.

What happened afterwards was that Jack was taken to a hospital. His mother and his mistress were appalled. Gabrielle, who was sixty-four in 1958, had recently come to find comfort with Nin and her family in Orlando, but Jack needed her now. He was still bound by his pledge to support her, and the books had provided the money. Joyce herself, realizing that Jack was more of a son than a husband, suggested a place for them to move together.

Joyce Glassman:

He had been living with his friend Henri Cru [in New York City], and then he said what he wanted to do was move his mother up near New York, but not in the city. He wanted to live out of the city, and he wanted a real house.

I had known someone who had grown up in Northport, out on Long Island, and I had heard a lot about it. It was like a fishing town. It had kind of an interesting character. There were clammers there. It was like New England a little bit.

So Jack and I and Robert Frank drove to Northport one day and looked it over, and Jack went in to see several real estate agents and rented this brown-shingled house.

Then he moved his mother in there and didn't come into the city very much and became rather withdrawn and got involved and swept up with things that were going on in Northport. He was very much lionized, particularly by all the kids. He was hanging out with all these high school kids.

Finally, he invited me to come out. And I was upset because we had not been in communication that much. I went out to see him. It was on a Sunday, and I took a Long Island train, got out at Northport Station, and there was a bus there. I got on the bus, and it was full of middle-aged people carrying little paper bags. The bus took off, and it kept going and going and going, and it went through the gates of this estate-looking place, and then it stopped and there were all these people walking around looking very disturbed. I realized that I had ended up in a mental institution. It made me feel very strange.

I waited and got another bus back, and then got into Northport and found Jack's house. I walked into this house that was full of kids. I mean, I was twenty-two, but there were these people there who were sixteen and seventeen, these Long Island kids. They were all taking Jack off for an afternoon of swimming and visiting somebody's beach house. I went along, and there was this beach house on the water with this great golden rug and all these sunburned kids standing around and Jack, absolutely bombed out of his mind, not knowing where he was. Kids saying to me, "What's it like to live in the city?" Like I was an old lady.

Then we came back to Jack's house and his mother made this big meal that everybody ate except Jack. He ended up with his head in his plate. I went upstairs and we talked for a while. He felt very constrained in his mother's house.

Michael McClure:

His mother was a very protective individual. I never met Jack's mother, but I saw an incredibly beautiful photograph of Jack and her together. What an incredible thing! I've seen photographs of dominant mother monkeys with their male offspring, who are called "princes" in that condition. That is the photograph of a dominant female anthropoid with her prince. And their faces are so much alike. That's the kind of photograph you see in very highly specialized primate ethology texts. By that I don't mean anything ironic, I mean it was beautiful—but such a classic situation. A classic, not only human, but a classic anthropoid—a classic primate situation existed there.

Gabrielle became the guardian at Jack's door, the censor of his mail and telephone calls, the manager of his money. He re-established his writing room, which was like a monk's cell. A friend who visited from California catalogued its contents: a table with an electric typewriter, a chair, a roll of teletype paper feeding into the typewriter, a spotlight aimed at the table, a crucifix.

Just as he had done a decade earlier Jack now alternated between Gabrielle's house and his friends in the city. In 1948 he had been deeply involved in his first novel and in making notes for his second, *On the Road*. No similar task lay before him now.

In January, 1959, Robert Frank and Alfred Leslie recruited Jack into the production of a short, black-and-white film that would give cinematic expression to the Beat phenomenon. The script for the action was based on the third act of Jack's abandoned play, *The Beat Generation*, which by now he recognized was unfit for production.

In the finished film Jack explains what the viewer is seeing much as he might have narrated a home movie. The last act of Jack's play had described a real event—the visit of a liberal clergyman to the Cassady household in San Jose. The cleric was wholly unprepared to deal with Neal and his friends. Allen and Gregory played themselves, and the artist Larry Rivers portrayed Neal, "Milo." David Amram, who also acted, composed a charming tune for a poem that Jack, Allen, and Neal had collaborated on in 1949. *Pull My Daisy*, a bit of doggerel with a sexual connotation, became the movie's theme-song and its title.

David Amram:

Alfred Leslie called me over to a loft on Third Avenue. I think it was where Alfred lived. Robert Frank was there, Franz Kline was there, telling Alfred and Allen Ginsberg and some other people that maybe it took time to get recognized for a lot of people. And if you do get recognized, that can go as fast as it comes, and that, basically, recognition is not what it's all about, that there's something else called carrying out work, having that achievement, and having what you do be fine enough to transcend in other people's souls. Everybody was listening, because Franz Kline was really appreciated.

Frank was there, Kline was there—a friend of mine named Dan Cowan, who was a French horn player and used to come to Jack's parties and play the viola. He was like a real kind of Queens, New York, philosopher-genius-sideman. A really wild guy, who would play with different symphonies and shows for a living, but you'd always find him the rest of the time reading *avant-garde* literature, or painting, or reading poetry.

258

All these people being together was really something. And it just happened, because everybody was hanging out. It wasn't a press-person sending out a release saying, "We're now going to have a gathering of underground biggies," because everything was underground.

Nobody wanted to be underground, that's just the way it was. You were underground whether you wanted to be or not. There wasn't any particular prestige in that, you know. And there were thousands of people like that. There were also a lot of people who weren't artists at all, and never claimed to be. They just hung out with everybody. They were more or less in the same bag. They weren't so much aesthetes. Most of the people were out of work. I guess you'd call them dropouts. They didn't finish high school. They were just people who said, "Man, I wanna relax and find out the meaning of life." They were street philosophers, various types of total dropouts. Before, I'd never heard that expression, "drop-out." I don't think they were even dropping out. I think what happened is, they decided to quit trying to fight their way in. That's really what it is. They retired as in-fighters. They said, "Man, we don't even want to struggle to adapt ourselves to this crap." They had no outlet or dreams. There was no sense of community, except for scattered groups like ours. That's why those of us who survived and continued to pursue our dreams are happy today and have a cold eye for nostalgia merchants. The fifties were "el drag-issimo."

If you even sold anything, you were considered to be selling out. There was still a lot of that stuff where all the good artists had to be suffering every second. That's the biggest thing people of my generation have had to overcome, myself included: to realize, first of all, if you don't become a millionaire at what you're doing, that's not a disgrace either, but on the other hand, you should be trying to do your best and to take care of yourself so you can live long enough to be effective. And that the idea of the artist starving to death and being a hero is just like some super-sick idea from the nineteenth century where the artists were a certain class who were the entertainers and flunkies of another class. And that people who perpetuated this idea in the U.S.A. are people who believe in a class system who ain't got no class!

259

Jack talked a lot to me about what he felt about writing and the whole literary scene in New York. It killed him that his books were just being ignored and being tossed off as inconsequential. That whole thing about being the King of the beatniks was such a manufactured label to criticize everyone who didn't want to marry Eisenhower's grandchildren. The beatnik label had nothing to do with him or any of us. The word entered the vocabulary long after we had started to form our lives.

Anyway, we were sitting around the Third Avenue loft and Jack had made this tape called "Pull my daisy." It was this wild story he was telling about spending some time at someone's house—it was actually Neal Cassady. It was pretty interesting. It sounded like Jack telling one of his fantissimo tales. We were listening to it and Robert Frank said, "What do you think of that?" I said, "Well, that's all right." That's not a very articulate answer, but there wasn't much you could say. It was just Jack bombed out, making up this crazy story of his adventures. But he always did that, and it was always a gas.

Robert Frank said, "We're going to make a movie out of it." I said, "No kidding?" He said, "Yeah, and you're going to be Mezz McGillicuddy." Then he handed me a script, which had been typed from Jack's spontaneous ramblings. I still have a copy.

It was really weird because this became the film's scenario. Then nobody saw Jack until the film was almost over. Making *Pull My Daisy* was just like our jazz-poetry readings. Insane. Twelve hours a day with everybody showing off, flipping out, getting stoned, bombed, and improvising. Alfred Leslie started trying to direct while everybody kept cutting up and doing all these dumb things. Nobody got paid. Alfred Leslie's studio lights kept going out when they would turn on the camera lights. So he turned that around by putting slugs in the fuse box, an old Lower East Side trick. It almost burnt out the whole building, but it kept the lights on, since Alfred's cockroach-infested studio was like a cellar without them. Every once in a while, Robert Frank would just start laughing so hard the tripod would shake. When he was taking still pictures just at the time he was talking you'd

hear this *click*! He had timing like Muhammad Ali.
Ba-BOOP! He knew just when to click the camera, 'cause
he could really see. He was a super-perceptive guy, and
he was the soul of *Pull My Daisy*. Alfred Leslie had a
great style, just in terms of getting people excited. Even
though what he was doing might have seemed total
insanity to the average 1959 film-maker, it turned out to
be the most fun of any film I ever worked on. Now it is
considered to be a statement of the times. We were just
having fun. Jack came around once or twice.

When the thirty hours had been edited to twenty
minutes, we went over to Jerry Newman's studio. Jerry
Newman was the guy who recorded Dizzy Gillespie,
Thelonius Monk, up at Minton's on a home recorder in
the late 1940's and called a tune "Kerouac." It used
standard changes, but they didn't want to pay the
author's and publisher's royalties, so Jerry called it
"Kerouac." When we did the narration for *Pull My Daisy*,
we put on earphones and I played the piano, behind
Jack, which I didn't use in the picture. He wanted all that
spontaneous, too. I said, "No, man. For a movie it's
better—everything else is so raggedy—when you do what
you do that's gonna tie it all together, and I'll do something behind what you've done that'll fit in, that won't
step on what you're doing." Jack agreed it would be
better that way. After he did the narration, I cut the
piano music out, replacing it with a lot of silence, so you
just hear him. When there was music, it would really be
saying something. I composed music that I'm still proud
of today. I had played with Jack enough to know when
and where to play, and where to be out of the way and
let the music of his reading say it all.

There was a part of the film where it was supposed
to be Larry Rivers playing the saxophone. He was doing
the acting. We dubbed in Sahib Shahab playing alto
saxophone watching Larry, and playing perfectly on the
first take, Arthur Phipps, who played with Three Bips
and a Bop, and Babs Gonzales played bass on that. There
was also a bassoon. Jane Taylor played that—a woman
bassoon player who really dug Jack's books. Al
Harewood played drums, Midhat Serbagi played viola,
Ronnie Roseman played oboe, he's now solo oboe with
the New York Philharmonic. I played French horn and

piano, and Anita Ellis sang.

The night we did the original narration at Jerry Newman's, we had this big party and ended up staying there about a day and a half or so. Jack was there and we finally got the music and narration done. Then we made up a bunch of songs that Jerry recorded. Someone has the tapes. It doesn't matter. We had the experience. Jack's narration, which was just brilliant, was all made up on the spot. I was there, tinkling away. He did the whole thing on the spot. Alfred and Robert had completely transformed his whole play. The film was great but it had nothing to do with what he originally had in mind. So he looked at it and made up a whole other narration on the spot that was just as hip. That's what he was like.

The Sunday reviewer of the *New York Times* had warned that the road Jack had taken in *On the Road* could only be traveled once, and as Jack's books came out, one by one, the critics enforced their colleague's decision. The *Times* dismissed *Doctor Sax* as "psychopathic," and then unleashed Kenneth Rexroth upon *Mexico City Blues*. Rexroth attempted a set-piece that would provide a new benchmark for excoriation, but bile drowned his wit.

With the inventory of unpublished works now quite low, Sterling Lord provided Jack with magazine work. Kerouac began a monthly column in *Escapade*, an early *Playboy* imitator with a distinct New York sensibility in the articles between its nude spreads. The magazine pieces meant steady money for Jack, Mémère, and their cat, Tyke. The prospect of anyone reading his work as "one vast book" was gone.

Friends, such as Lucien, were saddened by the pieces that he brought into town on the train from Northport.

Lucien Carr:

I think Jack's language tended to get cheaper as it went on, and by "cheap," I mean easily come by. I'm not talking about novels, I'm just talking about language. It became cheaper and cheaper, which is a shame. I mean, to a man who loved each word in the English language more than I love my father... it became, plastic blither-blither.

I'm not thinking of any books, specifically, I'm really thinking more of what Kerouac had to *say* as he went on, the words that came out of his mouth.

Much of what Jack wrote dealt with politics and current events, subjects for which he could not have been more ill-suited. He was unable to take journalism in the direction of art as Norman Mailer, for example, was later to do in his detailed portrayals of the way that large events affected him personally. An essay for *Escapade* on the folly of war was a striking display of Kerouac's grasp of the fine points of history, but its Buddhist moral was phrased in terms which might have suited a Unitarian sermon. He read the Berlin crisis, more or less correctly, as Russia's bid to bargain with the United States as an equal, and he managed to defend Soviet Chairman Khrushchev and Joe McCarthy in the same column indicting the media for distorting the two men's actions.

He was hardly in touch with the world. The harrassment by his youthful admirers continued. At one point a bunch of kids showed up at his door wearing club jackets lettered "DHARMA BUMS" across the back. When Mémère barred their way at the door, they would climb the eaves to reach his room, and they stole his notebooks as souvenirs. Every so often, such as during Mémère's regular visits to Nin and Paul in Florida, Jack would join the teen-agers and drink as he rode around Northport in their cars, a shamefaced ally.

On his visits to the city Jack became an embarrassing and distracting burden to Allen and the others. When he was too drunk to come into town, or when Mémère denied him the money, he waited until she was through watching television and had gone to bed, and then he would telephone them.

Peter Orlovsky:

I had just finished going through a heroin and cough syrup thing, so I would get very annoyed at him for getting drunk all the time, and I'd worry about his

263

drinking. Trying to get him straight, but doing it by getting mad or getting him resentful, rather than getting tender and sweet, or thoughtful.

He used to call me up on the phone a lot. We had two phones, so me and Allen could both hear, and he'd call up and speak on the phone for hours and hours from Long Island. He'd talk about going out with gangs of young kids who came to see him in Long Island. A bunch of them would drive in their cars to a restaurant or cafe. They would run out of their cars naked and stand in the cafe and rush back in their cars and drive away. Maybe to let him know what the latest funny business was, the latest tricks.

And he would talk about politics. Kennedy was coming along, and he'd talk to me about voting. Jack would always talk about disliking the Communists and getting up in a tree with a gun and shooting the Communists if it came to that, if he had to.

Allen spent hours and hours on the phone. Allen tried and tried and tried. Allen's very patient. It's hard to talk to someone when they're drunk a lot. They don't listen.

He'd come into the city once in awhile, and we'd see him, but he didn't want to come in because he thought he'd get too drunk for too long and get sick and pass out. He would just conk out and get sick, his body would break out into a rash, and he had phlebitis in the leg. So then he stayed home a lot and got drunk.

Whenever the telephone bill was larger than the money that Mémêre had set aside for it, she ripped the instrument's cord from the wall, leaving Jack alone entirely.

He was to travel again in the ten years of life that were left to him, but the trip that he planned in the summer of 1960 was his last break from home. He wanted distance and silence with which to consider what had happened to him. He would go west. To California, to Neal.

5 BIG
SUR

Smart went crazy.

—ALLEN GINSBERG

< Jack Kerouac in Tangier, 1957. Photo courtesy of William Burroughs.

The catalyst for Jack's final fall was a place, Big Sur, the wilderness on the California coast midway between San Francisco and Los Angeles. Thought by its residents and many others to be the most beautiful shoreline in the world, its fog-cloaked calm can be interrupted in any season by vast storms that sweep across the Pacific from the Arctic. Cypress-lined bluffs are broken by canyons that shelter fern-lined streams and secret waterfalls. The entire landscape is said to have been ripped away, eons ago, from the matching coast on the Chinese mainland. Except for the occasional homes of the wealthy, which cling to the cliffs high above, and the sight of a hiker or two, its emptiness is as striking as its wild loveliness. For Jack it was an isolation fatal to his motives.

The words had stopped. By July of 1960 Jack had found himself unable to translate what had happened to him since *On the Road* was published into a novel, and his inventory of unpublished novels had dwindled. If he remained true to his aim of "one vast book," he would have to tell the story of a man incapable of dealing with his own success, unable to begin a family of his own, to find peace, to tend his art.

Within a year Jack would be at work on his capstone novel, *Big Sur*, which would mark the chronological end-point of his legend. He would write more books: *Passing Through*, a companion to the novel he began just down from his fire-watch under Hozomeen, and published together with the earlier novel as *Desolation Angels*; the travel novel *Satori in Paris*; the unemotional reconsideration of his boyhood and young man-hood in *Vanity of Duluoz*. But *Big Sur* was his single work dealing with the effects of the fame which had destroyed him, and before he could write it he had to hit rock-bottom, to survive that experience and to go on, as Scott Fitzgerald had lived through *The Crack-Up* before finding the strength to finish *Tender is the Night* or to begin *The Last Tycoon*.

In June of 1960 M-G-M released its film of *The Subterraneans*, the only movie that has been made from one of Kerouac's books. The musical-comedy producer Arthur Freed had undertaken it as an art film, a black-and-white venture that would be true to its source. Anxious to cash in on the Beat craze, the M-G-M front office prescribed CinemaScope and Metrocolor, vetoed the interracial love affair which was the theme of the novel, and cast the lily-white Leslie Caron as Mardou opposite George Peppard (whose stance and profile were remarkably like Jack's) as the Kerouac figure, Leo Percepied. The bickering in the film between the frustrated writer, Leo, and his domineering mother was the only halfway accurate portrayal, though there was little expression of Jack's tender concern for Gabrielle. Interestingly, the scenes between Mrs. Percepied and her son echoed the original draft opening of *On the Road*, which Jack had shown to John Clellon Holmes in 1948 before discarding it.

Producer Freed and his colleagues at M-G-M had cele-brated when they secured rights to *The Subterraneans* for a single flat payment of $15,000, but the movie was devastated by the critics, and barely earned back its cost for the studio. What the film made plain was Hollywood's intention to raid the Kerouac myth at a bargain price, rather than pay attention to the considerable dramatic values of the single story which had been purchased.

M-G-M hired Andre Previn and a stable of excellent musicians (Gerry Mulligan, Carmen McRae, Shelly Manne, Red Mitchell, Art Farmer) to supply a jazz ambience. But screenwriter Robert Thom invented a pregnancy for Mardou and a happy ending: Percepied returns to her to give their child his name. Roddy McDowall portrayed Gregory, Jim Hutton was Allen and, in the most bizarre bit of skewed casting, the diminutive comedian Arte Johnson appeared as Arial Lavalina, the figure based upon the tall and elegant Gore Vidal.

The film followed the book's transposition of events from Greenwich Village to San Francisco's North Beach, and the sets were hardly more garish, the extras little more theatrical than the real North Beach had become. Ferlinghetti had been making his own experiments with jazz and poetry. Busloads of tourists poured onto the sidewalks near City Lights Bookstore each evening to sample the new Bohemia firsthand.

Neal was absent from the scene. Only a few months after Jack had rocketed to fame Cassady had cheated two narcotics agents in a deal intended to set him up for an arrest. The police knew quite well his reputation as Dean Moriarty of *On the Road*. A few months of silence followed the "Beat deal," then Neal was picked up and convicted on charges he denied and sentenced to San Quentin for a term of two to five years.

Neal's fear and hatred of prison was as intense as it had been when Luanne's story of the imaginary policemen had sent him fleeing into the night eleven years earlier. In San Quentin he continued to read Cayce and other mystics, and his old Catholicism came back in full force. He committed novenas and prayed for early release.

Jack and Neal's intense correspondance had faltered. Neal wrote to a journalist from prison, "...I'm not interested in Jack's book or all that phony beat stuff or kicks.... Jack and I, we drifted apart over the years. He became a Buddhist and I became a Cayceite. Yeah, he was impressed with me. Let's see if he was impressed enough to send me a typewriter." Neither understood the other's prison.

Allen sent a letter of appeal to the California Adult Authority, pointing out that Carolyn and the three children had been reduced to living on welfare. He said that Al Hinkle would be able to get Neal a job on the railroad again, and there were letters from James Laughlin of New Directions, Ruth Witt-Diamant of the San Francisco State College Poetry Center, and from Lawrence Ferlinghetti, who offered to publish Neal's autobiographical fragment, *The First Third*. Cassady was portrayed as a major literary figure, the progenitor of all of the recently famous poetry and prose, and in a sense, he was. In the fall of 1959, after his "787th straight nite behind bars," Neal was released.

The First Third was finally published by City Lights in 1971, and remains in print today. In 1958 Jack and Ferlinghetti began to correspond in earnest about the possibility of City Lights bringing out the remainder of Kerouac's rucksack *oeuvre*. Until that time Ferlinghetti's great success had been with his "Pocket Poets" series, which included work by Ginsberg, Corso, and others in small, square-format books that cost one dollar or less.

Lawrence Ferlinghetti:

I really didn't have a chance at publishing Kerouac's novels for quite a long time. Much later I could have published *Visions of Neal*. But we were such a small press that we didn't have the money to put out a great big book like that. I felt that really was out of our range.

But Jack was oriented to getting published in New York. We were just another little two-bit poetry press, printing a thousand copies or fifteen hundred copies of a little book of poetry. I read *Mexico City Blues* in manuscript and *San Francisco Blues*, too. By hindsight, now I can see there was a lot of opportunity to be a really big publisher right there, but we were struggling to have a bookstore.

I didn't used to think very highly of Jack's poetry. I had the manuscript of *Mexico City Blues* and could have published it, but it just didn't turn me on very much. I don't know why. I wasn't really tuned in to his voice

Lawrence Ferlinghetti, 1976. Photo by Lawrence Lee.

enough. Now I can see it was all the same voice. I think he was a better novel writer than a poem writer. I'm putting it that way because it seems to me that the writing he did was all one, whether it was in the topography of poetry or in the topography of prose. It was the same kind of writing. If it were read aloud it sounded the same. It was poetry and vice versa. Right there the line between poetry and prose broke down.

It's the same with Ginsberg. On the manuscript of *The Fall of America*, when I was editing that, Allen wrote and said, "Do any of these poems strike you as poems that are not as good as the others, and some that are weaker than the others?" I wrote back and said, "Allen, once one starts digging your voice, no matter what comes out of your mouth, it's going to be as good as any other part because it's your whole voice that's coming across. If mind is comely, then everything that comes out of mind is going to be comely." When the mind is interesting, then anything that comes out of the mind is interesting. The trouble with so many poets that follow Ginsberg's poetics is that they don't have essentially very interesting minds, so it comes out really boring.

Later I got tuned into Jack's voice more, so that no matter what he said or wrote, it added up and sounded great.

Sensing from their correspondence Jack's pain and discomfort in Northport, Ferlinghetti offered Kerouac the use of his cabin at Bixby Canyon, beneath the spectacular arched bridge near the northern limit of the Big Sur wilderness. It was a gesture of commerce coupled with camaraderie. Jack could travel north to see Neal and his city friends whenever he wanted to, and he and Lawrence would discuss the manuscripts that City Lights was interested in. The main idea, however, was for Jack to dry out and to begin a new novel in isolation.

Jack accepted immediately and Mémêre helped him pack his rucksack for the trip west, a journey he made in a first-class train compartment rather than by thumb.

Lawrence Ferlinghetti:

I was to meet him and take him directly to Big Sur, because he didn't want anybody to know that he was around. He didn't want to get involved and start drinking in San Francisco. But the next thing I knew, he turned up at the bookstore. He just didn't follow through on his original plan of letting me know secretly what time he was arriving. The next thing I knew he was over at Vesuvio's drinking, and it was early in the afternoon. He said, "I want to get out of town right away." So we called up down there. We had this date to meet Henry Miller for dinner. The same day he arrived in San Francisco we were supposed to meet Miller for dinner in Big Sur, and Miller came up to Ephraim Doner's house.

Doner lived in Carmel Highlands and Miller had come up from Partington Ridge for dinner. We started calling up about five in the afternoon to say, "We're leaving now, and we'll be there by seven." And so it got later and Kerouac was still drinking and like six o'clock, we called up, and Jack was still in Vesuvio's. "Oh, we're leaving now. We're leaving now." And it got to be seven, eight, and he was still calling up, and Miller and Doner were waiting for dinner. He never did make it that night.

So I took off and went to Big Sur. I got there in time to get squared away for the night in my cabin, and the next morning we found Kerouac sleeping in the open meadow. He hadn't been able to find the cabin. He had arrived by taxi in Bixby Canyon, which is eighteen miles south of Carmel, carrying his brakeman's lantern.

Then we left him at the cabin. Presumably he was going to stay there several weeks by himself, but he only stayed a few days before he got together with Cassady up in Los Gatos. My cabin, at that time, didn't have any electricity and there was no glass in the windows, just these big wooden shutters, so that if it were a cold day you had to close these shutters. Then it was dark inside and you only had a kerosene lantern. There's a lot of fog in Big Sur, and sometimes the fog lays there in the canyon day after day, and it can be very gloomy. So it really can be a downer to be there in the spring and the fall. It's only in January when it's clear.

Anyway, it was raining quite a bit and Jack's sitting

there in this cabin, so he didn't stay long. I remember he said he was hallucinating, and this is even when he still was in San Francisco, before he went down. Then he came back to town, San Francisco, and he was drinking a lot and he didn't eat, and he was talking about going to a psychiatrist.

Phil Whalen told him at the time, "Jack, you don't need a psychiatrist. You've just got sugar in your blood. You haven't had any solid food in days, and you're drinking nothing but sweet wine." He used to drink Tokay, like skid row. I used to bawl him out for it. "What kind of Frenchman are you, drinking this sweet wine?" And Phil Whalen told him, "You don't need a shrink, all you need is to get some food in your stomach and you'll stop hallucinating."

In *Big Sur,* Jack Duluoz's first stay at the cabin lasts for three weeks. If the novel is an accurate record of the time, Jack alternated between long spells of sitting in the dark little room with the windows shuttered against the damp, and walks along the creek that led to the sea through a canyon so narrow and wooded that sunlight would not have spilled through on a fair day. He imagined the trees talking to him, the rocks discussing their ancestry. Finally, he heard the sea say, "GO TO YOUR DESIRE DON'T HANG AROUND HERE," and he obeyed.

After reuniting briefly with Neal he returned to San Francisco and checked into an old hotel a cut or so above a flophouse. There he found a more manageable isolation. He could take the Municipal Railroad over Nob Hill to North Beach or visit with literary friends who were living in the very earliest communes, such as East-West House, the old mansion in the Western Addition where Phil Whalen and Lew Welch made their home.

But with wine at hand Jack's social excursions often turned into binges that were painful for his friends to watch. Within a few days it occurred to him to make the wilderness hospitable by recruiting friends to return with him to the cabin in Bixby Canyon. One of those who joined him was a stranger, Victor Wong, then in his late twenties, the eldest son of an eldest son of an eldest son in a Chinatown family with rich connections to

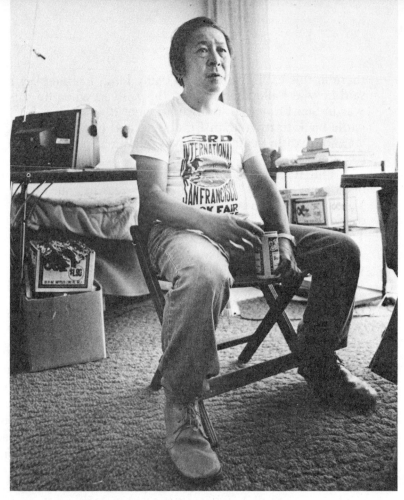

Victor Wong, 1976. Photo by Sarah Satterlee.

Sun-Yat-Sen and Chiang-Kai-Shek. When Ferlinghetti introduced him to Jack, Wong lived in two worlds only an alley
apart, Chinatown and North Beach.

Victor Wong:

When the Beat movement came along, I was already into
art, trying to get my intuitive going. One day Ferlinghetti
says, "Want to meet a friend of mine, this guy Kerouac?"
    I'd never read any of these books, any of the poems
Ferlinghetti had. If I had to, I would listen at a reading,
hear the people, observe the inflection in their voices. But
I hadn't read them, wouldn't want to.

I went with Lawrence to Japantown and into this place, up the second floor rear. There, around a kitchen table, sitting around talking and drinking Tokay, were Kerouac, Welch, and Whalen. Kerouac didn't like drugs, you know. Even beer. He liked muscatel, Tokay—wine like that.

So somebody said, "Let's go," and I went with them down to Big Sur. Right away. I grabbed just my shirt and underpants and my art stuff. I said, "How are we going to sleep?" Ferlinghetti says, "Never mind. I've got a lot of blankets and a fireplace."

We stopped along the way at Neal Cassady's place. He put a real spark into things, never stopped talking. By that evening, we were down at Big Sur. Neal went along. Phil was already there. A young kid named Paul Smith— young blond kid, a musician. Never saw him again. And Michael McClure, who'd just begun to write.

I was flabbergasted by the whole thing. I felt like a cameraman, really. These people weren't too real to me, but Kerouac was real, for some reason.

Everybody around him would be talking, and he'd just sit there. I asked him once if he was all right and he said, "I just have nothing to say."

He was going through a terrible time. He'd gotten famous. That *Subterraneans* movie had come out. He was in *Time* magazine. It made him very frightened, like, "Now that I'm a big person, how am I going to write those things that I wrote when I was not a public person? You expect me to write things that are just as good?" So it froze him.

When he came back out to San Francisco, I think he was cranking up to go out into the creative world again. We talked about being dislocated. I said, "You're having so much trouble creating again, why not go back to childhood and find an answer to the roadblocks? Go to Lowell?" He said that it was a very depressing town, said he didn't think that he could go back.

He always had an enormous knapsack, like a five-hundred-pound potato sack. He never showed anybody what was in there, but I noticed he had a big stack of cards with a rubber band. He had two of them. One was the American League and the other was the National League. He loved baseball, but he invented all the games.

He had a chart going back year after year, season after season, and all the fictitious people. I said, "How do you play the thing?" He said, "It goes on in my mind. You know, who comes up to bat, what he hit, the pitcher and all that."

That night we had the fireplace going, and we started drinking.

Michael McClure:

Everybody was sitting around, and we were all doing this, "Have you read this?" "Have you read that?" It was this big game at the time. "Have you read *Nausea*?" "No, but have you read ... ?"

Jack said, "This is just intellectual masturbation, this 'Have you read this?' 'Have you read that?' You must do something constructive. You must not ask questions and just sort of whip yourself up intellectually this way. You must give information. It doesn't matter whether the person has read what you're asking him or not, what matters is your perception of it that you can give to the other individual. For instance, you could say, 'I was recently conversing with William Burroughs and he told me that he had been reading a novel about the whale hunting industry, written in the late nineteenth century by a man named Herman Melville, and it concerned the quest of an elderly, one-legged whaling-ship captain, who was obsessed with the idea that a white whale named Moby Dick had become evil incarnate and his desire then became to crash through the mask of reality and find the great forces behind it, and he saw the whale as being one of the masks of reality.' How much better it would be if you said that rather than, 'Have you read *Moby Dick*?'"

Victor Wong:

As people got to drinking Jack took a book from his knapsack and started reading aloud. I said, "What the hell are you reading?" He said, "I'm reading *Dr. Jekyll and Mr. Hyde*."

But after a while I said, "You're not reading from that book." He wasn't. He was making up the whole

Goddamned thing as he was going on. It was incredible.

So then I started to join him, and it's getting darker and darker and people were falling asleep, and here there were just the two of us. For some reason there was just a vibration in the room. We went on and on. He'd make up a sentence, I'd make up a sentence. It just went on and on and on until I faded out and fell asleep. Maybe in my dream I heard him keep on going. And then later on, I read it all in his novel *Big Sur*. I don't know how he remembered all that.

The thing that was so interesting was, I'd never done anything like this before. Maybe that was his greatness, that he could suck the creativity out of people. He was doing it all the time.

Michael McClure:

Jack didn't like to listen to young Paul Smith, he liked to listen to Neal. It's funny, but here was another incessant talker around Jack, and Jack didn't like what the kid was saying. He liked Neal.

Neal had gotten busted, and Jack apparently felt some responsibility for Neal being busted, because he talked about Neal doing some things in an article he'd written for *Escapade*. He was just seeing Neal come out of jail, and he felt some responsibility for him being there. I hadn't seen Neal for a couple of years.

I thought Jack was sucking his arms up into his sleeves when he was around Neal. It was sort of like he became the little brother, like a "Peanuts" character. He really admired Neal. That was very curious. By that time, Jack had lost some of his personal grace through booze, too. I'm not talking about his writing ability, I just mean how one moves and how one stands and how one feels about his relationship to the world. Jack had already become physically less attractive and less graceful. He was starting to puff out.

Victor Wong:

Sometimes Jack was terribly daring. One day we were driving along the hills in Big Sur and I was sitting in the middle, he was sitting to my right, and Lew Welch was driving. Phil was in the back. The two of them, Jack and Lew, started arguing with one another. "Ahh, you son-of-a-bitch..." They were really going at it, coming around these mountain roads. They weren't drunk, they were just having this verbal argument. It was like children playing with words, but then they got really excited and hollering at each other.

Lew said, "God damn it, let's settle this right now," and he just came around the corner and pulled the brakes and they got out of the car. Luckily, in those days there weren't too many cars. They knelt and faced each other across the white line, and they started to pray with one another. They had their hands in the prayerful thing, and they settled it, got back into the car, and drove off. But shoot, if a car had come by at that time, it would just have totaled all of us. I was saying, "Jesus, they can't do that!" Phil in the back saying, "Leave 'em alone. They're all right." I said, "Oh shit, no, no, no, no." That scared the hell out of me. But he did it, and everything always came out all right.

One day we went to this bar-restaurant place down at Big Sur, and we sat around in the sun drinking. That was one of the times I wondered about Jack, because he was very quiet. McClure came over and asked him about some poem, and Jack was kind of pissed off, as if to say, "I can't even handle myself. How can I tell you what the hell you're supposed to write?" But the thing that was important was, that night we all started drinking.

In the middle of the night they all said, "Let's march down to the beach." We had to go through jungle, creeks, and all that, but for some damned reason, we were all hyped up by it. We all marched down single-file to the beach. We were all men there, all grown men, just going crazy. Grown men don't act that way. It was really shameful. They were all into their childhood, but into a very sweet part of it, not crazy.

Somehow, I don't know how—I don't think there was even a moon at the time—we stumbled all the way down to the beach on each other's shoulders, hanging on to each other all the way down. Of course, down by the surf it's much lighter. They recited poetry to each other on top of rocks.

278

Paul Smith had a cape on, and he recited Hamlet's monologue, the whole thing.

After we came back from Big Sur, Jack disappeared. We couldn't find him. Didn't see him for about a week. Then I said to Lawrence, "Where the hell is he?" And Lawrence said, "I think he's on a binge again."

For a few days of happiness, Kerouac's strategy had worked. He had company with him when the wind swept off the ocean and rattled the trees, but one by one, as the city pulled them back, the crowd dwindled, and Jack had followed rather than stay on alone.

Within a few days of returning to San Francisco, Jack was into his old pattern of recruiting acquaintances to join him for a drink. One drink led to many more, and Jack might announce to a barful of strangers that he was a famous novelist. "I'm Jack Kerouac!" he would shout.

Luanne Henderson:

That was the last time that I saw him, down on Grant Avenue. It kind of surprised me, but he had gotten very argumentative. As the evening wore on he was drinking, which hadn't been like Jack at all. He never had been a drinker to begin with, and he never had been argumentative. Now he was just being an ass, just being ornery.

On one occasion, Phil Whalen looked at Jack's saloon pallor and coaxed him into a walk to Washington Square Park in North Beach, where the two could sit in the sun together and talk. Jack brought along a gallon jug of Tokay wine and drank himself into unconsciousness. Whalen could do nothing to stop him.

Kerouac called one day on Ferlinghetti, who had a letter from Gabrielle saying that Jack's cat, Tyke, had died. Ferlinghetti broke the news to Jack as gently as possible, but he knew nothing of Jack's deep feeling for his pets or the connection between those emotions and the death of Gerard thirty years earlier. He was shocked by Kerouac's reaction: Jack disappeared into the Howard Street bars.

Victor Wong:

They found him in a flophouse and Lawrence took him up to his place. After that he came to me and said, "You know, I'm really in a bad place, and I need to get some wise person. Can I talk to your father?"

And I'm saying to myself, "Shit, here's this guy, he's drunk all the time and he's got these terrible clothes on, and he's unshaven. What will my father say?" I lived in a world that was so far away from him, that was so distinct, even though it's around the corner from the whole scene.

So I talked to Lawrence and we figured it out. I remembered that I had a maroon cashmere sweater which had little holes in it, but you couldn't see them too well. Lawrence shaved Jack, or he somehow shaved himself. Then we put this shirt on him and sweater.

My father was in this store on Jackson Street, a grocery store. But it was kind of dirty. Nobody ever went in there to buy stuff because it wasn't really a grocery store, it was my father's political office, like one of those ward offices in Chicago. In the back there's a fifteen-watt lamp up there with a shade so that only the person who sat in front of it had the light. But there was this couch there because people would come in to talk.

So we got Jack shaved, sprayed, and gargled, and he walks in there, but his face is still red. Obviously he's been drinking. So he sits there on this couch where all the politicians sit. My father says to me, in Chinese, "What is this?" I say, "This is a very noted poet. He's a very literary man. He's just as literate as you are in Chinese." He says, "Why do you bring him here?" This is all in Chinese.

Meanwhile, Kerouac is sitting there, and he doesn't know what the hell to do about it.

So I say, "Come on, talk to him. He's in trouble and he needs something from the Chinese that's wise."

My father turned around, turned his back to Jack and went back to writing his calligraphy. Went on for about ten minutes. Ten minutes in silence is a long time. I said, "Well, I'd better play it cool. If I say something it will prolong the damned thing." It would get too embarrassing and we would have to leave.

So I'm looking at Kerouac and he doesn't look at me. He's just looking at my father's back.

Finally my father turns around and says to Jack in his broken English, "What do you want?"

Kerouac says, "I'm not doing so well. I'm having troubles."

My father says, "What do you do?"

He says, "I write poetry."

So they banter back and forth, but finally my father said to him, "Obviously you like to drink."

He said, "Yes, of course."

And my father said, "You know, you should be like the Japanese monks, the Zen monks. You should go up in the mountains, drink all you want and write poetry."

Between Natalie Jackson's death-leap in 1956 and his imprisonment, Neal's city girlfriend was Jackie Gibson, an habituée of the North Beach scene from the earliest fifties. She was a commercial artist with a young son, and she attended Vedanta Society meetings. She also expressed a sincere interest in Buddhist texts and beliefs.

Since Neal's release from San Quentin, Jackie had been pressing Cassady to leave Carolyn in favor of her, and Jack's visit to the West Coast that summer inspired Neal to try a plan he had used before. Even before Kerouac arrived Neal had begun to read his letters to Jackie, telling her how much she had in common with Kerouac.

Jackie and Jack had been just missing each other for years. Kerouac had visited her apartment one day when she was out. She had arrived at more than one party in the mid-1950's to be told that Kerouac had left moments earlier.

When in 1960 Neal introduced the two and withdrew, they found enough in common to begin a friendship, which within a few weeks seemed to both of them to have become a romance. Her apartment became one of Jack's daytime refuges, and when she returned from the studio each day it seemed natural for Jack to stay on. They talked of marriage, and if Jack's notion of an elopement to Mexico was simply a fantasy, it was a

Lenore Kandel, 1976. Photo by Sarah Satterlee.

reality for Jackie. The stumbling-block was her son, Eric, who, while only four years old, applied strict standards to his mother's friendships. He considered Jack unfit as a prospective father, and he said so.

Jackie told her boss that she was going to marry Jack Kerouac, and the confidence found its way into both of San Francisco's highly competitive daily gossip columns, Herb Caen's and Jack Rosenbaum's.

Whenever they spoke of marriage Jack talked of staying in California and of sending Eric east to live with Mémère, a notion which the child understood clearly and resisted loudly.

To sort things out Jack planned a third trip to Ferlinghetti's cabin at Big Sur. Jackie and young Eric would come with him. Their companions would be the poet Lew Welch, a hard drinker himself who had once made his living as an advertising writer, and Welch's girlfriend Lenore Kandel, who would shortly outrage Berkeley bluestockings with the forthright eroticism of the poems in *The Love Book*.

Lenore Kandel:

I've thought of myself as a writer for as long as I can remember, and I remember once getting a strange flash at a party. I looked around. Everyone was a writer. I thought, "Everybody in this room is going to go from this room and write their version of this." It felt so surreal. Everything that happened was being looked back on *as* it happened.

The summer of '60, that's when I came to San Francisco and met Lew. I've always been an omnivorous reader, and I'd read Jack's books, the first one, the one that was written by "John" Kerouac. Well, I'd been in New York, and I rode out with a friend to L.A. I'd been meaning to come to San Francisco, and I decided to come here for a weekend and I stayed. I met Lew and all the people in that whole trip, and when Jack came into town, we all went to Big Sur.

He was in a very bad place, and he went there to clear his head. But it's a really elemental place, Big Sur, and it really burns. I guess it must be a little like an acid trip, a very heavy concentration of reality.

He'd been staying in that weird hotel that was his hideaway, down around Mission-and-something. We got him there, brought him back there. He didn't want anybody else to know about it, but I'm sure that other people did.

He also suggested it as a great place that you could go and hide and *make it*. I mean, the whole place he came from, where you go to a hotel! He wrote and did so many far-out things, but he still had this conservative —sneaky, almost—place inside him. Not sneaky, but where you've got to do these things outside of society rather than within it. It must have put a lot of conflict within him.

Going down to Big Sur was really a nice trip. Lew was a great driver, a great talker, the best talker I've ever known. Even if the facts were off, the story was great. He was talking, Jack was talking, and we were all singing.

But the lady he was involved with was in total chaos. I mean, he brought his own chaos, and it was city chaos, and he brought it to a place of high, natural elemental forces that just swept him in.

She stayed in the back, kind of slept. I think she would've dug being more in on it, but through some necessity of Jack's, he preferred to believe that she really wanted to be back there. The other three of us were running this talk-sing-drink-play on the way.

She had her little boy with her. I can't remember her name, but she had a beautiful face. I remember her face.

Jackie Gibson:

Jack and I were planning on getting married. We were all packed, had the tickets. These people were going with us, going to Mexico.

You see, you'd have to understand Jack and Neal's relationship. Remember the old M-G-M films? Jack and Neal were just acting out what they considered to be a reasonable relationship, based on their movie experiences. The buddies. The good guys. The crafty Americans who figure everything out.

My relationship with Neal was getting kind of shaky. In fact, it was the beginning of the end, about then. Neal just didn't know what else to do, so he called Jack in, to sort of hand me over. Mainly because I wanted to get married. Since he couldn't, I might as well marry Jack.

Jack went for it. I went for it, too, up to a point. It was a good meeting. The scene was really cool then. A lot of communication between people—people who identified with one another. It was a very communal time, a very accepting time.

We actually felt we were going to solve all the problems in the world, that this was some golden age or something. When it began to dawn on everyone that this wasn't happening, that everyone had their problems and wouldn't get past them, it was a disappointment, and everyone handled it differently.

We'd decided that we weren't going to get married

by the time that we went to Big Sur. Jack was drinking a lot of wine, a real binge before we went down. On the way down we stopped at Neal's house. I think Jack wanted Carolyn and me in the same room.

Carolyn Cassady:

Lew and Lenore Kandel and Jack and Jackie stopped by. Jackie's child was asleep in the car, and they left Jackie in the car and came in. I finally realized and said, "Don't be ridiculous. Bring them in." Jack was drunk, of course, but he was being very hedgy.

So then Lew said, "Ho boy, I'll go get the saucer of cream. Oh-ho-ho." And I said, "What's the matter with you guys? What do you think we're going to do, tear each other's hair out? How ridiculous." So she came in.

I'm surprised that Lew would think that instantly a rival woman would make you jealous. I mean, these are such square, conventional ideas, and here are all these people who are so far-out. They assumed that obviously, just like the movies, we were going to tear each other up.

I sat there and she sat there, and we jabbered away about kids and what-the-hell. And then Neal started stomping up and down, and in *Big Sur*, you'll read an

Jackie Gibson Mercer, 1976. Photo by Sarah Satterlee.

explanation for Neal's behavior which wasn't it at all. Jack is sitting here and in front of her he's asking me to go with him, right straight-out make. And I was disgusted with him. I mean, here's his girl, and Jack certainly had been treating me less than interested for a long time, and it was very crude. And Neal's stamping up and down, and Jack explains it in *Big Sur* that Neal's mad at him for something.

What it was, was Neal was doing his jealousy trip for Jackie. It had nothing to do with Jack making me, it was Jackie. He was trying to show Jackie. He was doing this because Neal's philosophy was: once his, always his.

Jack didn't get it. Jack didn't get it at all, that this was Neal's typical trip for getting the girl back that he's given away. He went through it a hundred times with Luanne, half of that as soon as Luanne got interested in somebody else after he'd thrown her out and said, "Don't bother me anymore." Then he'd go through this big, jealous trip to get you back again. And he did that to me with Jack.

So I knew what he was doing. And I don't know whether anybody else heard what Jack was doing with me anyhow, because he thought he was being awfully subtle, but whether they did or not, I don't know.

That's how they were. Maybe you can't take the genius without the other. I don't know. At least they taught me how to be detached. Now everybody can do their own thing, and it's up to me whether to take it or leave it. I learned that. You can be hurt if you're going to, and you can not be. It's their problem, not yours, really. They were instrumental in that lesson.

I never saw Jack again.

Jackie Gibson:

It went off okay. Neal was a little upset about it, but I wasn't too upset. I don't think Carolyn was too upset. I remember we almost started to get into an argument about something, Carolyn and me, and Jack thought that was terrific. And he obviously enjoyed that too much, so we cooled that. It upset Neal, I guess, because he didn't know what was going to happen.

When we got to Big Sur, it was pretty much okay. Then he started drinking quite a bit—but he wasn't really drinking any more down there than he had been in the city.

In *his* mind we hadn't really made a firm decision before we left the city that we weren't going to get married, and so we were just going to go down to Big Sur and relax for awhile and then come back to the city. He still felt pressure about making a decision about getting married, about being a father, about being a husband.

And when he made his decision, then he didn't want to be down there. The last night that we were there he didn't sleep all night, and the next day he really wanted to get back. Before that it was cool. We went to the ocean, we went fishing, we cooked the fish.

Lenore Kandel:

The night we got there, Jack just wanted out. He crawled in his sleeping bag. She immediately crawled in with him. I was watching the two of them in this one sleeping bag, and all Jack wanted to do was, like, go to sleep. He was

Carolyn Cassady, summer 1958. Photo courtesy of Carolyn Cassady.

tired. She just got in there and left her little boy. They were past the place of dealing with that, so Lew and I put the boy to bed.

That first night was really odd to me. The next day Lew wanted to go fishing and we took him out to the beach. It was strange, and Jack was sometimes very there. In the middle of his own chaos he really felt toward other people and did the best he could.

A lot of it was really within Jack, a lot of what happened. It wasn't something he said anything about, but we became aware of it.

He was into drinking and not eating. Lew, who was frequently into drinking and not eating, used to have regular breakdowns of the liver and would have to crawl in bed and eat milk-toast. He was very sensitive to where Jack was.

Lew tried to take care of him, like where he caught this great fish and was cooking it with a great rap and taking care with each step of it, this incredible, conversational fish thing. *Wanting* Jack to eat it. By then Jack was thinking, "This whole package is too elaborate."

He was beginning to wonder, "Is there something behind this?" The whole reality that he was dealing with grew suspect. He worked intuitively a whole lot, and then he could feel his intuition getting weird.

He didn't want to have this suspicious feeling. It was driving him. He heard the sounds of the ocean, and there were messages and frights. He loved Lew—there was a lot of love between them—and yet, he found himself suspicious of everybody's motivation.

I guess he found himself suspicious of me. Like he seemed to have an earth feeling, like I was a warm, caring thing, and then he started to wonder: was *that* for a purpose? Was that true as he had accepted it? Or was there something under it? Or was he going crazy, thinking that there was something under it?

You see, with the same care he considered things he started dissecting these levels, and if you've ever done that in any stage of consciousness or physicality, if you sit there and start dissecting levels, you'll drive yourself batty.

He had a warm care toward people, whoever it was that happened to be there. That was at least as true of him as the paranoia. But as an affliction becomes stronger it is a part of you. It's a very hard thing sifting out what's the true part. They were both him.

There's a strange line there, being any kind of a maker or channel. You've got to be really sensitive. You can't build a barrier around yourself. You have to leave yourself open to what comes in and what goes out, and sometimes the input can be very shattering.

When he was in Big Sur, I think that sensitivity, that listening place he had with all the people he met, also let in all these heavy vibes of the ocean, the earth. It's a very stark place there, and it just knocked him out.

And then the lady that was with him was in a pretty chaotic place. And there was this little boy of hers. Neither one of them could really handle it.

Jackie Gibson:

I don't know whether he felt that I was trying to drive him insane, or was driving him insane. *Big Sur* came out like there was intent to mess up his head, and that wasn't happening. As he said in the book, he thought Eric was a little warlock.

Four-year-old kids can be very perceptive, if they've been around adults. Jack didn't relate to children, period. The first thing that he wanted to do was to ship Eric back to his mother. That was one of the conditions, one of the things that we couldn't get around. When Eric didn't go for that Jack said he could go to a boarding school, and Eric didn't go for that, either.

Jack was very up front with him, which was a big mistake. If you're going to say things like that, you might as well say it behind their back, because Eric couldn't stand him. Eric did a lot of pushing, but he was just furious with Jack and didn't want to have anything to do with him. He felt like he was coming in and taking over.

Jack idealized his mother. She was very Catholic, and I think that that bothered him. I think he liked being there. He felt roots there. That was home. That was really the only home he ever had. I don't think he ever really established one of his own. I don't think that he felt he had established good relationships. He felt that his marriages had been big failures, and he wasn't sure his daughter was his daughter, and all that, which was just his head trip more than anything else. He needed his mother for ballast.

When he made the decision, I guess he didn't want to be down there. We couldn't go away and have a peaceful two days at Big Sur.

Jack's sleepless last night at the cabin with Jackie, her son, Welch, and Kandel is the climax of the novel *Big Sur*. It would be a full year before he sat down in Nin's kitchen in Orlando to write the book on a roll of teletype paper in the space of ten evenings, but for all his growing madness at the time of the experience itself, his recollection of that dreadful night is set out with the precision of total recall.

A torrent of voices (they fade into the sounds of the nearby creek when he tries to make out the words) advise Duluoz that Romana [Kandel] is a member of a Communist secret-murder society, that neighbors have poisoned the stream by Monsanto's [Ferlinghetti's] cabin with kerosene, that Dave Wain [Lew Welch] and Romana, who have purposely claimed his favorite sleeping spot in the soft sandbank, are lying awake, waiting for him to die.

"Can it be it was all arranged by Dave Wain via Cody that I would meet Billie [Jackie] and be driven mad and now they've got me alone in the woods and are going to give me final poisons tonight that will utterly remove all my control so that in the morning I'll have to go to a hospital forever and never write another line?—Dave Wain is jealous because I wrote 10 novels?—Billie has been assigned by Cody to get me to marry her so he'll get all my money?"

Duluoz and Billie move their makeshift bed several times, but he simply cannot sleep. Whenever he closes his eyes, the faces of hell appear.

"—Ma was right, it was all bound to drive me mad, now it's done—What'll I say to her?—She'll be terrified and go mad herself—*Oh ti Tykey, aide mué*—me who's just eaten fish have no right to ask for brother Tyke again—"

Suddenly the voices fall silent, and Duluoz has a vision of the cross. Again and again through the night, whenever the voices reach an unbearable roar, the cross appears. Duluoz imagines himself the prize in a battle between angels and devils. The voices confide that little 'Elliott' [Eric] is a warlock, but when Duluoz goes into the cabin to confront his torturer he finds only a child who has kicked off the covers. Tenderly, Jack pulls the blanket over the child's sleeping figure. Three times Duluoz drifts near sleep, and each time the child, asleep himself, thumps his foot, awakening Jack.

"Dawn is most horrible of all," wrote Kerouac, as Duluoz's friends go about the business of cleaning up Monsanto's cabin. Billie digs a pit for the garbage—"exactly the size fit for putting a little dead Elliott in it." Duluoz shouts at Billie, "[W]hy did you make it look like a grave? ... With the same quiet steady smile Billie says, 'Oh you're so fucking neurotic.'"

Duluoz sits down in a canvas chair on the porch, closes his eyes and, for only a minute or two, falls into a deep sleep. When he awakens, Billie and Romana are standing frozen nearby, startled to have found him at peace. "Blessed relief has come to me from just that minute."

Jackie Gibson:

The trip back was pretty good. He related to Lew easily. I guess you could say his spirits picked up. They talked a lot.

I was pretty estranged by then. By that time he had really put Eric down. He insisted on going into bars. None of us really drank much, and all the way back he'd insist on going into bars, sitting at bars, and I wouldn't go. I'm not going to take a child into all those highway bars. So I read most of the way back.

When the party reached the turn-off near San Jose that led to San Francisco, Jack insisted that Lew drive a few miles further, to the tract house where Helen and Al Hinkle now lived.

Helen Hinkle:

The last time I saw him was that time he arrived with a

291

sort of entourage. He fell on the floor in the kitchen and looked up and said, "Where is this place?" And then he said, "Got to piss," so I took him outside and held him up while he pissed.

Al Hinkle:

That's when he read the poem "Big Sur."

Helen Hinkle:

Oh, God. What poetry. It was beautiful to hear it spoken.

Al Hinkle:

Even drunk, it was.

Helen Hinkle:

Maybe it was even more so. It was absolutely lovely. The sounds of the sea.

6 A GLOOMY BOOKMOVIE

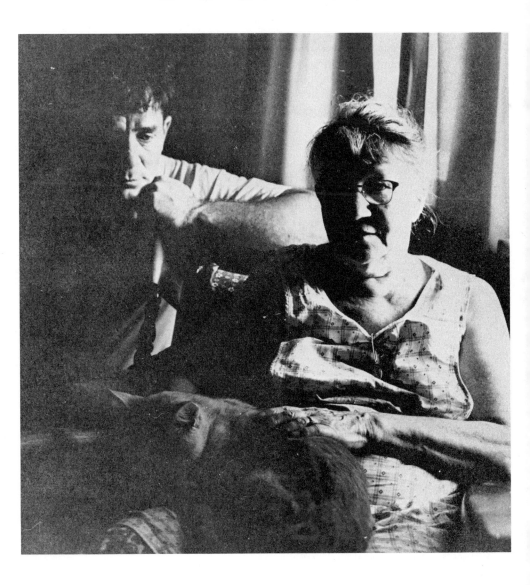

Gary said, "You old son of a bitch, you're going to end up asking for the Catholic rites on your deathbed." I said, "How did you know, my dear? Didn't you know I was a lay Jesuit?" He got mad at me.

—KEROUAC to ANN CHARTERS

◄ Jack and Mémère in Hyannis, Mass., August 1966. Photo courtesy of Ann Charters.

After the breakdown at Big Sur, Jack flew back to New York. Home again in Northport he tried to regain his health, working out like an athlete preparing for a major event. It was a year before he secured the strength to write *Big Sur*.

Gabrielle had returned to Nin in Florida, which she considered her home. Jack took a brief trip to Mexico City, worked on the new second section of *Desolation Angels*, carrying on beyond his sketches of 1956, and drank.

When *Big Sur* was published by Farrar, Straus, and Cudahy in September, 1962 it received excellent reviews, perhaps because it portrayed the "King of the Beats" brought low, perhaps because of its frightening honesty. The book, unlike those which had been published before, portrayed Duluoz as a man who could feel as well as observe.

Jack never had been really comfortable with Nin and her husband, and that October, when his thoughts turned to Lowell, he decided that the time had come to live in New England again.

John Clellon Holmes:

After *Big Sur*, Mémère wrote us a letter. She had never met my wife, Shirley, but she wrote us a letter. Jack was in trouble, they were in Florida, Jack was drinking too much. Mémère actually penned us a letter saying, "Please find Jack a place to live in Connecticut." We wrote back and said, "Christ, well, of course, if that's what he wants." And Jack arrived about three days later on the train.

Jack arrived completely sober on a late Sunday evening. He came here to find a house, to move Mémère into the house. He came alone, he had the money, and he was intent on finding the house.

I said, "Great, Jack. I'll drive you around." We researched it as far as we could.

I hadn't seen him for a year or two—we'd talked on the phone—so he got here and he started tipping, and I started tipping, and we got to feeling happy and reminiscing.

One week later—*one week* later—the project had gone out of his head. We sat all day, and there was no one better to talk to than Jack Kerouac, drunk or sober. He drank a quart of brandy every single day, and it was all Shirley could do to get food into him so he'd keep alive.

Then Saturday came and I said, "Look, Jack, God damn it, let's go look for a house for you. Your mother has written me personally saying 'Save my boy.' Her letter says, 'Save Jack. Please save him. He's going to pieces.'" So that day I said, "Look, Jack. Let's drink beer today and forget all this."

So he did. He shaved for the first time, he also bathed, and he looked handsome, as he always was, even when he was in bad shape.

So we went up to Deep River, we drove around looking at houses, and I could see him sweating in the back of the car, drunk sweats, manfully trying to handle it.

Nothing was right. We couldn't find anything. We tried too late and it was one of those projects that had a doomed feeling to it anyway. It wasn't going to work out.

So I took him to a bar up in Essex and we had beers, and he became very bellicose and started arguing with the bartender. He had nothing but beer and he started to become paranoiac and argumentative, and the project—the whole idea of getting out of the Florida situation that was clearly bugging them both—had vanished from his head.

We came back here and sat around while Shirley made some dinner, and then he started to drink hard liquor. Then he looked at me—one of the big looks—and said, "I've got to get out of here." I said, "What do you want to do?" He said, "Drive me to Lowell." I said, "Jack, I ain't gonna drive you to Lowell. I'll do anything for you, but I can't drive to Lowell. I'm not that good a driver, I hate the whole idea, it's a hundred miles up there..."

He drew back and I thought, "Oh, here it's gonna come: 'You're not a swinger, you don't love me,' that sort of thing." But I was so tired after a week of this that I wasn't going to give in because, simply, it would screw my life up.

And then he smiled the way he often did and said, "Maybe I can get a taxi." I said, "Jack, a taxi for eighty miles? You're out of your ding-a-ling, man." Shirley came in at that point and could see—Shirley's terribly perceptive and Shirley knew Jack very, very well and loved him—and said, "Are you serious?" And Jack was serious.

There were times when he had to move. He had to get out of someplace, he couldn't stand it. So Shirley went in there and phoned up somebody in New London and said, "We got a guy here who wants to go to Lowell, Massachusetts. Could you...?" Jack had plenty of money at that time, so we got him a taxi ride. The taxi came down here from New London and we fixed Jack up. I made him the biggest drink in the world. I gave him a quart jar, preserve jar, and I made him a brandy and soda that would take him all the way.

The taxi driver came in, took one look at Jack and blanched, because Jack was drunk by this point—that is, he'd stopped beer and now was on hard stuff. I took the taxi driver out in the hall and said, "Don't worry about this guy. He's okay. He's gonna drink all the way up, but he ain't gonna give you any trouble. He's gonna talk your ear off, but he's calm as a bunny."

So we put Jack in that taxi with his quart brandy and soda, and he talked the guy's ear off. I said, "Deliver this man to Lowell, get him there and don't worry about him." He was going back to Lowell to see G.J., who perhaps wasn't even there then. I don't know.

He homed in in his confusion to where he thought it would feel good.

G.J. Apostolos:

He'd come back to Lowell in the middle of winter in his sneakers and stay in a flophouse over the depot. He'd call up at four in the morning and say, "I'm here." It would be morning to night, drinking, drinking, drinking.

Jack was a beautiful kid. We really loved Jack. I don't know what happened to him. I can't connect the two people. I had to avoid him later. I couldn't take a week off. If I had to do it again, I would have gotten stiff with him more often when he was here. I couldn't keep up with him. But if I had it to do over again, I would spend more time with him.

John Clellon Holmes:

Jack wrote me a week later. He'd spend maybe thirty-six hours up there, and then he'd gotten someone to take him to Logan Airport to take a flight back down to Florida. He had no place to light.

Back in Florida, Jack spent considerable time in bars, depressed with his situation. Frustrated and confused, Jack and Mémêre moved back to Northport. There Jack took up with an earlier acquaintance, the painter Stanley Twardowicz, whom he'd met originally in the Cedar Tavern, a painters' hangout, in New York City in 1959. Twardowicz, whom Kerouac called "Stasiu," hung out with Jack in Gunther's, the fishermen's bar in Northport, and provided the manly yet intellectual companionship Jack was so deprived of in Florida.

"If I had my life to live over again," Jack told Stanley, "I'd be a painter." Several of Jack's paintings—one of the Pieta—still hang on the walls of Twardowicz's studio.

Twardowicz remembers Jack as still being severely restricted in his activities by Mémêre, though he did not object overly. Once Stanley helped him cash a five-dollar check Mémêre had written Jack, his allowance for the week. Twardowicz's studio became a sanctuary for Jack—kids still came calling at his house to see the beatnik author of *On the Road*—and he persuaded Jack to donate a duplicate copy of *The Town and the City* manuscript to the Northport Library, as well as participate in an interview for the library archives.

Still, Jack was an unhappy man. Though he allowed Stanley to act as guide and protector, Twardowicz could do nothing to stanch Kerouac's worsening alcoholism. One particularly drunken evening, Jack lay down on the streetcar tracks and refused to get up, determined to remain until he was run over. It was only after Stanley, searching desperately for some ploy to get Jack back on his feet, remarked, "Well, there's Jack Kerouac, back on the road," that Jack saw the humor of the situation and removed himself from danger.

Before a trip to Europe a couple of years later to research his family background—what became the novel *Satori in Paris*—Jack attempted to enlist Twardowicz as companion on the journey, even arranging for Grove Press (which had commissioned the project as a series of articles for *Evergreen Review*) to pay both of their expenses. But Twardowicz refused the offer at the last minute. "Jack was very disappointed that I didn't go, but what he wanted was a nursemaid, someone to take care of him, make sure he didn't lose his money, get beat up, fall in the gutter. I couldn't go on a trip like that."

Jack still made occasional forays into the city to see Allen and Lucien and the others who were still around.

Joyce Glassman:

I ran into him a few times, sometimes in the Cedar Tavern, and he was always friendly.

When I was married, which was in the fall of '63, I got a call one night saying it was Jack and he was in town and he really wanted to see me. He was over at a friend's. Could I come over and see him? And I said, "Well, you know I'm married now. Can I bring my husband?" And he said, "Oh, sure. Bring your little husband." (He was not little.)

I had told him about Jack, and he was willing to go, and we went over and it was a horrible scene. His friend was drunk in this very mean way. Jack was drunk. This guy was burning Jack with cigarettes. It was really horrible, a very depressing scene. Jack looked bloated.

My husband was killed a few months later in an accident, and I moved to my mother's house for a few months. I was all set to go to Europe. I got a call from

Jack as though he hadn't even remembered that I had been married or anything. I don't even know how he found me. A very sentimental sort of call, suddenly, after all these years.

He said, "You never wanted anything from me. You were the one. You never wanted any furs." I said, "Furs?" He said, "All you wanted was a little pea soup," and so on. Which was not all I wanted, but still, it was sort of maudlin, touching. I tried to explain to him what had just happened to me. It couldn't somehow penetrate his consciousness, and that was really the last time I spoke to him.

"Irene May":

I saw him after the Kennedy assassination. We were walking to the Ninth Circle and he said, "I can't walk that far without getting a drink." I asked, "Why not?"

"Because I break out into a sweat and I have to have another drink."

Peter Orlovsky:

One night Jack was dead drunk, and me and Allen tried to cheer him up, and we both blew him. He said, "What are you doing that for? I'm not gay, I'm not queer." I said, "Oh, we're just trying to make you happy, Jack." He couldn't even get a hard-on 'cause he was so drunk.

Jack and Mémère kept on moving. By late summer of 1964 they were back with Nin in Florida. Jack bought a house in Tampa, the scribbled-on walls of which were torn apart after his departure by his hangers-on of those days.

This Florida residency was punctuated by the trip to France recorded in *Satori*, a lonely, abortive sojourn that resulted in little of value. Jack stayed drunk, was treated badly (he felt) by his French publisher, and received his "satori," or enlightenment, from Raymond Baillet, the taxi driver who rushed him to the airport to catch his return flight. The illumination provided by Baillet proved to be as elusive as the point of the trip—not only was Jack unable to trace his ancestry, but he failed to mention in the book what it was Baillet had said to enlighten him. The trip lasted ten days.

In September Jack's sister Nin died in Orlando. The

300

remaining Kerouacs, Ti Jean and Mémêre, moved back up North, this time to Hyannis on Cape Cod.

The novelist Robert Boles, who knew him there, recalled his harangues against M-G-M for creating a scene for the film of *The Subterraneans* in which Leo slaps Mardou, and against the producers of the television series *Route 66* who, he believed, had usurped the central idea of *On the Road* (two men in a car), rather than buying it from him.

Boles arranged a meeting with Kurt Vonnegut, Jr., who lived in nearby Barnstable. Jack was drunk when he arrived and joined Vonnegut and the others in a poker game, playing black-jack (although that was not the game) and throwing other players' cards around the room.

At this point Jack was as far out of touch with his old friends of the fifties and sixties as he ever would be. The Vietnam war was becoming a public issue and psychedelic drugs were on their way to being a daily supplement to the diet of those younger and/or more adventuresome members of what the press would soon label the "counter-culture."

Jack was a drinker, but he wasn't averse to occasionally sampling a wonder drug brought to him by Ginsberg or Corso.

Gregory Corso:

Oh, he mighta had a shot of morphine, but then like that must have been so glorious in his head as to write about it. I think he was too scared to get hooked. He was never hooked. He got into lush, obviously. That's what killed him. He was into bennies, because of the writing. You write fast on speed. It was no speed-freak scene where he'd be shooting up methedrine or shit like that, it'd be popping of the pill. Many popped a pill to play football. Many popped a pill to drive their long trucks across the country. Drug-orientated, he was not. Lush-orientated, yeah.

He had peyote. He had it early in the ballgame and he didn't want. That's good. He handled it cool, man. He took it very early in the ballgame when nobody knew what that stuff was.

In the early sixties the journalist Dan Wakefield inter-viewed Tim Leary, who recently had published the first issue of *The Psychedelic Review* and had founded the League for Spiritual Discovery. In Ginsberg's apartment Leary told Wakefield that even a hard-nosed barfighter and alcoholic like Jack Kerouac had taken psilocybin and had found peace and poetic insights.

At that moment Jack burst in demanding more of the drug from Leary. Leary suggested instead that Jack use the drug to create. He gave Kerouac a pen and a sheet of paper. Jack scrawled a large "X." "Now," he told Leary, "give me some more of that psilocybin." In Ginsberg's memory the experience with Leary's psilocybin did supply Jack with an insight, the often-quoted line, "Walking on water wasn't built in a day."

Jack never considered psychedelics, or any drugs, as the answer to anything. In the forties and fifties he had seen enough of the damage junk can do; he saw it, as he saw most everything, as directly related to death, to dying. By the sixties death was close at hand, and he knew it.

Gregory Corso:

I was staying at Allen's and I was taking junk and I was very down and Jack came over. That's when I had gave birth to a child, and Jack said, "I just brought him something to die," and that she, all she wanted, the woman I married, was a replica of me. That was his view of it. I used to battle it all the time in my head. I said, "What do you mean? What do you mean? Wait a minute. I didn't bring up somethin' to die," and all that.

But there was good in that. He hit me with the heavy truth. You bring up a child to die. That's how he looked at it.

By the time of the active protests against the Vietnam war, Jack had almost totally withdrawn from public life. Allen and Peter were more active than ever in the anti-war movement, and while Jack had always maintained a general non-violent philosophy—he especially loved Gregory's poem "Bomb"—he nevertheless recoiled at what he saw as the protestors' invective against America, their own country. He couldn't abide their seeming lack of respect, he abhorred their desecration of the language, and he subscribed to William F. Buckley's *National Review*. Jack stayed drunk, cursing the new wave, the critics

302

who didn't recognize his genius, his old friends who had forgotten him. He was lonely and frightened, as he had always been, but now he was bitter, too, and it was the beginning of the end.

Peter Orlovsky:

One time Allen and I went to his house—we went a couple of times—and we couldn't get in and he wouldn't come out. And one time early in the sixties, '64 or '65, I went out by myself to see him. I had long hair, and his mother answered the door and she wouldn't let me in because I had long hair. She knew who I was, and she had liked me before, but she wouldn't let me in.

I should've cut my hair.

When he was getting drunk a lot in the mid-sixties, I wish I wasn't so dogmatic or so hung up on trying to stop him from drinking. I would have approached it from another, more tender or humorous angle, rather than a worrywart or worrisome type thing. And then we got into politics and Allen and I were taking the left side and he was taking the right side, and he was calling us Communists and we were defending the Communists in South and North Vietnam. Jack was taking the side of the rednecks.

William Burroughs:

It's generally construed that Jack underwent some sort of a change and became more conservative. But he was always conservative. Those ideas never changed. He was always the same. It was sort of a double-think. In one way he was a Buddhist with this expansionistic viewpoint, and on the other hand he always had the most conservative political opinions. He was an Eisenhower man and he believed in the old-fashioned virtues, in America, and that Europeans were decadent, and he was violently opposed to communism and any sort of leftist ideologies. But that did not change. It wasn't something that came on in his later years. It was always there, and there was no change in the whole time that I knew him. It didn't really fit in with the rest of his way of life, but it was there.

303

In the fall of 1966 Mémère suffered a severe stroke that partially paralyzed her. Jack needed help now, not only for himself, but for his mother as well.

He phoned Stella Sampas, the sister of his old friend Sammy. She had been a girlfriend in Lowell, briefly, and for years he had mentioned her to friends, telling them that she was waiting for him. In November of that year they were married, and almost immediately they moved back to Lowell, to the village of Pawtucketville.

John Clellon Holmes:

Jack called us from Hyannis the night he was married. This was in November of 1966. We had never met Stella then. During their wedding celebration he called us, and he put Stella on the phone. I had never met Stella—knew about her, of course—and he was drunk and happy. He sounded great.

I'd known about Stella during my entire friendship with him. It seemed to me to be a preordained kind of thing. She was the sister of his friend. He used to say, "She wants to marry me. She's gonna wait for me."

It was good for Jack. He did the right thing. At that point his mother had had a stroke; his life had become very very complicated. I'm not saying this is why he married Stella, but it was certainly a part of it. Stella's very capable, and clearly, that Kerouac ship needed someone to take hold. She certainly dealt herself a tough hand when she got into that. I think she was equipped for it.

Stella Sampas Kerouac:

Jack first asked me to marry him before he married his second wife, Joan. But I couldn't. I had a family to raise. I always followed Jack's career, read his books when they came out—and you know, no one in Lowell reads. I'd say, "Look at Jack Kerouac's new book," and they'd look at the cover, flip through it and say, "Very nice."

Jack loved Lowell. When we were there, we'd go down to the river off Moody Street, on the Lowell side, the low bank, not Pawtucketville, and Jack just had to run down and look at the water swirling. We used to all go swimming in that river. Sometimes we'd drive out to Centralville, where Jack was born, on Lupine Road, and attend St. Louis de France, where he was baptized. Other times he'd go to St. Jean-Baptiste.

But he hated the traffic. He loved to walk, he had to have his walks, and he got so angry about the traffic. The last time we were there he came back from a walk to the store and said he almost got killed. It made him so angry that you couldn't walk anywhere anymore.

Jack was doing fine in Lowell. He really was, not drinking much. He only went down to my brother Nick's bar once every couple of weeks. He looked up to Nick, Nick took care of him. He got along with all of my brothers. Once he went out one night with the old gang and had a great time. The next morning the owner of the bar they went to came in—he'd not been there the previous night—and found one man swinging a bottle over his head and shouting, "Whoopee!" He went to the phone to call the cops and the man started saying, "Stella Sampas, Stella Sampas," so he dialed our house instead and told me, "There's some crazy drunk in here, must have broke in during the night, keeps calling your name. Maybe you'd better come down and get him." So my brothers went down and got Jack out of there. He had a great time.

At one time we had therapists working with Mémère, a large woman and a man, who would come into the house and try to get her to exercise her limbs. I was behind Mémère with the wheelchair, in case she needed it, and they were "walking" her through the house, dragging her along, saying, "See, see, she's walking, she's doing fine. Look at her!" Jack was sitting and staring and he points at Mémère and says, "She's fainted, she's fainted—" Sure enough, they look at Mémère—me being behind I couldn't tell—and she had passed out. They had just been dragging her across the room. That was the last time we tried therapy.

It was bad for Jack, living in Florida. He had no real friends.

In Lowell, Jack was practically as isolated as he had been in Florida, and, though she was fairly incapacitated by her stroke, he was still operating under the stern eye of Mémêre. In 1967 his old pal from Northport, Stanley Twardowicz, had made arrangements beforehand with Jack to stop by on his way to Maine. He would be coming with his new girlfriend, and Jack was pleased, telling him to come on up and spend the night.

Twardowicz and Jack carried on as before, Kerouac obviously pleased to have some company, while Stella played hostess, making small talk with Stanley's woman friend and bringing out the refreshments. Mémêre remained invisible, in her room with the television. Jack took Stanley on a Cook's tour of Lowell that day, showing him Dracut Tigers field, Bartlett Junior High School, the Grotto, the Textile Lunch, the landmarks of the Duluoz Legend.

But that night, when it was time for bed, Twardowicz saw that Jack had arranged for Stanley and his lady to sleep in separate rooms. Stanley protested and Jack explained that it was his mother's house—unmarried couples could not sleep together under Gabrielle's roof. Twardowicz stormed out, declaring that that was fine, they'd sleep in his Volkswagen camper in the driveway.

Jack was extremely upset, and several times during the night came out and pounded on the side of the camper, shouting, "Come on out, stop fucking the blonde! Come on out and have a drink!" In the morning Twardowicz and his girlfriend had breakfast with Jack and Stella, and Jack kept apologizing. Stanley said that he understood and told Jack to forget it, it didn't matter. They drove on to Maine that morning, and it was the last time that Twardowicz saw Jack.

That year Jack wrote *Vanity of Duluoz*, his reworking of the years covered in *The Town and the City*. Written in a more ordinary, moderate style—like a letter to Stella, to whom the narrative is addressed—it lacks the passion and daring of the earlier books, but imparts events "truthfully," filling in some of the gaps in the earlier, more fictional treatment. He had promised Lucien Carr he never would write about the murder of David Kammerer, but included it in *Vanity of Duluoz* with only the most minimal disguising of the facts. He also took the opportunity in the novel to rant against the hippies and LSD, complaining about how nobody walked down the street anymore hands-a-pocket, whistling for no reason. It is a sentimental, crusty, defensive book, but it has its moments. As Allen Ginsberg remarked, "It has a sweet wit about it."

Vanity of Duluoz was Jack's first book since *The Town and the City* that exempted Neal from events in which he really had played a part. Jack and Neal had not been in touch since the time in 1964 when Neal arrived in New York with Ken Kesey and the Merry Pranksters, a meeting recorded on film and tape by the Pranksters in order to immortalize the bringing together of the old order and the new. An American flag had been spread on the couch but Jack took it off, folded it carefully and put it back down on the sofa. Jack felt Kesey had ruined Neal, that he didn't understand Cassady as he had, and the reunion was less than joyous.

Allen, however, had, of course, kept in contact with Neal and knew what was happening. Since Cassady's release from prison, he and Carolyn had divorced—a fact Jack refused to accept during his long-distance telephone conversations with Carolyn, imploring her to "put old Neal on the line." Neal had gone to live in the tiny settlement of La Honda with Kesey and his group, taking not only psychedelics, but amphetamines, to excess. It was after a long 1967 trip to San Francisco from Bellingham, Washington, that Neal and Allen spent a night together—with Neal's girl at that time—in a motel on Van Ness Avenue. Allen described Neal's skin as "cold, chill, sweaty and corpselike—the chemical cast of excess weeks amphetamine—" and Neal as being "irritable. I think it was the first time," Allen said, "I ever got out of bed with Neal voluntarily, in despair myself, finally, and walked the street, pondering over the miracle of deathly fate that had overtaken my youthful idealism in romance with him."

But Jack knew nothing of this, or refused to believe it. He preferred to think of Neal as he'd been in the forties, "Neal behaving well," as Lucien had put it.

Allen Ginsberg:

In the early fifties Jack and I were complaining that Neal had fallen silent, though he was bubbling on until '65 and '68 with Kesey. Just a phase. Youth over and beginning to approach death and silence.

Neal Cassady, 1966. Photo © by Ted Streshinsky.

Luanne Henderson:

It seemed through the years, as I watched Neal and we talked and everything, that as each year went by, he felt a little more drained and a little more drained. He was keeping up a façade. He was just keeping up a big act, and he was getting tired. He was really tired.

This is in his conversations to me, too. A couple of times I was on the Merry Pranksters bus with Kesey and all of them, but I wasn't living it with them. And he was just performing. He had to keep up his performance all the time, his flipping-the-hammer bit, and his satin shirts. And when we were alone he would just throw the hammer down, like he was just tired. He was performing all the time, and it seemed like he was going at a faster pace each year when I would see him. And he was getting physically down, physically he looked each year more tired to me. Every time I'd see him, he'd look a little more desperate.

The last time I saw him was just before he went to Mexico, before he passed away. I've never seen Neal like that in my life. It was really an upsetting visit. Neal and I had seen and said goodbye a thousand times, but that time, we went to a restaurant and had a cup of coffee, and he just took hold of my hand and he said, "Where am I going?" He said, "I'm so damned tired I don't want to go anywhere."

Neal never talked like that, or hadn't in years, anyway. He was always moving. Neal was a natural speed-freak to begin with, he didn't have to take anything. But of course, he did. I hadn't seen him quiet like that, or pensive, for a long, long time. Sometimes when we were alone we'd talk, but nothing like that. And then he told me, "Well, at least I've done one thing." He had just been down to see his grandchild, Cathy's baby, and he was extremely happy over that, that he had seen the baby.

But he—he talked just like he wasn't interested anymore. I can't quite put it into words. I tried to tell Allen the same thing, about the last time I had seen him, that he was just totally unlike himself.

At that point in our lives we weren't that close, and yet we were extremely close. We could always talk. But I was going this way, and having my own problems, and Neal was heading the other way, and except for offering to be there, which he knew I always was, there wasn't really very much to offer.

I couldn't say, "Let's run away," which I'm sure wouldn't have appealed to him. It would be taking on more problems. Or to get him interested in something. I'd tried that before.

Neal always lived like time was short. Time was always too short. From the time I met him he didn't have enough time.

In February of 1968 Carolyn telephoned Jack to tell him that Neal had died in Mexico. Neal had been staying in San Miguel de Allende and was found unconscious alongside the railroad tracks outside of town. He died soon thereafter in the local hospital, where the cause of death was determined as heart failure due to exposure. "We know time!" he had told Jack. Drugs and alcohol notwithstanding, it is not unfair to conclude that time had finally consumed Neal as easily as he had consumed it.

Afterward, Jack liked to pretend he didn't really think Neal was dead, even telling interviewers from *The Paris Review* that Neal would show up again someday and surprise everyone. It had been more than twenty years since their first trip together on the road. Even to Jack it was the *vision* of Neal that couldn't die—he was still out there, the Adonis of Denver, a shroud driving through the myth of the rainy night.

Soon after Neal's death Jack appeared on William F. Buckley's televison show "Firing Line". Grossly overweight and obviously very drunk, Kerouac was sarcastically patronized by Buckley, who mentioned that the recently published *Vanity of Duluoz* was perhaps Jack's finest novel. Kerouac proceeded to insult his fellow guests, poet and musician Ed Sanders, who told Jack that *On the Road* foreshadowed and sparked the Hippie movement only to have Kerouac respond, "As the Buddha said, 'Woe be unto those who spit into the wind, the wind'll blow it back,'"; and sociologist Lewis Yablonsky, whom Kerouac referred to as "Goldstein", which "error," as Jack half-heartedly tried to afterwards make out, Yablonsky took as a serious affront: "Don't get anti-Semitic with me, Kerouac!" he shouted. Jack provided one brief bit of flash when, apropos of nothing that was apparent, he staggered

310

to his feet and sang Slim Gaillard's line, "Flat-foot Floogie with the floy floy!" and flopped back down into his chair.

At the end of the year an old Lowell buddy, Joe Chaput, drove Jack, Stella, and Mémêre from Lowell to St. Petersburg, Florida, where the weather would be more beneficial for Mémêre's condition. The brutal Lowell winters were too hard on her now, and Jack, though he hated the thought of life on the west coast of Florida, obliged her as always.

Jack had always used the telephone to make sudden reconnections with old friends and lovers, and, if anything, the calls increased from Florida.

John Clellon Holmes:

He used to call me from Florida, but I never went down.

He was pathetically lonely, tragically lonely, down there, and got into all kinds of messes as a result. What could one do? What could one do?

He used to call me up and say, "God damn it, get on the plane and come down!" I couldn't do it. I had my own life. And yet, I should have heard the desperate note in his voice.

He called about five people. He called Carolyn—he called Allen—if he could find Allen—he called Lucien, he called me. When he felt lonely, he'd talk forever. He would literally talk for two hours on the phone.

I don't know what it cost him, but he wouldn't get off. I'd say, "Look, Jack. Great. I'll write you tomorrow," but no, he wanted to talk, just talk. He was alone. He was sitting there. I can imagine the very room, because I've seen the living rooms in Long Island, at least. His mother had gone to bed, the big television set was turned down but the pictures were still going on, and there he was. What to do? Drunk. Drink makes you feel that you have some kind of energy that you really don't have, and he felt cut off. There were people that he valued and he wanted to see—old friends, always—because he had a lot of new friends. Wherever he went he had new friends, but he never called them up.

Allen Ginsberg:

Long, strange, beautiful conversations. Insulting

conversations, sort of like Dirty Dozens. Making all sorts of vicious anti-Semitic remarks, until I realized he was just doing that to get my goat and see how I'd react, and see if I'd finally come out from under and strike back. And so finally, when I said, "Oh, fuck you, Kerouac. Your mother's cunt is full of shit and you eat it," he started laughing. You know, he was just toying with me to see if I had any ego to get insulted. It finally got my goat and I suddenly realized, "What am I taking this shit for?" And realized how funny it was, actually, that I was taking it very seriously and trying to deal with it rationally, instead of jumping to some sort of Dirty Dozens. You know, Signifying Monkey...

G.J. Apostolos:

You can't go back. Thomas Wolfe said it. You can't go back to it. Not to us, not to Mary Carney, even the landscape. But there'd be that phone call in the middle of the night. It was always snowing and cold. We failed him, his old buddies, but what could we have done?

Jack wrote very little during that last year in Florida. He was getting low on money, and in order to put a down payment on the house in St. Petersburg, Jack had agreed to take an advance from a publisher for a book he had not yet envisioned, something he had never done before. Allen convinced him that this was a bad idea and helped him sell some letters to Columbia University and the University of Texas at Austin to obtain the cash that he needed. Even though *On the Road* still sold well, it was expensive to support Mémère, pay off the mortgage, keep himself in booze. Stella had to take a job sewing after Robert Giroux rejected Jack's request that Farrar, Straus and Giroux publish *Vanity of Duluoz* in a Noonday paperback. Instead Giroux had sent Jack a copy of Ken Kesey's latest novel, as if to imply—as Jack interpreted it—that Kesey was the new boy, Jack was old hat.

He had two ideas for what the next book should be, speaking often to his new Florida friends of his desire to write a novel covering the ten years of his life since *On the Road* was published, and to Stella about the book that would fit between *Visions of Gerard* and *Doctor Sax*, a story set principally in

Leo's printshop. Only a few nights before his death, he had decided to call it *Spotlight Print.*

Because he needed the money, Jack resurrected *Pic*, his imaginary chronicle of a black boy in the South, padded it to novella-length and sold it to Grove Press. When Stella and Mémère talked him out of the original ending, in which the black boy who narrates the story hooks up with Dean Moriarty and Sal Paradise, Jack took his typewriter to Gabrielle's bedside, and she helped him write the final scene, in which a priest saves the boy from a wasted life on the road.

The last income that Jack saw from his writing came from a piece he called "After Me, the Deluge," a dreadful, prolix article—serious, to be sure—attacking the by-now entrenched counter-culture, publicly affirming his allegiance to the views of William F. Buckley, Jr.

Jack rarely went out of the house. He had no one but Stella and Mémère to talk to, and he sat with the shades drawn against the Florida sun, watching television with the sound off, playing Handel's *Messiah* on the phonograph, as loud as it would go. He was forty-seven years old.

Stella Sampas Kerouac:

If it hadn't been for Mémère's wanting to be in Florida, Jack would have stayed in Lowell. He wanted to go back just before he died. He went in and told Mémère, and she said no, she wouldn't go. Besides, winter was coming and it would have been too hard on her, so Jack said okay, he'd wait and we'd go back in the spring. "Who says you can't go home again?" he said. And then a few weeks later he died.

We'd been up all night before the day he died. We were watching television, "The Galloping Gourmet," about ten-thirty in the morning. I had just finished attending to Mémère and I was going to get Jack something to eat, but he wouldn't let me. He made me sit while he went and opened a can of tuna fish. He ate the whole can. Then he went into the bathroom. I heard some noise and I went in to see about it.

Jack was in there, the toilet was filled with blood. "I'm hemorrhaging," he said. "I'm hemorrhaging."

Jack didn't want to go to the hospital. He wanted the

Jack Kerouac and wife, Stella. Photo by James Coyne.

doctor to come over, but I called the ambulance. Jack kept insisting he didn't want to go, but he went.

G.J. Apostolos:

I didn't know hardly anybody at the funeral.

Scotty Beaulieu:

Jack's wake was a big mess, full of hippies and a whole crowd of people laughing and talking. It was so crowded and noisy you couldn't even get close to his coffin and have a little peace to pay your last respects. G.J. and I thought maybe we'd be asked to be pallbearers, but we decided not to say anything about it unless we were asked, and we weren't. We stayed for a little while, but we didn't go to the burial because of all the crowds.

Gregory Corso:

When I went to his funeral Stella said, "Gregory, you must have known he wanted to see you. Why didn't you come while he was alive?" I told her, "Well, I don't know people are gonna die. I don't know when they're gonna go."

When I saw Jack in the funeral parlor, where

everybody was paying a last visit to him, I had this idea
of picking up his body and throwing it across the room. I
thought it might have been a Zen thing that he would
have dug. Because he wasn't there, this was the body. So:
plunk! I don't know what they would have done to me,
maybe put me in the looney bin or something, 'cause you
just don't do things like that. You *don't*.

I'm glad I didn't do it. I'm not that impulsive, but it
was a thought that went through my head, to break it.

"Break this, Gregory. Break this bullshit hypocrisy of
funerals and all that. People mourning something that
ain't there."

Allen Ginsberg, 1976. Photo by Lawrence Lee.

That was the last shot I had with my friend, but it was when he was dead.

Allen wrote Carolyn: "Jack's funeral was very solemn. I went with Peter & Gregory & John Holmes in Holmes' car, saw Jack in coffin in Archambault funeral home on Pawtucketville St. Lowell . . . pallbore through high mass at St. Jean-Baptiste cemetery—Jack in coffin looked large-headed, grim-lipped, tiny bald spot top of skull begun but hair still black & soft, cold skin make up chill to finger touch on his brow, fingers wrinkled, hairy hands protruding from sports jacket holding rosary, flower masses around coffin & shaped wrinkle-furrow familiar at his brow, eyes closed, mid-aged heavy looked like his father had become from earlier dream decades—shock first seeing him there in theatric-lit coffin room as if a Buddha in *Parinirvana* pose, come here left his message of illusion-wink & left the body behind."

EPILOGUE

Luanne Henderson:

It was kind of a shock when I found out that *On the Road* had become a pattern for young people.

A friend of mine, a young boy about twenty-two years old, I guess, came up from Los Angeles with these two young girls, about eighteen—in their late teens—and this woman that was a friend of the boy, she had lived with me. She had told him about *On the Road*, and so forth. I'd never even talked to him about it at all, but he had related all this to these girls, and they had to come to meet me, so he brought them up to the house.

They were on their way to Denver to recreate the trip back to New York, and I couldn't believe that. How could anybody? It was just totally insane to me. You know, here are these two well-heeled young women from upper-middle-class families, money in their pockets and beautiful clothing, and they were going to Denver and go through with this. I don't care what they did, but I just couldn't imagine young people trying to recreate something out of a book like that. It was really a shock to me to find out what impact Jack's books were having on the younger generation.

Of course, I loved the book, but I guess in living it and being around Jack and Allen and all of them I didn't think about it as material for a book. I was quite convinced that John [Holmes] would finish his book, because they were all dedicated and disciplined. They weren't fly-by-night, you know, running around not getting anything accomplished. I just never thought of

Jack as being famous, or Allen as being famous. We were all just doing a thing, and that was the extent of it.

Malcolm Cowley:

I think most of Jack's place will be for *On the Road*, and there'll be a little passage in the history of American literature on his revelation that there was a new underground generation with new standards. He was a precursor, of course, of the revolution of the 1960's. Strangely, that revolution of the sixties has receded, but *On the Road* keeps on being read.

John Clellon Holmes:

The tragedy—I shouldn't even call it that—but the irony is that he worked so hard to project, to put on paper and project in the world a vision, his own particular vision. Somebody else is going to have to judge how widespread it was, how encompassing it was. He'd worked really very selflessly out of his genius to get it down, and then when it came back to him, when it was accepted, from his point of view, for the wrong reasons, he didn't know how to handle it.

I'm not sure that if you handle fame, you deserve it. He deserved it because he was a great writer, in my opinion, but there was nothing in his personality that could handle it, that could be judicious about it, that could say, "Well, I understand they're not talking to me, they're talking to their idea of me." That's what made him good.

Jack had tremendous areas of—I'm loath to call it ignorance, but they were. But that's what made him good.

If he'd known how the world worked he never would have broken his heart over it.

Lucien Carr:

He ain't dead to me by a long jack shot. And I mean it, not only in terms of a *man*, but in terms of someone that scribbles, scribbles, scribbles, a scrivener, a writer. Jack is very important to me, and he's just as alive today as he ever was. Unfortunately, he can't come down here and in San Jose. Until recently AL HINKLE still worked for the Southern Pacific Railroad. BOB BURFORD pursues his business and artistic interests in Denver. His sister, BEVERLY, lives near Denver with her husband, a Republican politician, raising horses on their ranch. ED WHITE is a sucessful Denver architect. That city's striking arboretum is his work. "IRENE MAY" works for a magazine publishing company in New York City. GREGORY CORSO has recently moved his poetic practice from Paris to San Francisco. Novelist GORE VIDAL is now regarded as one of America's leading literary essayists.

MALCOLM COWLEY writes essays and criticism and serves as an editorial consultant from his home in suburban Connecticut. PETER ORLOVSKY, who has begun to compose and sing as well as reading and publishing poems, remains Allen Ginsberg's close companion. MICHAEL Mc-CLURE is now a playwright as well as a poet. LAWRENCE FERLINGHETTI's City Lights Publishing retains its front-rank position among America's small presses. ROBERT DUNCAN has become one of America's foremost poets. PHILIP WHALEN now writes from the viewpoint of a Zen monk. GARY SNYDER, who lives in the Sierra Nevada mountains, won the Pulitzer Prize for Poetry in 1976. LOCKE MCCORKLE is the senior aide to Werner Erhard, the secular guru of est, Erhard Seminars Training.

JOYCE GLASSMAN is an executive editor with a major New York trade publisher. DAVID AMRAM's career ranges from jazz gigs to guest-conductor stints with major world symphony orchestras, usually in performances of his own classical and mixed-genre works.

VICTOR WONG became familiar to San Francisco television audiences as a reporter-photographer on that city's public television news program, Newsroom. Today he teaches art to children. LENORE KANDEL lives in San Francisco's Noe Valley, reading and writing. JACKIE GIBSON MERCER married a jazz musician and remained in San Francisco.

STELLA SAMPAS KEROUAC remains in St. Petersburg, Florida, where Gabrielle—Mémêre—died in 1972, the year her son Jack would have turned fifty.

CHARACTER KEY TO THE DULUOZ LEGEND

Dan Wakefield once wrote that the names Jack chose for the characters in his books were like "funny hats." In most cases they were either thinly disguised and therefore easily recognizable to those intimate with the situations described, or they drew upon one or more outstanding—to Jack's eye—aspects of that person's character.

Throughout Jack's career publishers feared that the real-life counterparts of his fictional characters would bring suits based upon what the fictions contained. (None did.) In some cases—for example, the Cassady children or a number of poets and musicians in New York and San Francisco—the names stand for real people who have been recruited into the works as supernumerary characters, in much the way a film director might offer friends non-speaking roles as dress extras. (However, the friends were not necessarily consulted about their cameo roles.) In other cases, especially those of the characters who appear again and again under a variety of pseudonyms, the real persons were so important to Jack as he set about transforming his life into fiction that he could not exempt them. In this latter case, the friends and lovers used in this way are roughly akin to a stock company of actors. The fictional shadows speak and act, but in ways which Jack has devised for them and which serve his artistic purposes. If this is understood, the standard disclaimer which preceded each of his novels is entirely accurate. For the same reason the key that follows is not intended as an absolute identification of those named below with the characters and actions of the Kerouac characters who share some of their memorable traits. Additionally, there is no implication that the persons upon whom Jack based his characterizations actually behaved in the manner he ascribed to their fictional counterparts.

TITLE ABBREVIATIONS

The Town and the City (TC); *On the Road* (OR);
Satori in Paris (SP); *Maggie Cassidy* (MC); *Tristessa* (T);
Visions of Gerard (VG); *Desolation Angels* (DA);
Visions of Cody (VC); *Vanity of Duluoz* (VD);
Big Sur (BS); *The Subterraneans* (SUB);
The Dharma Bums (DB); *Book of Dreams* (BD);
Lonesome Traveler (LT); *Doctor Sax* (DS).

NOTE: Alphabetical cross-reference of real and fictional names. Actual names appear in capital letters, fictional names in upper and lower case.

Julian Alexander (SUB) = ANTON ROSENBERG
Ange (VD) (DS) = GABRIELLE L'EVESQUE KEROUAC
Annie (SUB) = LUANNE HENDERSON
ALAN ANSEN [Poet friend of Jack's in New York] = Austin Bromberg (SUB), Rollo Greb (OR), Irwin Swenson (BD) (VC)
GEORGE APOSTOLOS [Boyhood friend of Jack's] = G.J. Rigopoulos (MC) (DS), G.J. Rigolopoulos (VD), Danny "D.J." Mulverhill (TC)
Alex Aums (DA) = ALAN WATTS
GEORGE AVAKIAN [Musicologist and record producer, a friend of Jack's at Horace Mann] = Chuck Derounian (VD)
George Baso (BS) = ALBERT SAIJO.
HENRY BEAULIEU [Boyhood friend of Jack's] = Scotcho Rouleau

(TC), Paul "Scotty" Boldieu (DS), Scotcho Boldieu (VD).
Dick Beck (BD) = BILL KECK
Roger Beloit (SUB) = ALAN EAGER
Charlie Bergerac (DS) = LEONA "LEO" BERTRAND
Lucky Bergerac (DS) = HAPPY BERTRAND
Vinnie Bergerac (MC) (DS) = FRED BERTRAND
Ernest Berlot (TC) = FRED BERTRAND
Charles Bernard (SUB) = ED STRINGHAM
FRED BERTRAND [Boyhood friend of Jack's] = Vinnie Bergerac (MC)
    (DS), Ernest Berlot (TC)
HAPPY BERTRAND [Father of Fred Bertrand] = Lucky Bergerac (DS).
LEONA "LEO" BERTRAND [Mother of Fred Bertrand] = Charlie
    Bergerac (DS)
Jimmy Bisonette (MC) = CHARLIE MORRISETTE
Phil Blackman (VC) = PHIL WHITE
Blacky Blake (DA) = BERNIE BYERS
CAROLINE KEROUAC BLAKE [Jack's sister] = Catherine "Nin"
    Duluoz (DS), Nin (DB) (MC)
PAUL BLAKE [Husband of Caroline Kerouac] = Big Luke (DB).
PAUL BLAKE, JR. [Son of Paul and Caroline Blake] = Little Luke
    (DB)
Ron Blake (BS) = PAUL SMITH
Deni Bleu (LT) (VD) (DA) (VC) = HENRI CRU
Paul "Scotty" Boldieu (DS) = HENRY BEAULIEU
Scotcho Boldieu (VD) = HENRY BEAULIEU
Remi Boncoeur (OR) = HENRI CRU
IRIS BRODIE [Friend of Jack's in New York] = Roxanne (SUB)
Austin Bromberg (SUB) = ALAN ANSEN
Peter Browning (BS) = ROBERT LAVIGNE
Rosie Buchanan (DB) = NATALIE JACKSON
Ed Buckle (BD) = AL HINCKLE
Helen Buckle (VC) = HELEN HINCKLE
Slim Buckle (VC) = AL HINCKLE
WILLIAM F. BUCKLEY, JR. [Schoolmate of Jack's at Horace
    Mann] = William F. Buckley, Jr. (VD)
William F. Buckley, Jr. (VD) = WILLIAM F. BUCKLEY, JR.
Biff Buferd (VC) = BOB BURFORD
BEVERLY BURFORD [Bob Burford's sister, she knew Jack in San
    Francisco as well as Denver] = Babe Rawlins (OR)
BOB BURFORD [Friend of Jack's in Denver, former editor of *New
    Story* Magazine] = Ray Rawlins (OR), Biff Buferd (VC)
DAVID BURNETT [Son of Whit Burnett, a friend of Jack's in New
    York] = Walt Fitzpatrick (SUB)
WHIT BURNETT [Poet and editor, with Martha Foley, of *Story*
    Magazine] = Bennet Fitzpatrick (SUB)
JOAN VOLLMER ADAMS BURROUGHS [Wife of William S.
    Burroughs] = Jane (SUB) (OR), Mary Dennison (TC), June (VD)
JULIE BURROUGHS [Daughter of Joan Burroughs] = Dodie (OR)
WILLIAM BURROUGHS, JR. [Son of Joan and William S.
    Burroughs] = Ray (OR)
WILLIAM S. BURROUGHS [Novelist, author of *The Naked Lunch, The
    Soft Machine, Nova Express* and others] = Will Dennison (TC),
    Wilson Holmes "Will" Hubbard (VD), Old Bull Lee (OR), Frank
    Carmody (SUB), Bull Hubbard (DA) (BD)

323

BERNIE BYERS [Chief Ranger at Marblemount Forestry Station, Washington State, when Jack worked as lookout on Mt. Hozomeen] = Blacky Blake (DA)
Reinhold Cacoethes (DB) = KENNETH REXROTH
Camille (OR) = CAROLYN CASSADY
BILL CANNASTRA [Lawyer friend of Jack's who was decapitated in New York subway] = Finistra (VC)
Frank Carmody (OR) = WILLIAM S. BURROUGHS
MARY CARNEY [High school girlfriend of Jack's] = Maggie Cassidy (MC) (VD), Mary Gilhooley (TC)
CESSA CARR [Wife of Lucien Carr] = Nessa (VC)
LUCIEN CARR [Friend of Burroughs in St. Louis and of Burroughs, Kerouac, and Ginsberg at Columbia and later in New York City] = Kenny Wood (TC), Julien Love (BD) (VC), Sam Vedder (SUB), Damion (OR), Claude de Maubris (VD)
CAROLYN CASSADY [Married to Neal Cassady for twenty years, a graduate of Bennington College, she is the author of *Heart Beat: My Life with Jack & Neal*] = Camille (OR), Evelyn (VC)
CATHY CASSADY [Daughter of Neal and Carolyn Cassady] = Emily Pomeray (VC), Amy Moriarty (OR)
JAMIE CASSADY [Daughter of Neal and Carolyn Cassady] = Gaby Pomeray (VC), Joanie Moriarty (OR)
JOHN ALLEN CASSADY [Son of Neal and Carolyn Cassady, named after Jack and Allen] = Timmy Pomeray (VC), Timmy John Pomeray (BS)
NEAL CASSADY [Model for the main character of Kerouac's most famous novel, *On the Road*, railroad brakeman, "Adonis of Denver," author of *The First Third*, autobiographical fiction] = Dean Moriarty (OR), Cody Pomeray (VC) (DB) (DA) (BS) (BD), Leroy (SUB)
Maggie Cassidy (MC) (VD) = MARY CARNEY
Cecily (VD) = CELINE YOUNG
BILLY CHANDLER [Boyhood friend of Jack's killed in World War II] = Dicky Hampshire (TC) (DS) (VD)
Jay Chapman (VC) = JAY LANDESMAN
Charlie (VC) = CHARLIE MEW
HAL CHASE [Friend of Jack's at Columbia and in Denver] = Chad King (OR), Val Hayes (VC), Val King (VC)
DUKE CHUNGAS [High school football buddy of Jack's] = Bruno Gringas (DS), Telemachus Gringas (VD), Duke Gringas (VC)
Timmy Clancy (VD) = JIM O'DAY
MARGARET COFFEY [High school girlfriend of Jack's] = Pauline "Moe" Cole (MC) (VD)
Pauline "Moe" Cole (MC) (VD) = MARGARET COFFEY
Ricci Comucca (SUB) = RICHIE KOMUCA
Paddy Cordovan (SUB) = PETER VAN METER
GREGORY CORSO [Poet, author of *Gasoline, Long Live Man, Elegiac Feelings American* and others] = Yuri Gligoric (SUB), Raphael Urso (DA) (BD)
Warren Coughlin (DB) = PHILIP WHALEN
ELISE COWEN [Friend of Joyce Glassman's, girlfriend of Allen Ginsberg's in New York during the mid-fifties] = Barbara Lipp (DA)
HENRI CRU [Friend of Jack's at Horace Mann School and later in California and New York] = Remi Boncoeur (OR), Deni Bleu (LT) (VD) (DA) (VC)

Elliot Dabney (BS) = ERIC GIBSON
Willamine "Billie" Dabney (BS) = JACKIE GIBSON MERCER
CLAUDE DAHLENBURG [Friend of Jack's in San Francisco] = Paul
    (DA), Bud Diefendorf (DB)
Damion (OR) = LUCIEN CARR
Al Damlette (T) = AL SUBLETTE
Mal Damlette (BS) = AL SUBLETTE
David D'Angeli (DA) = PHILIP LAMANTIA
Francis Da Pavia (DB) = PHILIP LAMANTIA
Lafcadio Darlovsky (DA) = LAFCADIO ORLOVSKY
Simon Darlovsky (DA) (BD) = PETER ORLOVSKY
Dave (*Kulchur* Magazine story "Dave") = DAVID TERCERO
GUI DE ANGULO [Photographer and artist, daughter of the anthropolo-
    gist Jaime de Angulo] = Gia Valencia (DA)
Claude de Maubris (VD) = LUCIEN CARR
Mary Dennison (TC) = JOAN VOLLMER ADAMS BURROUGHS
Will Dennison (TC) = WILLIAM S. BURROUGHS
Chuck Derounian (VD) = GEORGE AVAKIAN
DAVID DIAMOND [Composer friend of Jack's in New
    York] = Sylvester Strauss (SUB)
Diane (VC) = DIANA HANSEN
Richard di Chili (DA) = PETER DU PERU
Bud Diefendorf (DB) = CLAUDE DAHLENBURG
Dodie (OR) = JULIE BURROUGHS
Denver D. Doll (OR) = JUSTIN BRIERLY
Geoffrey Donald (DA) = ROBERT DUNCAN
BOB DONLIN [Friend of Jack's in San Francisco] = Rob Donnelly
    (DA)
Rob Donnelly (DA) = BOB DONLIN
Catherine "Nin" Duluoz (DS) = CAROLINE KEROUAC BLAKE
Emil "Pop" Duluoz (VG) (VD) (MC) (DS) = LEO ALCIDE KEROUAC
Gerard Duluoz (VG) (DS) = GERARD KEROUAC
ROBERT DUNCAN [Poet, author of *Roots and Branches, Bending the
    Bow*, and others] = Geoffrey Donald (DA)
Ed Dunkel (OR) = AL HINKLE
Galatea Dunkel (OR) = HELEN HINKLE
PETER DU PERU [San Francisco acquaintance of Jack's] = Richard di
    Chili (DA)
Dusty (VC) = DUSTY MORELAND
ALAN EAGER [Tenor saxophone player, a well-known bop
    musician] = Roger Beloit (SUB)
Kyles Elgins (VD) = KELLS ELVINS
HELEN ELLIOT [Roommate of Helen Weaver] = Ruth Erickson (DA)
Elly (VC) = EDIE PARKER
KELLS ELVINS [Friend of William Burroughs in St. Louis and later at
    Harvard] = Kyles Elgins (VD)
Ruth Erickson (DA) = HELEN ELLIOT
Evelyn (VC) = CAROLYN CASSADY
Ben Fagan (BS) = PHILIP WHALEN
Alex Fairbrother (DA) = JOHN MONTGOMERY
LAWRENCE FERLINGHETTI [Poet and publisher, author of *A Coney
    Island of the Mind, Pictures of the Gone World*, and others] = Larry
    O'Hara [composite with Jerry Newman] (SUB), Lorenzo Monsanto
    (BS), Danny Richman (BD) (VC)

Finistra (VC) = BILL CANNASTRA
Bennet Fitzpatrick (SUB) = WHIT BURNETT
Walt Fitzpatrick (SUB) = DAVID BURNETT
Mardou Fox (SUB) = "IRENE MAY"
BEA FRANCO [Girlfriend of Jack's in California, "The Mexican
    Girl"] = Terry (OR)
WILLIAM GADDIS [Novelist, author of *The Recognitions* and
    J.R.] = Harold Sand (SUB)
Old Bull Gaines (DA) (T) = BILL GARVER
Harry Garden (DA) = LOUIS GINSBERG
Irwin Garden (VD) (DA) (BS) (BD) (VC) = ALLEN GINSBERG
BILL GARVER [Friend of Burroughs in New York and Mexico
    City] = Old Bull Gaines (DA) (T), Harper (VC)
George (DB) = PETER ORLOVSKY
ERIC GIBSON [Son of Jackie Mercer] = Elliot Dabney (BS)
EDDIE GILBERT [Friend of Jack's at Horace Mann School, he later
    embezzled a large sum of money and absconded to Brazil] = Jimmy
    Winchel (VD)
Mary Gilhooley (TC) = MARY CARNEY
ALLEN GINSBERG [Poet, author of *Howl, Kaddish,* and
    others] = Leon Levinsky (TC), Irwin Garden (VD) (DA) (BS) (BD)
    (VC), Carlo Marx (OR), Adam Moorad (SUB), Alvah Goldbook (DB)
LOUIS GINSBERG [Allen Ginsberg's father] = Harry Garden (DA)
JOYCE GLASSMAN [Jack's girlfriend in New York at time of the
    publication of *On the Road*] = Alyce Newman (DA)
Yuri Gligoric (SUB) = GREGORY CORSO
Alvah Goldbook (DB) = ALLEN GINSBERG
STANLEY GOULD [Friend of Jack's in New York] = Ross Wallenstein
    (SUB), Shelley Lisle (BD)
Ed Gray (VC) = ED WHITE
Rollo Greb (OR) = ALAN ANSEN
Guy Green (BD) = ED WHITE
Tim Grey (OR) = ED WHITE
Bruno Gringas (DS) = DUKE CHUNGAS
Duke Gringas (VC) = DUKE CHUNGAS
Telemachus Gringas (VD) = DUKE CHUNGAS
Dicky Hampshire (TC) (DS) (VD) = BILLY CHANDLER
DIANA HANSEN [Neal's wife in New York] = Inez (OR), Diane (VC)
Harper (VC) = BILL GARVER
ALAN HARRINGTON [Novelist and essayist, author of *The Immortalist*
    and others] = Hal Hingham (OR)
Elmo Hassel (OR) = HERBERT HUNCKE
JOAN HAVERTY [Jack's second wife; he wrote *On the Road* while
    living with her in New York] = Laura (OR)
Val Hayes (VC) = HAL CHASE
Ruth Heaper (DA) = HELEN WEAVER
LUANNE HENDERSON [Neal's first wife and road companion of his
    and Jack's] = Mary Lou (OR), Joanna Dawson (VC), Annie (SUB)
AL HINKLE [Friend of Neal's in Denver and San Francisco, he accom-
    panied Jack on a trip across the country with Neal and Luanne
    Cassady] = Ed Dunkel (OR), Slim Buckle (VC), Ed Buckle (BD)
HELEN HINKLE [Wife of Al Hinkle, she also traveled with Jack, Neal,
    and Luanne, and spent a month with William and Joan Burroughs in
    New Orleans] = Galatea Dunkel (OR), Helen Buckle (VC)

326

Hal Hingham (OR) = ALAN HARRINGTON
MASON HOFFENBERG [Friend of Jack's in New York, co-author of
the novel *Candy*] = Jack Steen (SUB)
JIM HOLMES [Early friend of Neal Cassady's in Denver] = Tom Snark
(OR), Tom Watson (VC)
JOHN CLELLON HOLMES [Novelist, author of *Go*, *The Horn*, and *Get
Home Free*] = Tom Saybrook (OR), Balliol MacJones (SUB), James
Watson (BD), Tom Wilson (VC)
Bull Hubbard (DA) (BD) = WILLIAM S. BURROUGHS
Wilson Holmes "Will" Hubbard (VD) = WILLIAM S. BURROUGHS
Huck (BD) (VC) = HERBERT HUNCKE
HERBERT HUNCKE [early friend of Kerouac, Burroughs, Ginsberg,
et al, in New York, author of *Huncke's Journal*] = Junky (TC),
Elmo Hassel (OR), Huck (BD) (VC)
Inez (OR) = DIANA HANSEN
Jack (BD) = JACK KEROUAC
Jack (TC) = PHIL WHITE
NATALIE JACKSON [Girlfriend of Neal's in San Francisco, she commit-
ted suicide in 1956, recorded in *The Dharma Bums*] = Rosie Bu-
chanan (DB), Rosemarie (BD)
SANDY JACOBS [Friend of Jack's in San Francisco] = Joey Rosenberg
(BS)
Jane (SUB) (OR) = JOAN VOLLMER ADAMS BURROUGHS
RANDALL JARRELL [Poet and critic, author of *Poetry and the Age*, he
was poet-in-residence at the Library of Congress in Washington, D.C.,
when he had Gregory Corso and Kerouac as houseguests] = Varnum
Random (DA)
Jeanne (TC) = CELINE YOUNG
FRANK JEFFRIES [Friend of Jack's in Denver, he traveled with Jack
and Neal from Denver to Mexico City, recorded in *On the
Road*] = Stan Shepard (OR), Dave Sherman (VC)
Joanna (VC) = LUANNE HENDERSON
Earl Johnson (VC) = BILL TOMSON
Helen Johnson (VC) = DOROTHY TOMSON
Roy Johnson (OR) = BILL TOMSON
June (VD) = JOAN VOLLMER ADAMS BURROUGHS
Junky (TC) = HERBERT HUNCKE
DAVID KAMMERER [Friend of Burroughs and Carr in St. Louis and
New York] = Waldo Meister (TC), Franz Mueller (VD), Dave
Stroheim (VC)
LENORE KANDEL [Poet, author of *The Love Book*, *Word Alchemy*,
and others] = Ramona Swartz (BS)
Johnny Kazarakis (MC) (VD) = JOHNNY KOUMENTZALIS
BILL KECK [Friend of Jack's in New York] = Fritz Nicholas (SUB),
Dick Beck (BD)
GABRIELLE L'EVESQUE KEROUAC [Mémère, Jack's
mother] = Marguerite Courbet Martin (TC), Sal's "Aunt" (OR), Ange
(VD) (DS)
GERARD KEROUAC [Jack's brother] = Gerard Duluoz (VG) (DS),
Julian Martin (TC)
JACK KEROUAC = Peter Martin [and elements of other Martin
brothers] (TC), Jack Duluoz (SP) (MC) (T) (VG) (DA) (BS) (VC),
Leo Percepied (SUB), Ray Smith (DB), Jack (BD)
LEO ALCIDE KEROUAC [Jack's father] = George Martin (TC), Emil

"Pop" Duluoz (VG) (VD) (MC) (DS)
Chad King (OR) = HAL CHASE
Val King (VC) = HAL CHASE
RICHIE KOMUCA [Tenor saxophone player, primarily a studio musician based in Los Angeles] = Ricci Comucca (SUB)
JOHNNY KOUMENTZALIS [Track star at Lowell High School during the late 1930's] = Johnny Kazarakis (MC) (VD)
PHILIP LAMANTIA [Poet and surrealist, associate editor of Parker Tyler's magazine *View*] = Francis Da Pavia (DB), David D'Angeli (DA)
JAY LANDESMAN [Editor of *Neurotica* Magazine] = Jay Chapman (VC)
Laura (OR) = JOAN HAVERTY
Albert "Lousy" Lauzon (MC) (DS) = ROLAND SALVAS
Arial Lavalina (SUB) = GORE VIDAL
ROBERT LAVIGNE [Artist friend of Jack's in San Francisco, it was he who introduced Allen Ginsberg to Peter Orlovsky] = Levesque (DA), Robert Browning (BS)
Rose Wise Lazuli (DA) = RUTH WITT-DIAMANT
Old Bull Lee (OR) = WILLIAM S. BURROUGHS
Leroy (SUB) = NEAL CASSADY
Levesque (DA) = ROBERT LAVIGNE
Leon Levinsky (TC) = ALLEN GINSBERG
Lu Libble (MC) (VD) = LOU LITTLE
Barbara Lipp (DA) = ELISE COWEN
Shelley Lisle (BD) = STANLEY GOULD
LOU LITTLE [Jack's football coach at Columbia] = Lu Libble (MC) (VD)
Julien Love (BD) (VC) = LUCIEN CARR
Big Luke (DB) = PAUL BLAKE
Little Luke (DB) = PAUL BLAKE, JR.
Balliol MacJones (SUB) = JOHN CLELLON HOLMES
MICHAEL MCCLURE [Poet, novelist, essayist, dramatist, author of *The Beard,*September Blackberries*, and others] = Ike O'Shay (DB), Patrick McLear (DA) (BS)
LOCKE MCCORKLE [Friend of Gary Snyder's in Mill Valley, he rented the cabin behind his house to Gary and Jack in 1956] = Sean Monahan (DB), Kevin McLoch (DA)
Jimmy McFee (MC) = JIM O'DAY
Patrick McLear (DA) (BS) = MICHAEL MCCLURE
Kevin McLoch (DA) = LOCKE MCCORKLE
Arthur Ma (BS) = VICTOR WONG
Roland Macy (BD) = ED STRINGHAM
NORMAN MAILER [Novelist and essayist, author of *The Naked and the Dead,* and others. At one time he was married to Adele Morales, former girlfriend of Jack's] = Harvey Marker (DA)
Roland Major (OR) = ALLAN TEMKO
Justin Mannerly (VC) = JUSTIN BRIERLY
Harvey Marker (DA) = NORMAN MAILER
George Martin (TC) = LEO ALCIDE KEROUAC
Julian Martin (TC) = GERARD KEROUAC
Marguerite Courbet Martin (TC) = GABRIELLE L'EVESQUE KEROUAC

Peter Martin [and elements of other Martin brothers] (TC) = JACK KEROUAC

Carlo Marx (OR) = ALLEN GINSBERG

Mary Lou (OR) = LUANNE HENDERSON

"IRENE MAY" [Model for the main female character in *The Subterraneans*, Jack's girlfriend in New York in 1953] = Mardou Fox (SUB), Irene May (BD)

Waldo Meister (TC) = DAVID KAMMERER

MÉMÊRE [Jack's mother, GABRIELLE L'EVESQUE KEROUAC] = Margaret Courbet Martin (TC), Sal's "Aunt" (OR), Ange (VD) (DS)

JACKIE GIBSON MERCER [Mistress of Neal's in San Francisco, later girlfriend of Jack's during time of *Big Sur*] = Willamine "Billie" Dabney (BS)

JAMES MERRILL [Poet and novelist, author of *The (Diblos) Notebook*] = Merrill Randall (DA)

CHARLIE MEW [Friend of Neal and Jack's in San Francisco] = Charlie (VC)

Allen Minko (VC) = ALLAN TEMKO

Irving Minko (BD) = ALLAN TEMKO

Sean Monahan (BD) = LOCKE MCCORKLE

Lorenzo Monsanto (BS) = LAWRENCE FERLINGHETTI

JOHN MONTGOMERY [Poet and pamphleteer, author of *Kerouac West Coast*] = Henry Morley (DB), Alex Fairbrother (DA)

Adam Moorad (SUB) = ALLEN GINSBERG

BREW MOORE [Bop saxophone player, based primarily on the West Coast] = Brue Moore (DA)

Brue Moore (DA) = BREW MOORE

DUSTY MORELAND [Friend of Jack and Allen's in New York. Allen often referred to her as an "ignu," a person of high intelligence] = Dusty (VC)

Amy Moriarty (OR) = CATHY CASSADY

Dean Moriarty (OR) = NEAL CASSADY

Joanie Moriarty (OR) = JAMIE CASSADY

Henry Morley (DB) = JOHN MONTGOMERY

CHARLIE MORRISETTE [Friend of Jack's in Lowell, first husband of Caroline Kerouac] = Jimmy Bisonette (MC)

Franz Mueller (VD) = DAVID KAMMERER

Danny "D.J." Mulverhill (TC) = GEORGE APOSTOLOS

Nessa (VC) = CESSA CARR

Alyce Newman (DA) = JOYCE GLASSMAN

JERRY NEWMAN [Record producer friend of Jack's in New York] = Larry O'Hara [composite with Lawrence Ferlinghetti] (SUB)

Fritz Nicholas (SUB) = BILL KECK

Nin (DB) (MC) = CAROLINE KEROUAC BLAKE

OMAR NOËL/JEAN FOURCHETTE [Boyhood friend of Jack's, he purportedly amused his buddies by masturbating in front of them] = Ali Zaza (DS), Zouzou (TC), Zaza Vauriselle (MC)

JIM O'DAY [Boyhood friend of Jack's, they hitchhiked together from Lowell to Boston to join the Marines in 1942] = Timmy Clancy (VD), Jimmy McFee (MC)

Larry O'Hara [composite with Jerry Newman] (SUB) = LAWRENCE FERLINGHETTI

Larry O'Hara [composite with Lawrence Ferlinghetti] (SUB) = JERRY
    NEWMAN
Ike O'Shay (DB) = MICHAEL MCCLURE
LAFACADIO ORLOVSKY [Brother of Peter] = Lafcadio Darlovsky
    (DA)
PETER ORLOVSKY [Poet, longtime companion of Allen Ginsberg,
    author of *Clean Asshole Poems and Smiling Vegetable
    Songs*] = George (DB), Simon Darlovsky (DA) (BD)
Edna "Johnnie" Palmer (VD) = EDIE PARKER
Alex Panos (TC) = SAMMY SAMPAS
EDIE PARKER [Jack's girlfriend at Columbia, they were married while
    Jack was being held in custody at the Bronx jail as an accessory after
    the fact in a murder case] = Judie Smith (TC), Edna "Johnnie"
    Palmer (VD), Elly (VC)
Paul (DA) = CLAUDE DAHLENBERG
Leo Percepied (SUB) = JACK KEROUAC
JAMIE PERPIGNAN [Friend of Neal's in San Francisco] = Perry
    Yturbide (BS)
Cody Pomeray (VC) (DB) (DA) (BS) (BD) = NEAL CASSADY
Emily Pomeray (VC) = CATHY CASSADY
Gaby Pomeray (VC) = JAMIE CASSADY
Timmy Pomeray (VC) = JOHN ALLEN CASSADY
Timmy John Pomeray (BS) = JOHN ALLEN CASSADY
Merrill Randall (DA) = JAMES MERRILL
Varnum Random (DA) = RANDALL JARRELL
Babe Rawlins (OR) = BEVERLY BURFORD
Ray Rawlins (OR) = BOB BURFORD
Ray (OR) = WILLIAM S. BURROUGHS, JR.
KENNETH REXROTH [Poet and essayist, author of *Assays, Natural
    Numbers, 100 Poems from the Chinese, 100 Poems from the Japanese,*
    and many other books] = Reinhold Cacoethes (DB)
Rhoda Ryder (DB) = THEA SNYDER
Danny Richman (BD) (VC) = LAWRENCE FERLINGHETTI
G. J. Rigolopoulos (VD) = GEORGE APOSTOLOS
G. J. Rigopoulos (MC) (DS) = GEORGE APOSTOLOS
Gerard Rose (BD) = ANTON ROSENBERG
Rosemarie (BD) = NATALIE JACKSON
ANTON ROSENBERG [friend of Jack's in New York] = Julian
    Alexander (SUB), Gerard Rose (BD)
Joey Rosenberg (BS) = SANDY JACOBS
Scotcho Rouleau (TC) = HENRY BEAULIEU
Roxanne (SUB) = IRIS BRODIE
VICKI RUSSELL (alias of Priscilla Arminger) [Friend of Jack's in New
    York] = Vicki (VC)
Japhy Ryder (DB) = GARY SNYDER
ALBERT SAIJO [Friend of Jack's in San Francisco, he traveled from
    there to New York with Jack and Lew Welch in 1959] = George Baso
    (BS)
Whitey St. Clair (MC) = RED ST. LOUIS
RED ST. LOUIS [Boyhood friend of Jack's, he introduced Jack to Mary
    Carney] = Whitey St. Clair (MC)
Sal's "Aunt" (OR) = GABRIELLE L'EVESQUE KEROUAC
ROLAND SALVAS [Boyhood friend of Jack's] = Albert "Lousy" Lauzon
    (MC) (DS)

CHARLES SAMPAS [Brother of Sammy and Stella Sampas, columnist for Lowell *Sun*] = James G. Santos (MC)

SAMMY SAMPAS [Important early friend and influence on Jack; brother of Stella Sampas, Jack's third wife, he was killed at Anzio during World War II] = Alex Panos (TC), Sabby Savakis (VD)

STELLA SAMPAS [Jack's third and last wife, sister of Sammy Sampas] = Stavroula Savakis (VD)

Harold Sand (SUB) = WILLIAM GADDIS

James G. Santos (MC) = CHARLES SAMPAS

Sabby Savakis (VD) = SAMMY SAMPAS

Stavroula Savakis (VD) = STELLA SAMPAS

Tom Saybrook (OR) = JOHN CLELLON HOLMES

Stan Shepard (OR) = FRANK JEFFRIES

Dave Sherman (VC) = FRANK JEFFRIES

Lionel Smart (VD) (MC) (VC) = SEYMOUR WYSE

Judy Smith (TC) = EDIE PARKER

PAUL SMITH [Spent several days with Kerouac at Ferlinghetti's cabin, Big Sur, 1960] = Ron Blake (BS)

Ray Smith (DB) = JACK KEROUAC

Tom Snark (OR) = JIM HOLMES

GARY SNYDER [Model for the main character in *The Dharma Bums*, poet and essayist, author of *Myths & Texts*, *Earth House Hold*, *Turtle Island* and others] = Japhy Ryder (DB), Jarry Wagner (DA), Gary Snyder (VD)

Gary Snyder (VD) = GARY SNYDER

THEA SNYDER [Gary Snyder's sister] = Rhoda Ryder (DB)

Jack Steen (SUB) = MASON HOFFENBERG

Sylvester Strauss (SUB) = DAVID DIAMOND

ED STRINGHAM [Friend of Jack's in New York where he worked for *The New Yorker* Magazine] = Charles Bernard (SUB), Ronald Macy (BD)

Dave Stroheim (VC) = DAVID KAMMERER

AL SUBLETTE [Friend of Jack's in San Francisco] = Mal Damlette (BS), Al Damlette (T)

Ramona Swartz (BS) = LENORE KANDEL

Irwin Swenson (BD) (VC) = ALAN ANSEN

ALLEN TEMKO [Architectural critic and professor, a friend of Jack's in New York and Denver] = Roland Major (OR), Irving Minko (BD), Allen Minko (VC)

DAVID TERCERO [Mexico City drug dealer] = Dave (*Kulchur* Magazine story "Dave")

Terry (OR) = BEA FRANCO

BILL TOMSON [Friend of Neal's in Denver and San Francisco, he introduced Neal to Carolyn] = Roy Johnson (OR), Earl Johnson (VC)

DOROTHY TOMSON [Wife of Bill Tomson] = Helen Johnson (VC)

Tristessa (T) = ESPERANZA VILLANUEVA

DON UHL [Friend of Neal's in Colorado] = Ed Wall (OR), Ed Wehle (VC)

Raphael Urso (DA) (BD) = GREGORY CORSO

Gia Valencia (DA) = GUI DE ANGULO

PETER VAN METER [friend of Jack's in New York] = Paddy Cordovan (SUB)

Zaza Vauriselle (MC) = OMAR NOËL/JEAN FOURCHETTE

Sam Vedder (SUB) = LUCIEN CARR

Vicki (VC) = VICKI RUSSELL
GORE VIDAL [Novelist, essayist, and playwright, author of *Burr, The City and the Pillar, Myra Breckenridge*, and many others] = Arial Lavalina (SUB)
ESPERANZA VILLANUEVA [Friend of Burroughs and Kerouac's in Mexico City] = Tristessa (T)
Jarry Wagner (DA) = GARY SNYDER
Dave Wain (BS) = LEW WELCH
Ed Wall (OR) = DON UHL
Ross Wallenstein (SUB) = STANLEY GOULD
James Watson (BD) = JOHN CLELLON HOLMES
Tom Watson (VC) = JIM HOLMES
ALAN WATTS [Theologian, author of *The Way of Zen* and other books] = Arthur Whane (BS), Alex Aums (DA)
HELEN WEAVER [Girlfriend of Jack's in New York] = Ruth Heaper (DA)
Ed Wehle (VC) = DON UHL
LEW WELCH [Poet, author of *Ring of Bone, How I Work As A Poet*, and, in collaboration with Kerouac and Albert Saijo, *Trip Trap*] = Dave Wain (BS)
PHILIP WHALEN [Poet and Zen priest, author of *On Bear's Head, The Kindness of Strangers*, and others] = Warren Coughlin (DB), Ben Fagan (BS)
Arthur Whane (BS) = ALAN WATTS
ED WHITE [Friend of Jack's at Columbia, an architect; it was White who interested Jack in the concept of "sketching"] = Tim Grey (OR), Guy Green (BD), Ed Gray (VC)
Dr. Williams (DA) = WILLIAM CARLOS WILLIAMS
WILLIAM CARLOS WILLIAMS [Poet and novelist] = Dr. Williams (DA)
Jimmy Winchel (VD) = EDDIE GILBERT
RUTH WITT-DIAMANT [Former Director of the San Francisco Poetry Center] = Rose Wise Lazuli (DA)
VICTOR WONG [Son of a San Francisco Chinatown politician, he accompanied Jack on a trip to Big Sur] = Arthur Ma (BS)
Kenny Wood (TC) = LUCIEN CARR
SEYMOUR WYSE [Jack's closest friend at Horace Mann School, he first interested Jack in jazz] = Lionel Smart (VD) (MC) (VC)
CELINE YOUNG [Girlfriend of Lucien Carr's at Columbia] = Jeanne (TC), Cecily (VD)
Perry Yturbide (BS) = JAMIE PERPIGNAN
Ali Zaza (DS) = OMAR NOËL/JEAN FOURCHETTE
Zouzou (TC) = OMAR NOËL/JEAN FOURCHETTE

THE DULUOZ LEGEND

BIBLIOGRAPHY OF BOOKS BY JACK KEROUAC

Title & Publisher	Date Written	Date Published	Time & Place Chronicled
Visions of Gerard (NY: Farrar, Straus & Giroux)	Jan. 1956	1963	1922-26 Lowell, Mass.
Doctor Sax (NY: Grove Press)	July 1952	1959	1930-36 Lowell, Mass.
Maggie Cassidy (NY: Avon)	1953	1959	1938-39 Lowell, Mass.
The Town and the City (NY: Harcourt, Brace & World)	1946-49	1950	1935-46 Lowell/N.Y.
Vanity of Duluoz (NY: Coward, McCann)	1968	1968	1939-46 Lowell/N.Y.
On the Road (NY: Viking)	1948-56	1957	1946-50 N.Y./ Denver/S.F./ New Orleans/Mexico & across the United States
Visions of Cody (NY: New Directions; N.Y.: McGraw-Hill)	1951-52	1960; 1972	1946-52 N.Y./S.F. Denver & across the United States
The Subterraneans (NY: Grove)	Oct. 1953	1958	Summer 1953 N.Y.
Tristessa (NY: Avon)	1955-56	1960	1955-56 Mexico
The Dharma Bums (NY: Viking)	Nov. 1957	1958	1955-56 West Coast & No. Carolina
Desolation Angels (NY: Coward-McCann)	1956, 1961	1965	1956-57 West Coast Mexico/Tangier/ Europe/N.Y.
Big Sur (NY: Grove)	Oct. 1961	1962	1960 S.F./Big Sur
Satori in Paris (NY: Grove)	1965	1966	June 1965 Paris & Brittany
Mexico City Blues (NY: Grove)	August 1955	1959	
The Scripture of the Golden Eternity (NY: Totem Press)	May 1956	1960	

Pull My Daisy (NY: Grove)	March 1959	1961
Book of Dreams (SF: City Lights)	1952-60	1960
Lonesome Traveler (NY: McGraw-Hill)	Compiled 1960	1960
Pic (NY: Grove)	1951; 1969	1971
Scattered Poems (SF: City Lights)	1945-68	1971
Two Early Stories (NY: Aloe Editions)	1939-40	1973
Old Angel Midnight (London: Booklegger/ Albion)	1956	1973
Trip Trap (Bolinas: Grey Fox)	1959	1973
Heaven & Other Poems (Bolinas: Grey Fox)	1957-62	1977
San Francisco Blues	April 1954	Unpublished
Some of the Dharma	1954-55	Unpublished
Pomes All Sizes	Compiled 1960	Unpublished

SELECTED CRITICAL AND BIOGRAPHICAL WORKS ABOUT JACK KEROUAC

Charters, Ann. *Jack Kerouac: A Bibliography*. New York, 1967; Revised edition, 1975.

_____ *Kerouac*. San Francisco, 1973.

Cook, Bruce. *The Beat Generation*. New York, 1970.

Duberman, Martin. *Visions of Kerouac*. Boston, 1977.

Feied, Frederick. *No Pie in the Sky*. Berkeley & Los Angeles, 1964.

Gaffie, Luc. *Jack Kerouac: The New Picaroon*. Brooklyn, 1977.

Gifford, Barry. *Kerouac's Town*. Santa Barbara, 1973; Revised edition, Berkeley, 1977.

Ginsberg, Allen. *Visions of The Great Rememberer*. Northampton, Mass., 1974.

Hipkiss, Robert A. *Jack Kerouac: Prophet of the New Romanticism*. Lawrence, Kansas, 1976.

Holmes, John Clellon. *Nothing More To Declare*. New York, 1967.

Jarvis, Charles. *Visions of Kerouac*. Lowell, Mass., 1974.

Levy-Beaulieu, Victor. *Jack Kerouac: A Chicken-Essay*. Toronto, 1977.

Montgomery, John. *Jack Kerouac: A Memoir*. Fresno, 1970.

_____ *Kerouac West Coast*. Palo Alto, 1976.

Tytell, John. *Naked Angels*. New York, 1976.

INDEX

Mailer, Norman, 263
Markfield, Wallace, 163
May, Irene, 174-176, 177, 182, 251-253, 300, 321
Melody, Jack, 59, 60, 145, 177
Melville, Herman, 42, 43, 66, 74, 276
Mémêre, *see* Kerouac, Mrs. Gabrielle Ange L'Evesque "Mémêre"
Memory Babe (Kerouac), 244-245
Mercer, Jackie Gibson, 281-283, 284-288, 289-290, 291, 321
Merry Pranksters, the, 307, 309
"Mexican Girl, The" (Kerouac), 187
Mexico City Blues (Kerouac), 47, 190, 211, 222, 245, 246, 262, 270
Miller, Henry, 272
Millstein, Gilbert, 170-171, 228, 238, 239, 240, 253
Mitchell, Red, 268
Montgomery, John, 201, 204
Muir, John, 202, 213

New American Poetry, 223
New World Writing, 186, 187, 189
New World Writing No. 7, 201
Newman, Jerry, 176, 261, 262
Nietzsche, Friedrich, 64, 96, 161

"October in the Railroad Earth" (Kerouac), 164
O'Day, Jim, 30
Old Angel Midnight (Kerouac), 207
Olson, Charles, 199
On the Road (Kerouac), viii, ix, xi, xii, 9, 23, 70, 76-77, 80, 81, 87, 89-90, 98, 107, 109, 114, 119, 120, 121-122, 137, 146, 152, 154, 156, 157-158, 159, 160, 161, 168, 169, 170, 172-173, 186, 187, 188, 189, 205, 206, 219, 224, 226. 227-228, 231, 232, 233, 234, 238-239, 240, 241, 242, 243-244, 245, 248, 251, 252, 253, 258, 262, 267, 268, 269, 298, 301, 310, 312, 317
Orlovsky, Peter, 190, 191-194, 197, 200, 224, 225, 263-264, 300, 302, 316, 321

Pareto, Vilfredo, 37
Parker, Charlie, 112, 154
Parker, Edie, *see* Kerouac, Mrs. Edie
Passing Through (Kerouac), 267
Patchen, Kenneth, 199

Penn, William, 17
Perkins, Maxwell, 79, 122
Phipps, Arthur, 261
Pic (Kerouac), 159, 245, 313
Piccolo, Luigi, *see* Little, Lou
Pius X, Pope, 5
Pius XI, Pope, 5
Pomeroy, Wardell, 55-56
Ponteau, 166-167
Porter, Arabelle, 186, 187, 188
Proust, Marcel, xi, 103, 155, 206, 233
Pull My Daisy (motion picture), 245, 258, 260-262

Railroad Earth, The (Kerouac), 167-168, 245
Reed, Dickie, 99
Rexroth, Kenneth, 194, 196, 197-198, 199, 201, 210, 215, 221-222, 262
Rimbaud, Arthur, 36, 42, 213, 248
Rivers, Larry, 258, 261
Robbe-Grillet, Alain, 245
Robinson, Carolyn, *see* Cassady, Mrs. Carolyn
Roseman, Ronnie, 261
Rosenbaum, Jack, 282
Rosset, Barney, 225, 245
Russell, Vicki, 59, 60, 61, 145, 177

Salvas, Roland, 9-10, 15, 16-17, 320
Sampas, Nick, 305
Sampas, Sammy, 16, 17, 24, 26, 28-29, 30, 31, 32, 304
Sampas, Stella, *see* Kerouac, Mrs. Stella Sampas
San Francisco Blues (Kerouac), 186, 270
Sandburg, Carl, 80
Sanders, Ed, 310
Saroyan, William, 29
Satori in Paris (Kerouac), 245, 267, 299, 300
Schopenhauer, Arthur, 96
Scripture of the Golden Eternity, The (Kerouac), 207, 209
Sea Is My Brother, The (Kerouac), 32, 33, 35, 42-43, 76, 159
Serbagi, Midhat, 261
Shahab, Sahib, 261
Simpson, Louis, 224
Six Gallery, 194, 195, 198, 199, 204
"Slobs of the Kitchen Sea" (Kerouac), 174
Smith, Paul, 275, 277, 279

338